Public Culture

Institute for
Public Knowledge

T0326704

Public Culture

Institute for
Public Knowledge

Volume 28, Number 2
May 2016

Climate Change and the Future of Cities:
Mitigation, Adaptation, and Social Change on an Urban Planet

Coming Attractions

Volume 28, no. 3:

Bharat Venkat traces a history of tuberculosis research to ask how cures come together and come undone; Megan Vaughan explores the development of counseling technologies in contemporary Africa and their effect on the subject; Shannon Cram unravels the politics of permissible exposure for US nuclear workers; Natasha Schüll considers online poker as a technology of self-management; Anthony W. Fontes maps the expanding geographies of extortion in postwar Guatemala; Ayşe Parla and Ceren Özgül examine the nexus of property, citizenship, and the nation-state through the Gezi Park protests in Turkey; Shamus Khan interviews noted sociologist Saskia Sassen about her conceptualization of the "global city" and "subterranean power"; and more . . .

Call for Contributions

Public Culture aims to publish original research of the highest caliber, and we welcome your submissions. We value strong writing, clear argumentation, imaginative theory, and an engaging prose style. *Public Culture* reaches an audience that transcends scholarly disciplines and extends beyond the academy. We seek work that persuades through evidence, logic, and analysis and that presumes no shared theoretical proclivities, political values, or specialized vocabularies.

Brief opinion-oriented pieces (of 500–3,000 words) run at the front of each issue in the Forum section. Full-length articles (of 6,000–9,000 words) based on original research are at the core. We also feature in-depth discussions with leading contemporary thinkers. Typically, we are familiar only with scholarly labor's final results, published books and articles, or occasional lectures. The interviews we publish call attention to the backstage of intellectual practice. In addition to original research essays, opinion pieces, and conversations, *Public Culture* welcomes translations of previously published, groundbreaking essays.

Our sister publication, *Public Books* (www.publicbooks.org), welcomes proposals for review essays about books (fiction or nonfiction), films, exhibitions, or plays, as well as profiles of intellectuals or literary scenes, visual essays, and multimedia work. Authors interested in submitting to *Public Books* should send proposals of 500 words or fewer to editorial@publicbooks.org.

....

Public Culture, 20 Cooper Square, Suite 517, New York, NY 10003; phone: 212-998-7866; fax: 212-998-8468; e-mail: info@publicculture.org; Web: www.publicculture.org.

Climate Change: Adaptation, Mitigation, and Critical Infrastructures

Eric Klinenberg

On October 22, 2012, an African easterly wave formed in the Caribbean Sea and quickly grew into a tropical storm with frightening potential. It was the hottest year in recorded human history (though that record has subsequently been shattered), and the seawater was unusually warm. Strong winds whipped the wet Caribbean air into a frenzy as the storm moved north and west, and by October 24 the system had become a hurricane. Meteorologists named it Sandy and predicted it would sweep through the Caribbean islands and make landfall somewhere on the eastern seaboard of the United States.

Sandy turned out to be more dangerous than anyone initially anticipated. The "superstorm" intensified and grew as it moved across the Caribbean, ultimately covering an area more than one thousand miles in diameter, making it one of the largest hurricanes in American history. Its winds were punishingly severe, yet the weather system was painfully slow, and the steady, relentless storm seemed to pause so that it could inflict extra damage on nearly everything in its path. Sandy hit the Atlantic coast on October 29—the worst possible moment. Not only was there a full moon with high tides, but there was also an early winter storm with arctic air moving into the northeastern region from the other direction, and the two systems collided to form what journalists called a hybrid "Frankenstorm."

As the primary target of the attacks on September 11, 2001, New York City had spent billions of dollars over the course of the following decade shoring up its security systems and preparing for a catastrophe. Terrorism was not its only con-

Funding for much of the research and the production of this volume comes from the Robert Wood Johnson Foundation, which provided support for a large project on international models of climate change adaptation.

Public Culture 28:2   DOI 10.1215/08992363-3427415

cern. Under Mayor Michael R. Bloomberg, the city also became a leader in planning for climate change, issuing high-profile reports about adaptation and mitigation and beginning the process of making the city more weather-resistant. In August 2011, New York City braced itself for the arrival of a severe storm system, Hurricane Irene, but was largely spared when the storm spun off to the north and west. The experience was something like a dress rehearsal for city officials and emergency managers, but it also gave residents a false sense of security and only bolstered the collective confidence that has historically served Gotham so well.

Sandy laid waste to New York City's spirit of invulnerability and to much of the city's vital infrastructure as well. The storm surge, which reached fourteen feet, toppled the city's flood protection systems. Subways filled up like bathtubs. The sewage system flooded and 11 billion gallons of soiled waters overflowed into rivers and streets. The communications system broke down, leaving more than 1 million residents and businesses without phone or Internet service. The power grid failed, massively, with outages lasting nearly a week in Lower Manhattan and much longer in parts of Brooklyn, Staten Island, and Queens. Several hospitals and nursing homes were evacuated. Tens of thousands of residents were displaced from their homes, some permanently. Officials estimated the economic toll at around $60 billion. Miraculously, in the United States fewer than one hundred people died.

I had been doing research and writing about extreme weather events in cities for nearly two decades when Sandy hit. This current period, which a growing number of scholars are calling the "age of extremes," has been punctuated by significant disasters that change the way we understand risk, vulnerability, and the future of cities. Superstorm Sandy was neither the deadliest nor the most expensive catastrophe in recent US history, and in global terms its impact was far less severe than other twenty-first-century disasters, from the Indian Ocean tsunami in 2004 (which killed more than two hundred thousand people) to the pan-European heat wave of 2003 (which killed around seventy thousand people). Yet Sandy is important for other reasons: not only did it reveal the surprisingly fragile physical and social infrastructure of one of the world's wealthiest and best-protected metropolitan areas; it also directly affected the political, economic, and media elite of the United States, where the fossil fuel industry has had its greatest success promoting climate change denial and policy stagnation on all variety of environmental matters. Today a wide range of people and institutions that have the capacity to shape public opinion, social policy, and urban planning see the world differently than they did before Sandy hit. They are looking for new ideas—about how to reduce greenhouse gas emissions, how to protect vulnerable people and places, and how to rebuild cities, communities, and critical infrastructures so that the systems we depend upon don't fall apart when we need them most.

The research articles in this issue, all published here for the first time, were developed through a multiyear ethnographic research project on climate change adaptation and mitigation, around the world, conducted by some of the most innovative scholars working on climate, culture, and cities today. The hypothesis that guided our project was that the best techniques for safeguarding cities and critical infrastructure systems from the threats related to climate change have multiple benefits, strengthening the networks that promote health and prosperity during ordinary times as well as mitigating disaster damage. Our research involved a blend of fieldwork, interviews, photography, and policy analysis. Some of the articles aim to assess whether the emerging models for adaptation work as well in practice as they do in theory and to identify challenges for importing different strategies to different parts of the world; others step back from immediate policy debates to analyze the underlying cultural and political ecological dynamics that shape the ways we make sense of emerging climate concerns.

The geographical scope of the articles here is wide, but they focus on a few major themes. Energy production—past, present, and future—is at the heart of global warming, so we feature several articles about emerging systems that planners, policy makers, and private corporations are introducing as substitutes for coal and oil. In an ethnographic study conducted in Mexico, anthropologists Cymene Howe and Dominic Boyer track the messy politics of a large-scale project to harness wind power as a source of renewable energy, showing how the project's champions ignored local social inequities and the political grievances of the people whose lives would be immediately affected by the new system. "We cannot fail to use energy transitions as opportunities to rethink dominant political, economic, and social institutions" (217–18), they argue. "To ignore this dimension is to imperil our ability to dislodge carbon's dominion and the many inequalities that carbon modernity helped to cement between the global North and South and between metropoles and resource-rich hinterlands" (218).

In an exciting collaborative essay, sociologist Colin Jerolmack and photographer Nina Berman go to Pennsylvania to document the ways that fracking—which policy makers around the world have positioned as a bridge from oil and gas to renewable energy—fragments the body politic, undermining the sense of common purpose and shared vulnerability required to address climate change. And in a short essay, Valeria Procupez chronicles a series of lengthy blackouts in Buenos Aires, where rapid urban development and rising energy consumption has taxed the local power grid beyond its capacities, rendering much of the city susceptible to outages in all weather, but particularly during its frequent summer hot spells. Neither in Buenos Aires nor at the national level, she shows, is there a coherent policy in place for updating the energy system; instead, a number of discrete entities take up independent projects, and the state's stated objectives—reducing emissions, developing renewable energy, establishing rational use protocols, and limiting consumption—are little more than rhetoric.

If converting energy systems is the main challenge of climate change mitigation, coping with extremes of water—sometimes too much, sometimes too little—is perhaps the most vexing problem of climate change adaptation. In a polemical but persuasive article, ethnographer Liz Koslov maps out the implications of sea level rise for the billion or so people who live in flood zones and urges scholars and policy makers to begin planning for the inevitable: a massive retreat from low-lying coastal and riverine regions. Although her fieldwork is in Staten Island, New York, where thousands of residents are asking the state to subsidize their relocation to higher ground and return their former neighborhoods to Mother Nature, Koslov provides a global tour of sites where inhabited land may soon prove uninhabitable. In another essay, the political ecologist Daniel Aldana Cohen takes us inside the fight over water management and rationing in São Paulo, identifies reasons why climate justice projects have not fit well into traditional campaigns for public goods, and speculates about how that might change as water becomes scarce. And, drawing on fieldwork on the other side of the planet, Gökçe Günel takes a critical look at another extreme: fantasies of infinite water produced through new technologies and desalination facilities in the Arabian Peninsula.

Global warming means that future states and societies will have to change more than their power and energy systems; in coming decades they'll also have to update the critical infrastructures that make urban settlements possible, from transit networks to food supply chains and climate security systems that protect against heat waves, hurricanes, and floods. This issue includes articles on urban infrastructure adaptation in a range of settings. In Bogotá, Austin Zeiderman introduces the concept of "adaptive publics" to signal the emerging constituency clamoring for policies to cope with climate change in the city. Like Cohen, Zeiderman is interested in how entrenched progressive political actors with redistributive economic agendas integrate technical adaptation projects into a broad program of social inclusion. He charts the rise of "metrological citizenship," whereby citizens demand both an assessment of their ecological vulnerability and a set of social infrastructure developments that will protect them.

In Singapore, Jerome Whitington observes a different version of climate politics at work. Water management, flood control, and coastal protection have always been vital to the welfare of the island city-state. In recent years, Whitington argues, government officials have framed conventional population security policies as climate change adaptation strategies but have failed to plan for the kinds of large-scale ecological transformations that, to use his term, "pluripotential climate futures"—nonlinear transformations that arise in the conjunction of human and nonhuman systems—could bring (417).

Andrew Lakoff is also interested in the ways that global warming alters the relationship between ecosystems and human-built systems. Drawing on new research in California, Lakoff chronicles the fascinating role of the delta smelt, a two- to three-inch translucent fish with a lifespan of roughly one year, in political fights over water management and new infrastructure in the parched state. His essay tracks the two-decade-long struggle, conducted by an alliance of fishery biologists, sport fishermen, and environmental advocacy groups, to protect the delta smelt and other native fish populations as policy makers attempt to circulate water to different constituencies. The negotiations Lakoff analyzes take up difficult questions: "What values are at play in efforts to sustain the existence of nonhuman life in a setting of intense competition over a diminishing and essential resource? What forms of knowledge are developed to gauge the health of threatened species, and what techniques are used to regulate the provision of water in the name of species protection?" (239–40). But they also reveal the ways that climate change adaptation policies necessarily intersect with other political concerns and interest groups, and even small, nonhuman actors can play powerful roles in shaping designs for vital systems work.

After Sandy, the Rebuild by Design competition became an important source of ideas for these projects, in the United States and throughout the world. An initiative of President Barack Obama's Hurricane Sandy Rebuilding Task Force, the competition attracted 148 entries from multidisciplinary, international teams that included architects, landscape architects, engineers, climate scientists, social scientists, and community organizers, among others. The federal government selected ten finalists, and after a nine-month process of research and extensive outreach, each team partnered with local stakeholders (governments as well as civic groups) and submitted formal proposals to a jury. There were six winning projects, all of which received federal funds for support and are currently in various stages of development. I was the research director for the competition, and part of our work involved assembling an international network of distinguished experts on the politics of designing for the climate changes to come. The group includes Fernando de Mello Franco, secretary for urban development, City of São Paulo; Mindy Thompson Fullilove, professor of clinical psychiatry and public health at Columbia University; Maarten Hajer, chief curator of the 2016 International Architecture Biennale Rotterdam; Henk Ovink, principal of Rebuild by Design and special envoy for international water affairs for the Netherlands; and Edgar Pieterse, South African Research Chair in Urban Policy and director of the African Center for Cities. For this issue, each of them talked to Cohen about their experiences with design. I'm excited to publish these conversations here.

Collectively, the articles and interviews in this issue help establish a research agenda for the social study of climate change adaptation, one that focuses on struggles over infrastructure provision, on the problems of forced migration and resettlement, on the politics of design, on the relationship between extant and emerging social movements, on the cultural consequences of new energy projects and public policies, and on the thorny questions of whose vulnerability and security will matter as cities, nations, and international agencies face up to the challenge of global warming That reckoning is inevitable; the only question is when it will begin. We hope this special issue of *Public Culture* advances the conversation.

Fracking Communities

Colin Jerolmack and Nina Berman

On a picture-perfect September morning in 2013 in the northern Pennsylvania hamlet of Trout Run, Cindy Bower noticed something unusual as she peered out the sunroom windows at the placid pond located a stone's throw from her rustic home: the tranquility was ruptured by the staccato tapping of one of her stained-glass sun catchers against the window. "They have never done this before in the fourteen years that we have had a house here," she reported. "I had to take one of them down, and I may have to remove more because the vibration is unsettling." Something is "definitely shaking the earth," Bower concluded, "and it is new."[1] Though she could only speculate on the source ("Is it mini earthquakes?"), Bower was certain it had something to do with the drilling and hydraulic fracturing of nearby gas wells. Within a quarter mile of her house, along a winding "tar and chip" (unpaved) road called Sugar Camp, earthmovers leveled the side of a mountain to build a well pad, two massive drilling rigs manned by dozens of workers operated around the clock, pipeline rights-of-way scarred a forested tract of state game land, tractor trailer caravans routinely snarled traffic and caused the road to buckle, and a fifty-foot plume of fire shot out of a flare stack for days. While the Bowers put a covenant on their property to enshrine its Arcadian character, and though the gas company placed mesh netting along the perimeter of part of their yard in an attempt to prevent the trucks exiting their neighbor's well pad from driving on it, Bower was powerless to stop

Text by Colin Jerolmack; photographs by Nina Berman. Direct correspondence to Colin Jerolmack, 295 Lafayette St., Floor 4, New York, NY 10012; e-mail: jerolmack@nyu.edu. Jerolmack thanks Eric Klinenberg and an anonymous reviewer at *Public Culture*, participants in Northwestern University's Culture Workshop, Nina Berman, Ralph Kisberg, Jooyoung Lee, Alexandra Murphy, and Iddo Tavory for comments.

1. All names in this article are real and used with permission. The stories and quotations presented herein were gathered from in-person interviews and direct observations carried out between 2011 and 2013.

Public Culture 28:2 DOI 10.1215/08992363-3427523

the "noise, the light pollution, and the smells" of industry from trespassing on her property. She felt "under siege" in a place they built to be their refuge and talked about "escaping" to upstate New York.

Whether or not the rattling of her sun catcher against the windowpane really was caused by shale gas extraction, it is important to understand Bower's underlying state of anxiety and uncertainty because it hints at how the process colloquially known as "fracking" can disrupt and transform everyday life in the rural communities situated on the front lines of America's "energy revolution" (Gold 2014).[2] Though fracking may help reduce carbon emissions and provide a shot in the arm for small towns struggling to find a place in the postindustrial economy, it imposes an industrial infrastructure onto agrarian and woodland communities (McGraw 2012). Many residents are ambivalent about whether the net balance of the changes wrought is positive or negative. But our investigations in more than two dozen municipalities across three northern Pennsylvania counties (Lycoming, Bradford, and Susquehanna) make clear that choices by individual landowners to lease and develop their property produce "spillover effects" that harm their neighbors' quality of life and degrade communally shared resources like forests and roads.

Many of the predominantly rural communities where fracking takes place have weathered prior boom-and-bust cycles and socioecological disruptions from other extractive industries (e.g., coal and timber). Moreover, this essay is hardly the first to document the environmental and community impacts of fracking (see, e.g., Perry 2012; Wilber 2012). Yet there is something distinct about how fracking reshapes the rhythms of community life and people's relationship to the land that has received scant attention. To access the gas, energy firms must lease the mineral rights, sometimes for thousands of dollars per acre, from landowners, who are also entitled to royalties if gas is extracted from under their land. Companies routinely operate right in lessors' backyards. In this way, fracking is more *intimate*, more dependent on personal approval (rather than, say, local governments), and potentially offers more direct financial benefits than many other environmentally risky land uses (e.g., a landfill or coal mining).[3] In regions like Appalachian Penn-

2. Some industry proponents reject the word *fracking*; others apply it only to the specific process of injecting high volumes of pressurized water, sand, and chemicals into a drilled well. We use *fracking* as it is used in everyday conversation: to refer to the entire process of preparing a well pad, drilling and cementing a gas well, fracking, and removing the briny "flowback" and "produced water" (wastewater).

3. New York is the only state where municipal bans on fracking have been determined to be legal, though the 2014 state supreme court decision became irrelevant after Governor Andrew Cuomo instituted a statewide ban.

sylvania where it is common for land to be passed down through generations and where property rights are sacrosanct (Perry 2012), when "landmen" fanned out across back roads seeking to convince landowners to lease their properties, many potential lessors took for granted that the decision to allow shale gas development on their premises (or not) was strictly a personal matter. There were no public town hall debates or referenda about whether "the community" should allow drilling, and while every natural gas installation requires a bureaucratic assessment of its *particular* impact on the environment and public safety, it is in the *aggregate* that personal land-use decisions can produce consequences that have an impact on almost everyone—even if they do not host natural gas infrastructure on their property or receive lease bonuses or royalties.

While the jury is still out on whether shale gas extraction can mitigate climate change or revive rust belt America, it seems that fracking has initiated a "tragedy of the commons" in historically communal locales: lessors keep all the money earned for themselves, while any negative impacts (e.g., traffic or water contamination) are shared, which incentivizes everyone to lease. Although Garrett Hardin (1968) claimed that private property counteracts atavism and resource depletion by internalizing costs, in this case exercising one's right to do what one will on one's own land undermined the potential of others to enjoy that same right and eroded common-pool resources. This social dynamic also weakened long-standing community norms of sovereignty and reciprocity and left some residents with a profound sense of alienation from their property, neighbors, and place. Because state and federal governments have leased public land for drilling, fracking entails our collective alienation from large portions of the literal commons as well.

The Gas Boom, Climate Change, and the Fracking Controversy

Shale gas has quickly become one of America's most important, and lucrative, energy sources. While it has long been known that vast reserves of natural gas (and oil) lay locked in layers of shale a mile or more underground, most of it remained inaccessible until this century, when the process of hydraulic fracturing—also known as fracking—was combined with horizontal drilling. It is hard to overstate the profound economic, sociopolitical, and environmental impacts wrought by this technological innovation.

President Barack Obama announced in his 2012 State of the Union speech that the United States has enough natural gas to supply domestic energy needs for one hundred years and support more than six hundred thousand jobs by the end of this decade. In just ten years, the United States has gone from anxious handwringing over peak oil to preparing for becoming an oil and gas exporter (Dernbach and May 2015). In just twenty more years, the dream of energy independence could finally become a reality (Anderson 2014). Moreover, fracking is generally credited with helping the US economy rebound from the "Great Recession," lowering fuel prices at the pump, and reducing millions of consumers' electricity and heating bills (Gold 2014; however, a glut of oil and gas has depressed prices so much that the industry and the locales dependent on it are now experiencing a serious economic downturn, including over seventy-five thousand layoffs in the past year [Helman 2015]).

The president and many others (including, controversially, the Environmental Defense Fund) also frame fracking as a tool in the fight against climate change since natural gas combustion emits about half as many pounds of carbon dioxide (CO_2) per million Btu of energy as coal does (Energy Information Administration 2014). Cheap and abundant supplies of natural gas are incentivizing energy companies to switch from coal- to gas-fired power plants and have emboldened the White House to enact the stricter air emissions standards that are slowly but steadily shuttering coal plants. Indeed, between 2007—just before the shale gas boom began—and 2012, the United States experienced a 12 percent reduction in CO_2 emissions (Gold 2014: 265); studies estimate that "between 35% and 50% of the difference between peak and present power sector emissions may be due to shale gas price effects" (Broderick and Anderson 2012: 2).

The ostensible environmental benefits of natural gas become murkier, however, if the calculus is expanded beyond an accounting of domestic CO_2 emissions. Global coal consumption continues to grow, and the meteoric rise of fracking in the United States was accompanied by a sizable increase in coal exports, suggesting that the shale gas boom may be offshoring some coal combustion rather than displacing all of it (Broderick and Anderson 2012). Furthermore, because methane (the primary component of natural gas) is a greenhouse gas whose potency is more than twenty times that of CO_2 over a hundred-year period, even a relatively small rate of methane leakage (i.e., 3 percent) from the production and distribution of shale gas could "offset or even reverse the entire apparent greenhouse gas benefit of fuel switching from coal to natural gas" (Dernbach and May 2015: 12). Some experts say that leakage rates are currently above that threshold (Brandt et al. 2014).

Of course, the most well-known environmental controversy surrounding fracking pertains to its potential to contaminate people's drinking water (see Darrah et al. 2014; Vengosh et al. 2014). Because of the 2010 documentary *Gasland*, which played a central role in shaping the public discourse surrounding fracking and in fomenting antifracking mobilization (Vasi et al. 2015), when people think about

Figure 1 Jodie Simons and Jason Lamphere of Monroeton, PA, demonstrate how their tap water ignites due to high concentrations of methane. Photograph by Nina Berman

the risks of fracking they likely envision flaming faucets (fig. 1). Although the Environmental Protection Agency's latest assessment (EPA 2015) of the impact of shale gas extraction on water resources "did not find evidence" of "widespread, systemic impacts on drinking water," it does conclude that "in certain cases" drinking water has been contaminated by methane migration "via the production [gas] well" and by surface spills of hydraulic fracturing fluid and "produced water" (wastewater). It also notes that the discharge of treated wastewater "has increased contaminant concentrations in receiving surface waters" (ibid.).[4]

4. There are also contentious debates over potential health impacts from fracking. Although no peer-review study has established a causal link between fracking and disease, "all phases of hydrocarbon gas production involve complex mixtures of chemical[s]," many with "significant toxicity" (Bamberger and Oswald 2012: 52), and Cuomo cited "significant health risks" as the reason for his ban on fracking in New York (Hill 2014). Perhaps counterintuitively, the proposed culprit in most reports of health impacts is *air* pollution, resulting from gas wells, compressor stations (which serve as nodes for area wells that pressurize the gas), and diesel engines venting volatile organic compounds— including known toxins such as benzene and formaldehyde—into the atmosphere next to residences, communal gathering places, and parks (Hill 2014).

Individual Choices, Collective Consequences, and the Tragedy of the Commons

It is difficult to know how many cases of well water contamination from shale gas extraction exist because in most cases where oil and gas companies offer a settlement to landowners affected (in exchange for being indemnified), they require them to sign a nondisclosure agreement (Phillips 2012). Our own research in northern Pennsylvania has chronicled over a dozen families' cases in which high levels of methane found in their water wells either were determined by the Department of Environmental Protection (DEP) to be caused by the drilling of a nearby gas well or resulted in a cash settlement.

Considering that more than 15 million Americans in eleven states live within one mile of a fracked well and that there are almost eight thousand active gas wells in Pennsylvania alone (Hill 2014), water well contamination appears to be a relatively rare event. However, when it does occur it completely upends lives and reveals how personal land-use decisions can create environmental impacts that extend beyond the lessor's fence posts and infringe on neighbors' property rights.

Most lessors understood that there were some risks when they signed. However, small landowners often reported that one reason they felt secure leasing was because they knew their property was not large enough for energy companies to install a gas well or other infrastructure on it—at most, a horizontal lateral would be drilled a mile or more below the surface. But what they seemed unable to anticipate, let alone control, was that gas wells on neighbors' properties that were thousands of feet away could visit harm upon their water supply. The situation of Cassie Spencer, formerly of Paradise Road in Wyalusing, is a case in point.[5] After two gas wells were drilled over a half mile away, she reported that her and her two neighbors' water wells became infused with explosive concentrations of methane. Her tap water fizzed like soda. Chesapeake, the gas company that operated the two gas wells—which the DEP cited for multiple violations[6]—provided Spencer's family with bottled water and placed a vent over their water well but denied responsibility. Once the Spencers and their neighbors sued Chesapeake, the water deliveries ceased. Spencer reported bathing herself and her five-year-old daughter with the door open because, with no bathroom windows, she was afraid the house could blow up, and a methane monitor had to be installed in the basement to warn if the buildup of gas in their home reached explosive levels. Moreover, because

5. For more on this case, see Berman 2011.

6. Violations include "failure to properly control or dispose of industrial or residual waste to prevent pollution of the waters of the Commonwealth" and "site conditions [that] present a potential for pollution of the waters" (StateImpact 2015b).

Figure 2 Methane-laced water from Jodie Simons's kitchen faucet in Monroeton, PA. Photograph by Nina Berman

they felt unsafe using the methane-laced water for any household purpose (fig. 2), a huge "water buffalo" storage container had to be installed right next to their doorway (fig. 3). The estimated value of their house plummeted from $150,000 to $29,000, and the place that was once their sanctuary became a disaster area that they sought asylum from. Chesapeake eventually paid damages to the Spencers and their neighbors and bought their properties ($1.6 million was paid out in total), but the Spencers moved out with heavy hearts because the home they had left behind was where they had hoped to reside their "whole lives."

It was a similar situation for four families living on Green Valley Road outside Hughesville. Although no development took place on their small plots of land, their spigots bubbled with methane after a gas well in their neighbor's yard up the hill was drilled (the DEP concluded that defective cement casing of the gas well had caused the contamination).[7] Forced to purchase bottled water and eat off of paper plates, these families bore the collateral damage of their neighbor's faulty gas well. Ironically, the water well of the family whose property hosted the gas well was unaffected. It is important to note that, as with the Spencers, even

7. Copies of DEP reports are available from Jerolmack. To view the violations associated with this well, see StateImpact 2015a.

if the four families had refused to lease their land, their water still would have been affected. Indeed, part of their justification for leasing was that they would shoulder some of the burden of others' decisions to lease even if they did not, so they may as well get some economic benefit. It is precisely this logic that propels the tragedy of the commons. Even Bower, who placed a conservation easement on her land and claimed that she was "dead against" leasing and "didn't need the money," eventually signed a restricted ("nonsurface disturbance") lease, explaining that she could not stop the drilling in her area and so should at least get some recompense for her troubles.

Although water contamination cases dominate the headlines, other less catastrophic but far more pervasive spillover effects dominated most residents' everyday concerns. Chief among them was traffic. It takes over one thousand truckloads just to deliver the water needed to frack one well, and a single well pad can host as many as eighteen to twenty-four gas wells (McKenzie et al. 2012). Thus when water was being withdrawn from streams and rivers or when a well was being fracked, dozens of big rigs clogged residential streets and idled all day (or night) in close proximity to farmers' fields, houses, and schools (fig. 4). Roads were

Figure 3 Cassie Spencer looking at the "water buffalo" installed at her house in Wyalusing, PA. Photograph by Nina Berman

Figure 4   Water trucks lining up at night at a water intake system in Wyalusing, PA.
Photograph by Nina Berman

routinely closed for hours or days to facilitate the safe passage of trucks to and
from shale gas operations; sometimes they were closed indefinitely. More traffic
jams and detours ensued when the trucks left as work crews scrambled to apply
a new layer of asphalt to roads not equipped to handle the volume and weight of
the trucks. Though during permit hearings gas companies commonly provided
an estimate of the amount of truck trips that residents could expect as part of the
development of a *particular* well pad, there was no mechanism in place to monitor
or regulate the *aggregate* amount of traffic created by fracking operations. With
multiple operators each running their own truck caravans to service individual
wells, the public's ability to access and enjoy roads—perhaps one of the most
unappreciated common-pool resources when traffic is flowing smoothly—was
diminished.[8]

While choked roads and detours palpably disrupted the habits of rural living,
they sometimes also conspired with other more insidious spillover effects to pro-

8. To view a video of truck traffic, see "Heavy Fraffic" 2011.

Figure 5   Methane flares from shale gas wells in Springville, PA. Photograph by Nina Berman

duce psychosomatic disruptions such as anxiety, loss of agency, and a deep-seated sense of estrangement from one's surroundings (cf. Perry 2012). For instance, what Bower said she found most "unnerving" was being deprived of dark skies and quiet (fig. 5). A drilling rig from a neighboring property, lit up like a Christmas tree, towered several stories above her red barn. After the gas well was fracked, flames from the flare stack created a din so intense that she had to close all of her windows and sleep with earplugs. The entire valley around her was flooded with so much light that the stars disappeared. "I miss the dark," Bower lamented. "Will it ever look like night again?"

Over the past several years, fracking had made Bower's sleepy hamlet of Trout Run—and dozens of other nearby rural settlements—feel more like a construction site or an industrial park. The contrasts could be jarring: just around the bend from pastures, unspoiled forests, and a lake popular with anglers, diesel fumes mingled with the mist coming off the mountains, a security guard shack and a portable toilet marked the entrance to a driveway, big rigs squeezed past each other on hairpin turns, a field served as a makeshift parking lot and storage facility, apple trees were coated with so much dust kicked up from the truck traffic along an unpaved road that the fruit was brown, cranes hoisted steel piping over tree stands, and a humble farmhouse sat a stone's throw (literally) from a massive above-ground water impoundment pond and three well pads that alternately hosted a hulking drilling rig, a flare stack belching fire and roaring like a jet engine, and trailer homes for the dozens of workers who temporarily lived on-site (fig. 6).

The effect was particularly surreal at night. The drilling rigs were so large and so brightly illuminated that some said it looked like Cape Canaveral, and the flare stacks produced an atmospheric orange and gold halo slightly reminiscent of the aurora borealis (fig. 7). "I mean, if it were not a pristine environment being ruined," Bower remarked of the scene, "you could say it is beautiful in its own eerie way."

Like the traffic, the smells, noise, and light pollution from fracking do not stop at the property lines of those who hold or profit from gas leases. Everyone experiences a diminished capacity to access peace and quiet, unbroken vistas, dark skies, unhurried country roads, and the sounds of nature. As Hardin (1968: 1248) noted, our regulation of the pernicious effects of the tragedy of commons "in matters of pleasure" such as sight- and soundscapes is negligible. Some

Figure 6 The view from a porch overlooking a drilling rig on a neighbor's dairy farm in Rome, PA. Photograph by Nina Berman

Figure 7 Flares from natural gas wells light up the night sky in Franklin Forks, PA. Photograph by Nina Berman

residents viewed the degradation of these previously taken-for-granted rural "goods" as a price worth paying for progress, but for others the loss was so disconcerting that their surrounds became alien to them and their attachment to place withered. So, while material spillover effects such as water contamination sometimes led to the physical displacement of residents from their homes, the despoiling of less tangible common-pool resources could prompt a psychological displacement. Bower found herself in a constant state of unease ("It's quiet now, but who knows how long it will last?") and sometimes unable to sleep because of worry. She also began spending more time at her upstate New York cottage and was considering abandoning her cherished home even though her property had not been tangibly affected in any way. Adron and Mary Delarosa (formerly) of Springville decided to pack up and leave their organic farm because they could not abide a planned compressor station next door in addition to the four gas wells already present within a mile of their homestead. For them, fracking did not just degrade their quality of life; the spillover effects brought about such global changes to their experience of place and community that it introduced a different way of life—one that they wanted no part of.

Fracking as a Way of Life

In writing about Appalachian communities decades ago, Kai Erikson (1976: 86) argued that residents live in an "uneasy suspension" between the "contrary leanings" of self-centeredness and group-centeredness. On the one hand, Appalachians have a fierce respect for individual liberty and are apt to distrust the government and any other forms of authority that try to impose limitations upon them. On the other hand, their feelings of attachment and obligation to kin and community can be so strong that they do not develop a "satisfactory self-image as a single individual" (ibid.: 84). Whether or not a distinct Appalachian culture persists in places like rural Pennsylvania, one certainly sees evidence of the "contrary leanings" of self-interest and communalism (which today we are apt to pair under the label "libertarianism"): government distrust is rampant, individual sovereignty is seen as a God-given right, and people often say they just want "to be left alone"; yet residents routinely preach self-sacrifice for the collective good and anchor their lives in the church and other voluntary associations.

The advent of fracking has forced the inherent tension between these self- and group-oriented proclivities to bubble to the surface in rural Pennsylvania. The tradition in many of these locales is to "live and let live" and resolve any disputes that arise through "informal norms of neighborliness" rather than through appeals to legal entitlements (Ellickson 1991: viii). However, the spillover effects of individuals' choice to lease their land (the "live" in "live and let live") can affect their neighbors' and communities' quality of life to such a degree that it contravenes the folkway of letting others live. As a result, both communalism *and* individual autonomy / property rights can be infringed by personal land-use decisions.

The stakes of fracking—financial, environmental, or otherwise—can be so high that neighbors and kin now routinely filter everyday interactions through legal-rational frameworks. For example, next-door neighbors who either never knew or never cared about the location of the boundary between their respective properties began researching deeds at the courthouse to ensure that no one else wound up with a dime of their rightful lease bonus. In one case, a couple who lived in a simple mountainside ranch house near Salladasburg had given a nearby hunting camp permission to construct a gravel access road through their property because, as they reported, it was the neighborly thing to do. The couple made the permission permanent through an easement just to ensure that, should they ever move, the new occupants could not deny access to the hunting camp. But the couple reconsidered when the camp leased its property for drilling and hundreds of big rigs and earthmovers began roaring up and down the driveway a mere dozen feet from their home. Their appeals to the hunting camp to disallow the trucks to use the access road on the grounds that it damaged their property and was against the spirit of the easement fell on deaf ears—camp members maintained that it was their legal right to use the driveway any way they saw fit.[9] Meanwhile, the couple had a friend who had inherited, along with her nine siblings, her parents' farm outside Hughesville, and she incorporated the property as a limited liability company after leasing it and set up monthly meetings in which someone took minutes and a lawyer was sometimes present to ensure that decision making and profits were fairly distributed among the ten of them.

Certainly, there were landowners who reaped a substantial windfall from leasing their property, and the presence of a new industry in rural towns suffering from decades of population decline and "brain drain" has fortified some declining businesses and opened up some new job prospects.[10] But by overlaying an industrial infrastructure based on individual lease agreements onto a rural setting, fracking is fundamentally altering neighbor and kin relationships, even in communities like the ones reported on here that were not sharply divided between supporters and opponents of fracking (cf. Wilber 2012: 165–204): one's right to do what one will with one's property increasingly infringes on others' ability to enjoy their own property or common-pool resources, and norms of neighborliness give way to legal doctrine. In some instances, residents tried—but largely failed—to make

9. The couple signed a nondisclosure agreement with the gas company upon being compensated for damages to their chimney and the foundation of their house.

10. Whether or not fracking is an economic "game changer" for communities that host it is debatable. Although Pennsylvania's gas "boom" peaked between 2011 and 2012, the state's unemployment rate remained 7.9 percent (almost identical to the national average), even though the unemployment rate fell in forty-three states in that time (Bureau of Labor Statistics 2015).

fracking compatible with customary ways of life. For example, it was common for landowners to collectively bargain as a single unit with gas companies so that all might be enriched together. Although this did ensure that stakeholders received commensurate leasing bonuses, only a fraction of lessors in any given unit were selected to host the natural gas infrastructure that generates continuous royalties; while their neighbors absorbed the spillover effects of that infrastructure, they did not share in the proceeds. Interestingly, some residents vexed by these disparities directed their animus mostly toward their neighbors rather than at gas companies. Perhaps since fracking is premised on voluntary leasing, these residents blamed unequal outcomes not on systemic factors but on their peers' actions.

Ironically, residents experienced insults to their sovereignty not only from others' leases but also from their *own* leases. George Hagemeyer of Trout Run, a retired custodian, hosted six gas wells on his beloved seventy-seven-acre property—mostly a grass field that he mowed religiously—which he inherited from his father. He reported at the outset that he was "thrilled" about having leased; however, over time he experienced a string of unforeseen indignities that challenged his control over his own backyard. First, the gas company placed a security guard shack and a portable toilet, along with nine warning signs, at the entrance of his unadorned gravel driveway. Then big rigs veered onto his grass. After fracking was completed, the gas company installed a security camera on the well pad and said he would be arrested if he went on it ("Arrested on my own property? I dare them!"). And it began using the pad as a parking lot. Hagemeyer said he learned about the gas company's plan to install a large radio tower in his yard from his sister, who happened to be at the township supervisors' meeting where the permit was approved, and he found out by reading a public notice in the *Williamsport Sun-Gazette* that the gas company had applied for a permit to withdraw up to 3 million gallons of water per day from his property.[11] But the clincher for him was when a guard reportedly stepped in front of his car with a stop sign one day and said he could not proceed to his house because they were moving heavy equipment. "This land is *mine*," Hagemeyer seethed, "and just because they've got a lease doesn't mean they can do anything they want."

But the truth was that Hagemeyer's lease—which had been "flipped" several times—allowed the company holding it to do most of those things. Even as Hagemeyer bought an SUV and started renovating his kitchen with the proceeds, he

11. "Notice is hereby given that on July 8, 2015, Anadarko E&P Onshore LLC has filed a Notice of Intent . . . with the Susquehanna River Basin Commission (SRBC) seeking approval . . . for the consumptive use of water for drilling and development of natural gas well(s) on the George E. Hagemeyer Pad" (*Williamsport Sun-Gazette* 2015).

lamented: "I wish I had never leased. What would my daddy say if he saw the way they use his land?" Even if hyperbolic (on other occasions Hagemeyer expressed more enthusiasm for leasing), the essence of Hagemeyer's lament was that he had become alienated from his property; he was no longer king of his humble fiefdom. What he and other lessors seemingly failed to realize was the extent to which the "guests" they invited onto their premises have the run of the place—in effect, lessors became tenants on their own property.

This Land Is Our Land?

Some recreationists reported a similar loss of liberty and feeling of alienation from land that once felt like their own upon returning to their favorite hiking trails and swimming holes after shale gas extraction had commenced in Pennsylvania's state forests and game lands. Since 2008, the governor's office has leased 138,866 acres of this "truly priceless public asset" (DCNR 2015) for shale gas development, bringing in $413 million in revenue. In all, approximately 700,000 acres of state forest are "available" for natural gas development—though the state has little say in and draws no rents from 290,000 of those acres because they are governed by private leases where the commonwealth does not own the subsurface rights.[12] The Department of Conservation and Natural Resources (DCNR 2015), which manages the state's 2.2 million acres of forests, has approved 232 well pads (each capable of hosting up to twenty-four wells) and 1,020 shale gas wells since 2008.

Many portions of public land now managed by the DCNR actually have a long history of resource extraction. Edwin Drake drilled the first oil well near Titusville in 1859, around the time that the Williamsport area was known as the "lumber capital of the world." Moreover, subterranean "orphan wells" and abandoned mine shafts are evidence of the state's legacy of gas and coal mining. Yet most mining operations were shuttered decades ago because they were small-scale and inefficient, and the lumber industry collapsed before the turn of the twentieth century. Since then, millions of acres of second-growth woodlands have swallowed up almost all traces of this extractive history and have been turned into protected public commons that collectively "represent one of the largest expanses of wildland in the eastern United States" (ibid.).

While the DCNR maintains that it is committed to the "environmentally sound

12. Mineral rights trump surface rights in Pennsylvania; thus the surface owner must allow subsurface access if someone else holds the mineral rights. This is referred to as "severed rights" or "split estate."

utilization of forest resources," it is hard to visit state forests under development like Tiadaghton and not see how shale gas extraction is at odds with the DCNR's efforts to retain their "wild character and . . . biological diversity" (ibid.). Tiadaghton is one of eight state parks designated as the Pennsylvania Wilds (2015), which are promoted as "home of the most spectacular, untouched and undisturbed wild lands east of the Mississippi." However, with over 51,000 of the forest's 146,539 acres leased for drilling, it is impossible to drive, walk, hunt, camp, or fish in the area without encountering industry.

As Jeffrey Prowant, the Tiadaghton district forester, eased his government-issued SUV onto a forest access road one spring morning in 2013, the bustle of the highway instantly gave way to a thick canopy of trees and a babbling brook. But in short order a caravan of water trucks with flashing warning lights forced Prowant to pull over to the side of the recently widened gravel road because they were kicking up so much dust. Helicopters buzzed low overhead, delivering equipment to mountaintop gas workers, and portable toilets and mounds of gravel occasionally appeared amid the foliage. Upon reaching a bend in the road where a 125-foot-wide grassy pipeline right-of-way coming down the mountainside intersected with a four-acre gravel well pad and a twelve-acre water impoundment pond surrounded by wire fencing, Prowant pulled over and remarked: "Prior to this, there was no—this was all forest. It was just unbroken forest." Pointing to a gravel road clogged with trucks hauling water and sand, he recalled: "There was no road. There was no pipeline" (fig. 8). After the security guard nodded at him and lifted the gate that controlled access to the gravel road, Prowant inched up the mountain. Pointing to a large well pad with some big rigs parked on it, he complained: "They don't have any other place to put 'em. But we're not a parking lot. We're trying to reduce the size of the pad, rehabilitate it, to some extent." He continued: "My feeling is, if they had to come back in ten years and do something, and they have a rehabilitated site, we got ten years of value for wildlife or some other [ecological] aspect." Yet he had seen no rehabilitation.

Figure 8 Pipeline right-of-way in Tiadaghton State Forest, PA. Photograph by Nina Berman

Between 2008 and 2012, shale gas extraction in Tiadaghton resulted in over 12 miles of new road construction and 44 miles of road modification (i.e., widening);

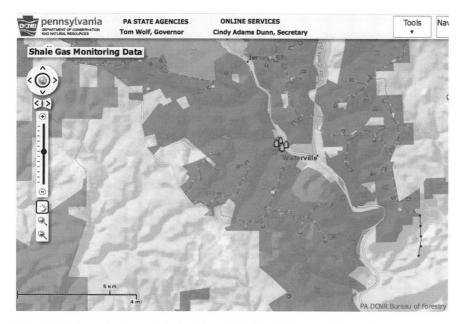

Figure 9 Shale gas development in Tiadaghton State Forest. The areas in blue are leased for drilling; the red lines are gas gathering lines (pipelines); the red dots are well pads. Map courtesy of DCNR

52 miles (or 144 acres) of gas pipeline right-of-ways (which equals .23 miles of pipeline for every square mile of forest); and 318 acres cleared for fifty-one well pads, three compressor stations, and twelve water impoundments (DCNR 2014). This equals the loss of over 586 acres of "core forest" (forested areas surrounded by more forest)—a reduction of as much as 10 percent within the leased portion of the Tiadaghton (fig. 9). This degree of forest fragmentation worried Prowant, and worries ecologists, because it created over 1,800 acres of "edge forests" that can attract invasive species, degrade the ecosystem services provided by core forests, increase riparian erosion and stream sedimentation, and drive out endangered plants and animals that only thrive in core forest (ibid.).[13]

Few would disagree that the "wild character" of the Tiadaghton "has been impacted" (ibid.) by shale gas extraction. Hikers of the Mid-State Trail, which traverses the entire length of Pennsylvania, now encounter well pads and must

13. Relatedly, the gas industry advocated the controversial Endangered Species Coordination Act, which would limit the ability of Pennsylvania state agencies to designate endangered species.

look out for gas trucks as they cross wide access roads. Mountaintop vistas of the meandering Pine Valley Creek are peppered with drilling rigs and the scars of pipeline clearances and well pads; the sounds of the birds and the rustling of the leaves are routinely drowned out by the clamoring of fracking operations; pine scent mingles with the pungent odor of diesel; and so on. But fracking operations take away more than the sensory experience of the wilderness. In some cases, they impede Pennsylvanians' ability to access their forests. In Tiadaghton, gas drilling necessitated the long-term closure of two public-access roads, including one that led to a popular vista. On a shorter-term basis, seventeen roads totaling over fifty-seven miles were closed to facilitate shale gas development (ibid.). While Prowant was adamant that "unless there's active drilling or some kind of active construction" gas companies could not impede public access even on well pads themselves, gas companies routinely policed people who encroached on their operations. Prowant was himself stopped as he stood in the woods next to a well pad while Colin Jerolmack took pictures. A security guard shouted: "Excuse me! This is XTO property! You must leave, and you cannot take pictures!" When Prowant replied that it was public property and that she could not stop anyone from walking in the woods or taking pictures, she demanded identification. It was only upon realizing that Prowant was the district forester that the guard sheepishly desisted, and she reported that her boss told her to write down the license plate number of any car that drove past and to disallow passengers from getting out of their cars.

Portions of the Tiadaghton have in effect become privatized, and an entire security apparatus has emerged to regulate access to land that is legally part of the commons and is a place where people have historically gone to escape the hassles of civilization and the scrutiny of others. Hunters, anglers, picnickers, campers, cyclists, and snowmobilers—anyone who visits "their" forest for recreation—can expect to find public-access roads inexplicably (and sometimes illegally) closed, to be recorded by surveillance cameras in places that are so remote they lack cell phone reception, to have to show identification and explain their presence to guards who determine whether or not they are allowed to proceed, to encounter fenced-off areas and signs that warn them (sometimes incorrectly) that they are trespassing, and to be chased off of areas (again, illegally) adjacent to gas installations. Indeed, Jerolmack experienced all of the above in the course of his ethnographic research.

With over 34 million acres of federal public land currently leased by oil and gas companies (Bureau of Land Management 2014), the industrialization and de facto privatization of large swaths of the Tiadaghton is a forewarning. If replicated

nationally, it could result in significant environmental degradation and enclosure of portions of America's most ecologically significant—and majestic—commons (fig. 10). In this way, even those of us not residing amid fracking operations may absorb the spillover effects from the government's decision to lease and develop (ostensibly) public land. As well, the tragedy of the commons engendered by private oil and gas leasing in rural communities works directly against the kind of collectivist politics needed to prevent our planet from lapsing into abrupt and irreversible climate change. This should be kept in mind when considering the role of fracking in mitigating global warming and moving us toward sustainability. For shale gas extraction to be "sustainable," it must do more than burn "cleaner" than coal: it should foster the resilience of common-pool resources *and* the communities that host it.

Figure 10 Water impoundment pond in Tiadaghton State Forest, PA. Photograph by Nina Berman

References

Anderson, Richard. 2014. "How American Energy Independence Could Change the World." BBC, April 3. www.bbc.com/news/business-23151813.

Bamberger, Michelle, and Robert E. Oswald. 2012. "Impacts of Gas Drilling on Human and Animal Health." *New Solutions* 22, no. 1: 51–77.

Berman, Nina. 2011. "'They Are Afraid Their House Could Blow Up': Meet the Families Whose Lives Have Been Ruined by Gas Drilling." Alternet, April 11.

Brandt, Adam R., et al. 2014. "Methane Leaks from North American Natural Gas Systems." *Science* 343, no. 6172: 733–35.

Broderick, John, and Kevin Anderson. 2012. "Has US Shale Gas Reduced CO_2 Emissions?" Working paper, Tyndall Manchester Climate Change Research Centre, Manchester, UK. www.tyndall.ac.uk/sites/default/files/broderick _and_anderson_2012_impact_of_shale_gas_on_us_energy_and_emissions .pdf.

Bureau of Labor Statistics. 2015. "Unemployment Rate for States." www.bls.gov/lau /lastrk12.htm (accessed November 9, 2015).

Bureau of Land Management. 2014. "Oil and Gas Statistics." www.blm.gov/wo/st /en/prog/energy/oil_and_gas/statistics.html.

Darrah, Thomas H., et al. 2014. "Noble Gases Identify the Mechanisms of Fugitive Gas Contamination in Drinking Water Wells Overlying the Marcellus and Barnett Shales." *Proceedings of the National Academy of Sciences* 111, no. 39: 14076–80.

DCNR (Department of Conservation and Natural Resources). 2014. "Shale Gas Monitoring Report." www.dcnr.state.pa.us/forestry/NaturalGas/monitoringreport /index.htm.

———. 2015. "Natural Gas Drilling on State Forests." www.dcnr.state.pa.us /forestry/stateforestmanagement/index.htm (accessed June 14, 2015).

Dernbach, John C., and James May. 2015. "Can Shale Gas Help Accelerate the Transition to Sustainability?" *Environment: Science and Policy for Sustainable Development* 57, no. 1: 1–15.

Ellickson, Robert C. 1991. *Order without Law: How Neighbors Settle Disputes.* Cambridge, MA: Harvard University Press.

Energy Information Administration. 2014. "How Much Carbon Dioxide Is Produced When Different Fuels Are Burned?" June 4. www.eia.gov/tools/faqs/faq .cfm?id=73&t=11.

EPA (Environmental Protection Agency). 2015. "Assessment of the Potential Impacts of Hydraulic Fracturing for Oil and Gas on Drinking Water Resources." EPA/600/R-15/047. Washington, DC: EPA.

Erikson, Kai. 1976. *Everything in Its Path: Destruction of Community in the Buffalo Creek Flood*. New York: Touchstone.

Gold, Russell. 2014. *The Boom: How Fracking Ignited the American Energy Revolution and Changed the World*. New York: Simon and Schuster.

Hardin, Garrett. 1968. "The Tragedy of the Commons." *Science* 162, no. 3859: 1243–48.

"'Heavy Fraffic' from the Documentary *Groundswell: Protecting Our Children's Water*." 2011. YouTube video, 2:45. Uploaded August 4. www.youtube.com /watch?v=KZZQxe6FiGA.

Helman, Christopher. 2015. "Itemizing the Oil Bust: Seventy-Five Thousand Layoffs and Counting." *Forbes*, March 16. www.forbes.com/sites/christopherhelman /2015/03/16/oil-layoffs-itemized-75000-and-counting.

Hill, Elaine. 2014. "Three Essays on the Impacts of Unconventional Drilling on Early Life Health." PhD diss., Cornell University.

McGraw, Seamus. 2012. *The End of Country: Dispatches from the Frack Zone*. New York: Random House.

McKenzie, Lisa M., et al. 2012. "Human Health Risk Assessment of Air Emissions from Development of Unconventional Natural Gas Resources." *Science of the Total Environment* 424: 79–87.

Pennsylvania Wilds. 2015. *Regional Visitors Guide*. pawilds.com/fileadmin/site content/PA_Wilds/Brochures/PAWilds_VG_brochure.pdf.

Perry, Simona. 2012. "Development, Land Use, and Collective Trauma: The Marcellus Shale Gas Boom in Rural Pennsylvania." *Culture, Agriculture, Food and the Environment* 34, no. 1: 81–92.

Phillips, Susan. 2012. "Chesapeake to Pay $1.6 Million for Contaminating Water Wells in Bradford County." StateImpact, June 21. stateimpact.npr.org/penn sylvania/2012/06/21/chesapeake-to-pay-1-6-million-for-contaminating-water -wells-in-bradford-county.

StateImpact 2015a. "Well: Harman Lewis Unit 1H." stateimpact.npr.org/pennsyl vania/drilling/wells/081-20292 (accessed June 1, 2015).

———. 2015b. "Well: Welles 1 3H." stateimpact.npr.org/pennsylvania/drilling /wells/015-20244 (accessed June 1, 2015).

Vasi, Ion Bogdan, et al. 2015. "'No Fracking Way!' Documentary Film, Discursive Opportunity, and Local Opposition against Hydraulic Fracturing in the United States, 2010 to 2013." *American Sociological Review* 80, no. 5: 934–59.

Vengosh, Avner, et al. 2014. "A Critical Review of the Risks to Water Resources from Unconventional Shale Gas Development and Hydraulic Fracturing in the United States." *Environmental Science and Technology* 48, no. 15: 8334–48.

Wilber, Tom. 2012. *Under the Surface: Fracking, Fortunes, and the Fate of Marcellus Shale.* Ithaca, NY: Cornell University Press.

Williamsport Sun-Gazette. 2015. "Public Notices." July 11.

Colin Jerolmack is an associate professor of sociology and environmental studies at New York University. He is currently writing a book about the impact of fracking on rural community life and is the author of *The Global Pigeon* (2013).

Nina Berman is a documentary photographer and associate professor in the Columbia University Graduate School of Journalism. She is the author of two monographs: *Purple Hearts — Back from Iraq* (2004) and *Homeland* (2008), which examine the aftermath of war and the militarization of American life. Her work has been exhibited at more than one hundred international venues, including the Whitney Museum of American Art 2010 Biennial.

Aeolian Extractivism and Community Wind in Southern Mexico

Cymene Howe and Dominic Boyer

Inaugurations

The October 2012 inauguration of the Piedra Larga wind park in Oaxaca's Isthmus of Tehuantepec was the last of President Felipe Calderón's many wind park ribbon-cutting ceremonies. When he served as Mexico's secretary of energy in 2003–4, Calderón helped to accelerate his country's commitment to wind energy. As he ended his presidential term, wind power counted for almost twenty-three hundred kilotons of carbon dioxide reduction in Mexico annually. Calderón's speech on that day was neither triumphant nor a swan song; instead, it pivoted between hope and precarity (fig. 1). He began with droughts, some of the most severe ever seen in Mexico and, to the north, in Texas. "This is climate change," he said to his audience of several hundred seated in front of him. "Carbon dioxide is like a sweater surrounding the earth," heating the ocean's waters and making for differently distributed weather. "However," he went on, "we cannot stop using electricity or building factories. Instead, we need to make electricity with less smoke. We need to reduce emissions." And here, in the heart of the isthmus, is where much of this effort is already taking place. In 2008 the region had two wind parks producing 84.9 megawatts of wind-generated electricity; four years later there were fifteen parks producing over 1,300 megawatts, a

The authors extend their profound appreciation to those who took time out of their lives to share with us their knowledge regarding renewable energy, wind power, and the political conditions of possibility as we endeavored to understand an evolving set of projects to avert further climatological harm. This research was made possible by a grant provided by the National Science Foundation (#1127246). We also wish to thank Eric Klinenberg and Stephen Twilley for their editorial stewardship, as well as the anonymous reviewers for *Public Culture* whose reflections sharpened this paper. Finally, for her careful bibliographic skills and editorial work on this essay, we thank Brijzha Boyer.

All translations from Spanish to English contained in this article are by the authors.

Public Culture 28:2   DOI 10.1215/08992363-3427427

1,467 percent increase that has made Mexico the second-largest wind power producer in Latin America (see GWEC 2016: 38, 53). Today the Isthmus of Tehuantepec represents the densest concentration of onshore wind development anywhere in the world.

New domestic conservation and sustainability legislation is rising across the world, and in 2012 developing countries passed twice as many environmental laws as wealthy nation-states did (*Economist* 2013). Suffering the effects of a changing climate, and facing diminishing oil reserves, Mexico has been both pulled and pushed toward adopting ambitious and comprehensive climate legislation that many experts consider groundbreaking (World Bank 2013). Thirty-five percent of Mexico's energy is legally mandated to come from clean sources by 2024, with 50 percent of that currently slated to come from wind power alone (GWEC 2015: 12). With incentives to develop renewable energy, the creation of a voluntary carbon market, a phaseout of fossil fuel subsidies, and a mandate that the largest carbon pollution sectors report their emissions, Mexico's climate laws are among the most extensive in the developing world. In 2012, before leaving office, Calderón signed the General Law on Climate Change, which formalized targets set in previous legislation, instituted a high-level climate change commission and national emissions registry, inaugurated the National Institute of

Ecology and Climate Change, and coordinated federal offices to develop holistic mitigation and adaptation planning.

The effects of climate change are being acutely felt in Mexico, often in locations where economic and labor prospects are already sparse, leaving rural and agrarian populations doubly vulnerable (Eakin 2006). Mexico's climate legislation and the growth of renewable energy infrastructures are initiatives for both mitigation and adaptation: securing an adaptive energy future through the forces of wind, solar, and hydroelectric power and mitigating the contaminative, warming effects of carbon loading the atmosphere. Accelerating renewable energy development is indicative of a growing awareness within Mexico's political and economic sectors that adaptation to changing weather and water conditions is crucial and that renewable resources, if usefully tapped, will not only result in less carbon contamination and green power but also further enhance the country's reputation as a leader in climate adaptation and mitigation in the developing world (Howe and Boyer 2015).

Aeolian Extractivism?

In an era increasingly defined by a troubled climate, and in which anthropogenic forces have an impact on our bio-, litho-, aqua-, and atmospheres in unprecedented ways (Crutzen and Stoermer 2000), we necessarily situate our case study within a wider context of global climate conditions, energy transition, and debates surrounding mitigation and adaptation. The transition from carbon fuels to cleaner energy forms is widely regarded as one of the most pressing environmental and social challenges facing humanity and other planetary life in the twenty-first century. However, it remains unclear how these goals can be achieved, especially given the proliferation of neoliberal economic and social policies across the world in the past three decades, policies that, in Mexico as elsewhere, openly question the legitimacy and effectiveness of state-led programs of development. We thus take Mexico as a critical, paradigmatic case. The Mexican government has produced unusually aggressive legislation to address climate change and support energy transition, and yet these projects remain susceptible to internal and external forces beyond the government's control, ranging from transnational investors' desire for profit to indigenous landowners' concerns about a "second conquest" that will deprive them of their land and livelihood. We wish to underscore that the commitment Mexico has made to climate remediation is laudable, especially given that the country was never compelled to do so by any international protocol. In their ambitious plan to address climate harm, however, Mexican officials and industry leaders have largely failed to link sustainable energy to more robust benefits for local populations, many of them living on the margins of the state and in places where the wind blows the fiercest. In this article, we find not only that there is "more to be done" in the reduction of carbon emissions but also that how that "more" is undertaken is of critical importance. Our core argument is that we cannot fail to use energy transitions as opportunities to rethink dominant political, economic, and social institutions. To ignore this dimension is to imperil our ability to dislodge carbon's dominion and the many inequalities that carbon modernity helped to cement between the global North and South and between metropoles and resource-rich hinterlands.

While the extractivist orientation of petropolitics has been well documented (see, e.g., Appel, Mason, and Watts 2015; Kashi 2008; Sawyer 2004; Sawyer and Gomez 2012), the politics of renewable energy remain relatively nascent. Sustainable energy projects have the potential to imitate the political and institutional logics informed by coal, oil, and gas (Mitchell 2011), or they might pursue different trajectories altogether. In many places in Latin America, including Mexico, efforts to address climate change must be understood against a backdrop of enduring economic and political marginalization, making low-carbon energy transition all the more precarious (Davis 2010; Giddens 2009; Howe 2015). Just as colonial and foreign corporate "extractivism" (Bebbington 2009; Gudynas 2009) has benefited affluent patrons and regions at the expense of others, we see a real danger that "green capitalist" renewable energy initiatives will emerge as new modes of resource exploitation legitimized by the urgency of climate change mitigation.

In our research we found that large-scale renewable energy projects in southern Mexico tended to prioritize the interests of international investors and federal officials over local concerns about cultural and environmental impact (see also Gómez Martínez 2005). Renewable energy projects that follow the same extractive frameworks that defined colonial and carbon modernity (Mitchell 2011) could very well result in backlashes against sustainable forms of energy production (Howe, Boyer, and Barrera 2015). This would only further stall low-carbon energy transition and climate mitigation, a result that the planet can ill afford. Failure to rethink an extractive model of energy production could likewise result in deepening geopolitical inequalities and lead, possibly, to a form of climatological imperialism in which the global South is tasked with rehabilitating the (much more historically contaminative) global North. Given these challenges, we suggest that Mexico faces a fundamental paradox in its transition to renewable energy: while the state and renewable power companies have initiated a potentially powerful intervention into climate mitigation and adaptation, if they fail to fully involve local populations and account for an ongoing legacy of exploitation, they risk undermining the positive contributions that low-carbon initiatives seek. The success of renewable energy transition in Mexico and elsewhere, we believe, will depend not only on technical and economic solutions for supplanting carbon energy use but also on whether new energy projects can be enacted more equitably and with greater attention to local resource sovereignty (McNeish and Logan 2012) than has been the case with fossil fuels. We offer in this essay a detailed case study of one such effort toward changing the paradigm of renewable energy development: the plan to build a community-owned wind park near the town of Ixtepec in the state of Oaxaca, Mexico.

The research we discuss here draws upon sixteen months of collaborative ethnographic fieldwork and approximately two hundred interviews with landowners, workers, fisherfolk, and activists in the Isthmus of Tehuantepec, as well as with municipal, state, and federal government officials, representatives of renewable energy corporations, development bankers, and financiers in the state capital of Oaxaca City and the nation's capital, Mexico City. In our study we draw upon local knowledge and local concerns to call attention to the dangers of allowing— whether in the name of urgency, expediency, or inevitability—renewable energy development to repeat the inequalities and translocal bias of carbon energy extractivism. Our project has focused on charting and analyzing the relationships among all stakeholders in wind power development in Oaxaca, and we have found that while *istmeños* are often referred to as "partners" (*socios*) in energy and climate change discourses among government officials and corporate representatives, oftentimes "partnership" amounts to local elites receiving land rents for a fraction of what similar rents might look like in the United States. Ambivalence regarding the local benefits of wind power has spread across the isthmus in recent years, in some cases leading to violence. In one dramatic case, a plan to build the largest (396 megawatts) wind park in Latin America collapsed after months of protests and a series of death threats (Howe, Boyer, and Barrera 2015). It is too early to speak of a "wind curse" parallel to the oft-cited "oil curses." But doubts are growing that wind development is anything more than another extractive enterprise foisted upon *istmeños* by northern elites. To rebalance the benefits afforded the windy isthmus, the community of Ixtepec is now trying to create the first community-owned wind park in Latin America. But, as we describe in some detail below, whether it will ever be permitted to exist remains an open question.

The first step toward understanding the tensions that surround the bid for community wind in Oaxaca is to analyze the foundational technopolitical instrument of Mexico's renewable turn: the policy regime of *autoabastecimiento* (self-supply).

Autoabastecimiento

In Mexico, there is only one way to receive electricity, and that is through the grid of the Federal Electricity Commission (Comisión Federal de Electricidad, or CFE). A parastatal corporation that holds a monopoly over the country's current, the CFE is tasked with supplying electricity to the entire nation, from lower-income residents (whose bills are subsidized) to commercial customers (who pay relatively high rates for their power). According to the director of the Energy Regulatory Commission (Comisión Reguladora de Energía, or CRE), which oversees the national energy sector, there are two distinct drivers of renewable energy in Mexico: the high (commercial) cost of electricity and the country's exceptional solar, wind, and hydroelectric resources. The CFE is required by law to buy the least expensive power available for its customers. Thus when the federal government considers the construction of a new power plant, a public tender is called by the CFE, and the winner is determined based on cost per megawatt hour offered. Effectively, renewable energy projects must compete against conventional energy sources on the basis of price, a difficult proposition given the relatively low market cost of fossil fuels.

To encourage private investors to develop electricity production from renewable sources, the CRE created different formulas in lieu of participation in the general tenders. Space in the substations was cordoned off for wind, and, in turn, private-sector developers and the CFE were allowed to enter into temporary public-private partnerships for the sole purpose of developing new high-capacity transmission infrastructure. Rather than invest directly in the development of wind parks, the CRE elected to allow the sector to be fully privatized. It saw this as a mandate of efficiency, insisting that private companies had better expertise to make optimal use of wind resources. However, more pointedly, the decision to pursue private models of renewable energy development is steeped in Mexico's neoliberal economic model that has dominated the country since the 1980s (Gledhill 1995; Ochoa 2001). Renewable energy, like other neoliberal ventures, makes states and populations vulnerable to the influence of corporate and capitalist interests in search of profit maximization rather than environmental or social benefits.

It is in this legislative, sociotechnical, and financial environment that Mexico's secretary of energy and other state-level officials promoted and instituted a model of self-supply energy production for the wind resources of the isthmus. Corporate self-supply, or *autoabastecimiento*, requires that the companies that purchase wind park electricity—such as Walmart, Coca-Cola, and CEMEX—are also co-owners of wind power plants. Companies buy power at a locked-in, lower-than-market rate, usually for a period of twenty years. The infrastructural advantage of *autoabastecimiento* is that the CFE is able to auction off space in substations and, often, to oblige wind park developers to augment or build the required technical extensions and infrastructural systems that carry electrons from place to place. *Autoabastecimiento* now rules the Isthmus of Tehuantepec, constituting about 75 percent of wind power development in the region. As a form of energy management and financing, it has led to at least three outcomes: it has ensured the dominance of private-sector ownership of Oaxacan wind power production; it has all but guaranteed that renewable electricity will be consumed solely by corporate partners; and it has compelled private developers and investors to augment electricity infrastructure that the state is not willing, or able, to subsidize.

In a twist on the neoliberal model, the Mexican government has obligated private companies to pay for infrastructural improvements usually undertaken by the state; if wind energy corporations want to get their power to the grid, in other words, they must finance that grid. The director of the CRE was very proud—as he repeated several times during our interview—that "Mexico, unlike the gringos, has no state subsidies for renewable energy." Instead, private energy companies are forced to take up the infrastructural slack. As one Mexico City journalist who has covered the energy sector for many years explained to us: "The [renewable energy companies] feel like they are getting a shitty deal from CFE. CFE makes them pay for their own transmission towers and for the substation . . . they aren't making much on these projects. But then again where else are you going to find this kind of wind?"

That wind, of course, blows over land. The state of Oaxaca, considered by many to be the indigenous "heart" of Mexico, is equally well known for its communal property regimes that date back to the Mexican Revolution (see Binford 1985). Although the federal government retains ownership, *ejido* (collectively managed land) and *bienes comunales* (communal property) are agrarian land designations that grant stewardship to specific groups of individuals. Providing resources to landless peasants (in the case of *ejidos*) and with the intention to preserve indigenous peoples' rights to their traditional lands (in the case of *bienes comunales*), each property regime was instituted to ensure the continuation of customary law (*usos y costumbres*) and pre-Hispanic forms of leadership as well as collective governance. In the isthmus both models were widely used through the 1980s, although several *ejidos* were semiprivatized through the Program for the Certification of Ejido Land Rights and the Titling of Urban House Plots (Programa de Certificación de Derechos Ejidales y Titulación de Solares Urbanos, or PROCEDE), a 1992 legal provision that certified land titles and registered individual landholders. The North American Free Trade Agreement (NAFTA), the Agrarian Law Reform, and PROCEDE, coupled with the 1992 Electric Energy Public Service Law, allowed local landholders to individually contract land with private interests (such as wind power developers) and gave private-sector companies the ability to participate in electric power generation.

Despite widespread privatization, some of the best land for wind development in Oaxaca continues to be maintained as communal property. While some *ejidos* have elected to adopt neoliberal land reforms and have signed private contracts with wind companies, others have refused. Although much of the resistance has been to wind power in general, the *comuna* (communal farmers) of Ixtepec has uniquely pursued an alternative "energopolitical" path (Boyer 2014).[1] The Ixtepec *comuna* has embraced the idea of wind development, but only as a community-owned endeavor, an unprecedented proposition in the *autoabastecimiento* heart-land. Partnering with a nongovernmental organization (NGO), Yansa, the *comuna* has articulated an ambitious plan to change wind power not only in Mexico but also across the developing world. In the sections that follow we offer a more detailed ethnography of this plan, the key characters involved in its formation, and the challenges they have faced in implementing it in the context of the *auto-abastecimiento* policy regime.

"This Isn't Denmark"

We first learned of the Yansa Ixtepec project in the course of background research and quickly sought a meeting with the NGO's founder, Sergio Oceransky. Yansa's model is to link wind power to social development targets in Ixtepec and two nearby villages whose land would also be affected by the wind park. The resources for social development would come from a unique partnership that Yansa had designed to connect the NGO, the *comuna*, development banks, and socially conscious investors (Hoffmann 2012).

Oceransky was born in Spain and became increasingly interested in how renewable energy could be harnessed as a tool for social development when he worked for a renewable energy center in Denmark, where community wind has been widely institutionalized. He had heard through members of his family (his mother is Mexican) about the "wind rush" in Oaxaca as well as the rising resistance to wind park projects. He traveled to Oaxaca in 2008, spoke with residents likely to be affected by wind parks, and then went to Mexico City to meet with the

---

1. *Energopolitics* refers to the ways in which energic forces and fuels shape and compel political power in particular directions (Boyer 2014).

industrial lobbying organization spearheading wind development in Oaxaca, the Mexican Wind Energy Association (Asociación Mexicana de Energía Eólica, or AMDEE). "Nowadays they've got a more polished message," Oceransky grinned. "But back then what I was hearing from them was really outrageous, blunt, even racist. They viewed the communities as villains, ignorant people ruled by local leaders who wanted bribes and were stopping progress. I told the president of AMDEE that in other parts of the world, like Denmark, communities were being engaged more constructively as partners in wind development." Oceransky's comment incited a scowl from the president, and the meeting quickly devolved and ended with a thinly veiled threat: "I don't know what you're going to do with all this information," said the AMDEE representative, "but I'd be careful. This isn't Denmark. Anyone can fall off his horse here."

Oceransky was in no way dissuaded, however. He started traveling frequently from his apartment in Mexico City to the isthmus, connecting with some of the activists working against the wind parks, who in turn had networks in the communities affected. "One of the first things was to try to shift their perspective on wind energy. For a lot of people it had become something evil, it meant giving your land to Spaniards," he explained. But Oceransky saw another potential future that he began to share across the *istmo*. He was convinced that community-owned wind was possible in Mexico, and his message began to gain traction. By chance, one of the activists with whom Oceransky had spoken shared a bus ride with a *comunero* (*comuna* member) from Ixtepec who mentioned that their *comuna* was already trying to convince the CFE to let it build a community wind park. The CFE needed to use Ixtepecan land in order to build a new substation to collect and evacuate wind park electricity to the high-voltage arteries of the national grid. When the CFE presented the *comuna* with its substation plans, some voiced the idea that Ixtepec should get a community wind park in exchange, to raise revenue for the *comuna*. But this proposal was quickly shot down. The CFE determined that the *comuna* would never be able to raise adequate capital for the park, and therefore when the time came to auction access to the Ixtepecan substation, the CFE ignored the *comuna*'s request. However, the idea did not disappear for some members of the *comuna*, or for Oceransky, and they have been collaborating ever since.

The Yansa Ixtepec Model

The basic elements of the Yansa Ixtepec partnership have been organized as follows. The partners would bid for the last two hundred megawatts of access to the Ixtepec substation in a public tender organized by the CFE. Assuming that they won the tender, Yansa would immediately form a community interest company (Yansa Ixtepec Compañía de Interés Comunitario, or Yansa Ixtepec CIC) that would own the wind park and negotiate a land lease agreement with the *comuna*. The estimated cost of building the park, consisting of thirty-four 3-megawatt turbines (production capacity of 102 megawatts total), is US$200 million. Construction funds would be raised through a mix of 70–80 percent development bank funding and 20–30 percent from socially responsible investors. Construction jobs would go to local residents, and, once operational, the park would sell its electricity directly to the CFE under a twenty-year contract. The total estimated annual surplus from the park (after servicing debts and interest payments to banks and investors) was Mex$50 million per year (US$3.81 million).

That surplus would be divided fifty-fifty between Yansa and the *comuna*. Yansa would use its half as seed funding for further community wind park projects elsewhere in the world. The *comuna*'s half would be further divided into approximately Mex$3 million in payments to the campesinos, a pension fund would be established, and the two other affected villages would receive funding for their own development targets. The remaining income (approximately US$1.25 million) would go into a community trust to finance social development. Oceransky saw the trust as a vital aspect of Yansa's work. "We want to make sure the whole community sees the benefits. Not just the old men who have traditionally run the *comuna*." To this end, the trust was designed to have over half the trustee positions held by women and two by youth members. The Yansa model included social interventions that pushed to decentralize traditional and masculine institutions of political authority by placing a portion of governance in the hands of women and youth. These political goals seemed to be uncontroversial; perhaps this was because a sufficient number of younger and female members of *comuna* families supported the initiative, or perhaps it was because it was simply unthinkable to the older *comuneros* that something as insubstantial as a wind park proposal could challenge the deep grooves of traditional institutions and relations of political authority. When the "normal *comuneros*" spoke to us about the wind park, their interest tended to gravitate toward two issues: what kind of work would be available and what kinds of rent payments they would receive.

The question of payments had a double life when it came to the CFE, too. On the one hand, the utility provided rental payments to the *comuna* for transmission lines. On the other hand, it was seen as inordinately tithing isthmus communities for the power that the grid provided. Well-circulated rumors claimed that the CFE charged customers more in the isthmus (although CFE officials in Mexico City denied this vehemently). The very mention of the CFE usually produced scowls and scoffs, since many residents and small business owners found themselves spending excessive amounts of their monthly income on electricity. One man complained to us, for example, that he was forced to shut the little convenience store he ran out of one window of his house because he could not afford refrigeration. Given the tiered pricing system the CFE used, just a few kilowatts more expended each month could push a consumer into a higher payment bracket, meaning that a new kitchen appliance might translate into a substantial difference in one's bill.[2]

That consumers are upset about the cost of electricity is by no means unique to the isthmus. But this frustration was inflected by what was viewed widely as the failure of wind parks to improve electrical access and service locally. Time and again we were told by local residents that they believed that wind parks would bring cheaper, more abundant power to them. But the regime of *autoabastecimiento* was designed only to export electricity from the isthmus to large industrial consumers elsewhere in Mexico. The only local grid enhancements were designed for what the industry describes as "evacuation," while even basic electricity service remained intermittent in more remote parts of the isthmus.

Visionaries

Much of the responsibility of organizing and informing the *comuneros* in support of Yansa Ixtepec fell on the shoulders of Oceransky's two closest allies, Daniel González and Vicente Vásquez, who belonged to the small group of *comuneros* who had been pursuing the possibility of a wind park even before Yansa arrived. The two of them were both retired professionals in their midfifties, both deeply disturbed by the federal government's neglect of Ixtepec and the isthmus, both very animated by issues of social justice and particularly indigenous rights. Each of them hoped to use wind power to change life in Ixtepec, making new opportunities available, especially for youth. Vásquez and González exemplify a certain class of *istmeño*: both educated and dedicated to their homelands. Their passionate work on behalf of Yansa Ixtepec demonstrates that it is not simply global elites, such as Calderón, who are invested in innovating new approaches to renewable power and the future of the planet's climate. Rather, local intellectuals like González and Vásquez are insisting on new collective models of energy generation and climate adaptation. In our conversations with them, as in our conversa-

2. A CFE agent explained, for example, that his home had four people, two televisions, a refrigerator, and one computer, using about five hundred kilowatt hours per month. If they were to go over that number, to 501 kilowatt hours, their bimonthly bill would go from Mex\$900 (US\$75) to Mex\$2,500 (US\$208) because they would lose their subsidy and move up to the next pricing bracket.

tions with Ixtepecan campesinos, questions of jobs and control over land were constant. But the ability to serve as an example to the rest of the world—by establishing the first community-owned wind park in Latin America—was a key motivator as well. Rather than have their communities simply serve as the land upon which foreign experts and capital would innovate, they believed in the potential of Ixtepec and Oaxaca to raise the bar, on a regional and global basis, for more equitable and inclusive projects of climate change mitigation.

Vásquez had spent most of his life working as a chemical engineer for the Mexican parastatal oil company Petróleos Mexicanos, or PEMEX, but returned to Ixtepec after his retirement and found himself depressed by the lack of possibilities for *el pueblo* (the people). He quoted Hermann Hesse and Karl Marx and told us that, more than anything, Ixtepec needed opportunities to thwart the *indolencia* (apathy) of large sections of the population. "What we're always thinking about," Vásquez told us, "is how to generate more opportunity. The plan is to potentialize things. . . . It's the difference between a *chamba* [job] and *trabajo* [work]. When I work, I'm working physically as well as intellectually. When I do a job, I'm doing it mechanically and don't care about the outcome because that makes no difference to me. This park could reach many, many people."

For González, it was as much a matter of reckoning with pasts as imagining alternative futures. González was the grandson of a rancher and a farmer; he fondly recalled visiting his grandfather's lands as a child. González spoke Zapotec in his youth even though for almost all of his professional life he worked in Spanish. He was teaching his grandson Zapotec now, taking him out to places around the isthmus where Zapotec was still the primary spoken language. González saw the wind park as a means of demonstrating how an indigenous community could become organized and collaborate directly with an NGO to take control of its future. The project was an avenue toward improved roads, reliable sources of water, educational opportunities for young people, pensions for the aged, and an opportunity for people to find real, meaningful work: *trabajo*, not *chambas*.

Although González was always quick to laugh, the undermining of indigenous rights in Mexico deeply troubled him. As a working attorney, he understood the *núcleos agrarios* (agrarian collectives) that formed *bienes comunales*, like the Ixtepecan *asamblea* (assembly), as having inalienable entitlement to their land. This was, for him, more than a moral claim, it was a matter of law. He acknowledged the privatization that occurred among *ejidos* following PROCEDE, but he drew a sharp distinction between *ejidos*, as social forms of the Mexican Revolution, and *comunidades de bienes comunales* (collective property communities), which were established to ensure that descendants of the first peoples of the Americas would maintain their traditional lands (see Kelly et al. 2010; also Cornelius and Myhre 1998; Haenn 2006). "*Ejidos* can now elect to privatize themselves," he explained, "but not, as a matter of law, *comunidades*." González understood that this was a controversial claim, since it involved an interpretation of the Mexican Constitution in which the rights of indigenous communities superseded those of the mestizo nation. His was, needless to say, not the dominant constitutional interpretation communicated to us by corporate participants in wind development in the isthmus who had devised somewhat suspect contracts with *bienes comunales*, only to later encounter strife and resistance. When González spoke of the significance of the Yansa Ixtepec partnership, he was very clear: "No [other] wind company anywhere in the world would offer their expertise in exchange for our land and share every peso equally. None."

Somos Paleros

In late September 2012, the possibility of sharing every peso equally came in danger of disappearing. We attended a long and complex *comuna* meeting in Ixtepec, and those gathered were tired, distracted, and cranky by the time Oceransky announced the bad news: the CFE had excluded them from even competing for access to the substation that lay *on their own land*. He described how the CFE had already given away the rest of the access to six foreign companies ("four of them Spanish") and was demanding US$7 million up front and Mex$548 million in the bank to participate in the competition. And the CFE wanted the tender winner to also pay to prepare the land for a new wind park nearby. Oceransky charged that the CFE was acting illegally and, moreover, violating its own norms. After hearing the litany of abuses, several *comuneros* called out, "¡Hay que demandarlos!" ("We have to sue them!"). The crowd stirred further as they discussed some of the forms of collective legal action that could be taken, including *amparo* (injunction), a unique provision of Mexican law that allows individuals and groups to seek protection from unconstitutional abuses of the government. "¡Lo vamos a hacer!" ("Let's do it!"), someone finally shouted.

A man named Isaias then stood up and asked permission to speak. Hardly pausing, he launched into a partly handwritten, partly improvised, thoroughly firebrand manifesto criticizing the authorities of the CFE, the government, and politicians of all levels, as "*antipatrióticos*" (sell-outs, traitors) doing dirty business with foreigners, heaping abuses on the peoples of the isthmus. Here is a taste of it:

> The Mexican government doesn't follow or recognize the international treaties because the *gachupines* [Spaniards] are giving them money

hand over fist, starting with the secretary of the interior, who gives them concessions, permission, and authorizations that streamline the whole process. They jump as quickly as the Spaniards want them to. They're mad, because they've come to loot us, and we've taken the time we need as a community to analyze our situation. Nowadays governments are used by violent capital that buy the wills of authorities who then threaten or do not hear what the *compañeros* [community, lit. comrades] tell them about their needs. They assault, deceive, and corrupt the people. These projects mean the dispossession and destruction of our environment, flora and fauna, all with the complicity of the federal government and the municipalities too.

Isaias switched into Zapotec, shouting, "We won't be misled mules, each animal running in its own direction," provoking widespread laughter, whoops, and hollers of recognition: "¡Palero! ¡Palero! ¡Somos paleros!" ("Leader! Leader! We are leaders!"). And, finally, bringing it home, he offered a proposal: "Either we have a community wind park here or no park at all."

The hatred of the CFE runs deep throughout the isthmus. As elsewhere, so many of the desired conveniences of modern life (artificial light, televisions, airconditioning) make people dependent on those who provide electricity. Understanding the depth of negative affect requires thinking in terms of the clientelist political and economic relations that still predominate in this part of Mexico. In the logic of *caciquismo*, or "boss politics," for example, one could at least expect some top-down redistribution of resources if one worked loyally for the *cacique*'s network (Knight and Pansters 2006). The political party networks, too, offer ways of translating the available power of labor into comparatively scarce currency. But the CFE only exchanged electricity for currency. It only accepted the form of value that was already in such short supply. The CFE was thus a deceiver, we heard again and again. It brought light, promising progress, mobility, and modernity, and then made that progress contingent upon further impoverishment, blacking out dreams, further condemning the people to hopeless marginality.

Squatter Grid

González, Oceransky, and others in the *asamblea* had begun planning legal strategy long before the CFE actually turned them away. We accompanied González and Oceransky to Oaxaca City to consult with an indigenous law specialist at the Oaxacan Ministry for Indigenous Affairs, where various legal scenarios were charted, assessed, erased, and rethought. In the end, the legal adviser was convinced that a complaint focused on being denied access to infrastructure was weaker than one focused on the subversion of residents' constitutional right to use their land the way they saw fit. An *amparo* was the right strategy, he assured everyone at the table: "It's faster, it'll put pressure on the CFE to deal with you. *El amparo tiene mas cojones* [An *amparo* has more balls]."

The legal argument mounted by the *asamblea* pivoted on the fact that the CFE had approached Ixtepec's *bienes comunales* with a request to *study the possibility* of building a new substation—reputedly the largest in Latin America—but it *never contracted* to do the actual construction. While the viability study was approved by the *comuneros*, who believed that it might generate jobs, the legal complaint maintained that the CFE never shared the study results with the community. More damning still was the fact that despite having no contract, and not having formally expropriated the forty-two hectares of land on which the substation would sit, the CFE went ahead and built it anyway. This might seem like a startling oversight on the part of the CFE, but it occurred at a time when government agencies and their corporate partners in wind development seemed generally uninformed about, or simply impatient with, *bienes comunales* decision-making procedures. Thus the legal argument being leveled against the CFE claimed that this was a case of exploitation and theft (*despojo*) on two grounds: first, the illegal occupation of *comuna* land by the substation, and second, the CFE's refusal to allow competitive access to the substation tenders.

Figure 2   Manila folder holding the documents for the Ixtepec *amparo* (injunction). Photograph by Dominic Boyer

The next week brought an important legal victory for Yansa Ixtepec. A judge in Salina Cruz issued an order of suspension to the CFE, demanding that the tender process cease while the evidence for the community's *amparo* claim was assessed (fig. 2). This was the first judicial injunction ever issued concerning a wind park in Mexico, and it did not go unnoticed by the Oaxacan wind industry. We had coffee with a senior manager of one of the major Spanish wind development companies about a week later; he launched into an unsolicited tirade against Yansa, telling us that Yansa was "ripping people off" since its numbers did not make sense—"How can they offer people 50 percent of their profits from electricity sales when the market rate in the isthmus is closer to 2 percent? Something is very fishy about that."

What happened next, or rather what did not happen, was a lesson for us in the parastatal power of the CFE. It simply ignored the judge's suspension order and proceeded with its tender process. González and Oceransky attended a meeting at the CFE in Mexico City in which the several companies that had been allowed to bid in the tender presented their business plans. At the beginning of the meeting, González stood up and waved a copy of the judge's suspension order saying that the tender could not proceed. But he was told by the presiding senior official that the CFE had not been informed of any suspension order and that it would certainly not accept a hand-delivered document from him.

On this very same day, far away in the isthmus, President Calderón helicoptered into the carefully orchestrated inauguration of the Piedra Larga wind park. At the end of his speech Calderón returned to the sky, having said nothing at all about the possibility of community wind power.

Impasse

Through an alchemy of pressures (judicial and legal), the CFE finally responded to the *amparo*, and the following year, in March 2013, canceled its tender. The CFE gave no explanation, admitted no wrongdoing, suggested no reconciliation. It was still unclear who would eventually get those last precious two hundred megawatts of access to the Ixtepec substation. When we met in Mexico City with one of the lawyers working on the case, he explained that the CFE's response "has been nothing really": "I think they are scared of touching the human rights issue." Indeed, the image of the CFE occupying indigenous land with its squatter grid was powerful and worrisome, especially when coupled with the fact that those same indigenous farmers were being barred from fully participating in the economic windfall of the parks that continued to be erected across the isthmus.

Later that summer, Vásquez, González, and Oceransky remained optimistic that some sort of political resolution would be found. Oceransky recalled that there had been informal talk early on of granting Ixtepec a special exemption for a community park. Even if it were only in gestural form, it would still be a way of bringing Mexico's indigenous communities more substantially into the process of renewable energy development. Officials in the Ministry of Energy (Secretaría de Energía, or SENER), we had found, were somewhat sympathetic to the community-owned park and shared their own (quiet) doubts about how wind development had been unfolding in the isthmus, particularly in the wake of the spectacular failure of the Mareña Renovables wind project (Howe, Boyer, and Barrera 2015).

Time will tell. When we left Mexico in July 2013, the *amparo* was not yet resolved, although optimism about a positive judgment remained. When we spoke with González in June 2014, with the case still unresolved, he assured us, "One more month. There's no turning back." As of this writing (August 2015), the *amparo* continues to be undecided. The future of wind power in Ixtepec remains unknown, brightened by hope, shadowed by doubt.

Conclusion

What we have sought to draw attention to in this article are the ways in which existing infrastructures of energy, political power, and capital resist the more revolutionary ambitions of renewable energy. Programs to alleviate climate change that depend on models like *autoabastecimiento*—favoring the interests of transnational capital and translocal governance over local interests and autonomy—can perversely pit marginalized political subjects against the climate remediation efforts that they otherwise say they support. This is by no means inevitable, as architects of energy transition like Hermann Scheer (2004) have argued at length. Indeed, for Scheer, the shorter supply chains of solar- and wind-derived electricity actually favor local political sovereignty and autonomy because they destabilize the translocal infrastructures and necessities of grid-based modernity (ibid.: 89).

Still, the complex supply chains and grids that Scheer critiques are emblematic of the challenges that lie ahead in imagining and enacting new energetic and political systems. Global flows of value, energy, and power reinforce one another, buttressed by intricate legal regimes, national and international, which are in turn only slowly becoming informed by scientific diagnostics of climate and ecology (Edwards 2010; Hulme 2009). Ornate webs of policy, infrastructure, and governance both actively enable climate change and actively resist energy transition, especially when those policies presume that the fossil fuel industry will facilitate that change. Even when states adopt bold energy transition targets, as Mexico has done, the methods of transition can turn out to be deeply problematic. The conditions of the Anthropocene, and the relative novelty of renewable energy forms, which continue to grow and transform, demonstrate the experimental plasticity of our era. And while renewable energy development and climate change mitigation are most commonly left in the hands of engineers, economists, climate scientists, and politicians, we might do better to think of energy transition and a decarbonized climate as problems that necessitate broader and more inclusive conversation and experimentation. We need to respect not just northern elites but also the creative experimental energies emerging in the global South, particularly in places where other extractivist curses have run rampant.

The potential of projects such as Ixtepec is multiple, combining qualities of social justice with sustainable energy production and sovereignty with climate mitigation; these experimental forms point toward new energy futures that are equal parts remedy *for* the climate and *against* histories of disenfranchisement. Thus the case of Ixtepec is not simply indicative of the future of Mexican energy and statecraft but rather offers a new imaginary of wind power and sustainability. While wealthy countries have been able to mount the capital investment and state subsidies required for utility-scale wind power generation, economic conditions have made this largely impossible in developing nations, even relatively prosperous ones such as Mexico. Cases such as Ixtepec, whether successes or failures, help us to think collectively through some of the potential pitfalls, missed opportunities, and feelings of betrayal that will likely result if the renewables revolution turns out to be more of the same. In a more positive light, community-owned wind parks (and other renewable projects) might inspire greater investment in renewable energy in Mexico and elsewhere. When hitherto marginalized populations can see themselves as directly and fairly benefiting from renewable energy projects—as they do in places such as West Texas or Denmark—rather than experiencing low-carbon energy production as a familiar form of land conquest and resource extraction, then we will have discovered more ethical principles and practices than those that have dominated large-scale energy production over the past few centuries.

And if the Yansa Ixtepec project is ultimately thwarted, we might ask: What does it mean for a country to be a global leader in clean energy development when that development is only tangentially concerned with the interests, hopes, and worldviews of the people in places where resources reside? Such a course toward "sustainability" is perhaps missing one of its greatest opportunities for positive social transformation along the way. Rather than a politics that manages new energy forms, what if we sought energy forms that generate a new politics?

References

Appel, Hannah, Arthur Mason, and Michael Watts, eds. 2015. *Subterranean Estates: Life Worlds of Oil and Gas.* Ithaca, NY: Cornell University Press.

Bebbington, Anthony. 2009. "The New Extraction: Rewriting the Political Ecology of the Andes?" *NACLA Report on the Americas* 42, no. 5: 12–20.

Binford, Leigh. 1985. "Political Conflict and Land Tenure in the Mexican Isthmus of Tehuantepec." *Journal of Latin American Studies* 17, no. 1: 179–200.

Boyer, Dominic. 2014. "Energopower: An Introduction." *Anthropological Quarterly* 87, no. 2: 309–34.

Cornelius, Wayne A., and David Myhre, eds. 1998. *The Transformation of Rural Mexico: Reforming the Ejido Sector.* La Jolla: Center for U.S.-Mexican Studies, University of California, San Diego.

Crutzen, Paul J., and Eugene F. Stoermer. 2000. "The Anthropocene." *Global Change Newsletter*, May, 17–18.

Davis, Mike. 2010. "Who Will Build the Ark?" *New Left Review*, no. 61: 29–46.

Eakin, Hallie. 2006. *Weathering Risk in Rural Mexico: Climatic, Institutional, and Economic Change.* Tucson: University of Arizona Press.

Economist. 2013. "Climate Change Laws: Beginning at Home." January 19. www.economist.com/news/international/21569691-domestic-laws-not-global-treaty-are-way-fight-global-warming-beginning-home.

Edwards, Paul. 2010. *A Vast Machine: Computer Models, Climate Data, and the Politics of Global Warming.* Cambridge, MA: MIT Press.

Giddens, Anthony. 2009. *The Politics of Climate Change.* Cambridge, UK: Polity.

Gledhill, John. 1995. *Neoliberalism, Transnationalization, and Rural Poverty: A Case Study of Michoacán, Mexico.* Boulder, CO: Westview.

Gómez Martínez, Emanuel. 2005. "Proyecto perfiles indígenas diagnóstico regional del Istmo de Tehuantepec" (Profiles of Indigenous Communities in the Isthmus of Tehuantepec Region). Oaxaca City, Mexico: Centro de Investigaciones y Estudios Superiores en Antropología Social, Unidad Istmo.

Gudynas, Eduardo. 2009. "Diez tesis urgentes sobre el nuevo extractivismo: Contextos y demandas bajo el progresismo sudamericano actual" ("Ten Urgent Theses on New Extractivism: Context and Demands under Contemporary South American Progressivism"). In *Extractivismo, política y sociedad* (*Extractivism, Politics, and Society*), edited by Jürgen Schuldt et al., 187–225. Quito, Ecuador: Centro Andino de Acción Popular (CAAP) and Centro Latino Americano de Ecología Social (CLAES).

GWEC (Global Wind Energy Council). 2015. *Global Wind Report: Annual Market Update, 2014*. Brussels: GWEC. www.gwec.net/wp-content/uploads/2015/03 /GWEC_Global_Wind_2014_Report_LR.pdf.

Haenn, Nora. 2006. "The Changing and Enduring Ejido: A State and Regional Examination of Mexico's Land Tenure Counter-reforms." *Land Use Policy* 23, no. 2: 136–46.

Hoffmann, Julia. 2012. "The Social Power of Wind: The Role of Participation and Social Entrepreneurship in Overcoming Barriers for Community Wind Farm Development; Lessons from the Ixtepec Community Wind Farm Project in Mexico." MA thesis, Lund University.

Howe, Cymene. 2015. "Latin America in the Anthropocene: Energy Transitions and Climate Change Mitigations." *Journal of Latin American and Caribbean Anthropology* 20, no. 2: 231–41.

Howe, Cymene, and Dominic Boyer. 2015. "Aeolian Politics." *Distinktion: Scandinavian Journal of Social Theory* 16, no. 1: 31–48.

Howe, Cymene, Dominic Boyer, and Edith Barrera. 2015. "Wind at the Margins of the State: Autonomy and Renewable Energy Development in Southern Mexico." In *Contested Powers: The Politics of Energy and Development in Latin America*, edited by John-Andrew McNeish, Axel Borchgrevink, and Owen Logan, 92–115. London: Zed Books.

Hulme, Mike. 2009. *Why We Disagree about Climate Change: Understanding Controversy, Inaction, and Opportunity*. Cambridge: Cambridge University Press.

Kashi, Ed. 2008. *The Curse of the Black Gold: Fifty Years of Oil in the Niger Delta*. Edited by Michael Watts. New York: powerHouse Books.

Kelly, John H., et al. 2010. "Indigenous Territoriality at the End of the Social Property Era in Mexico." *Journal of Latin American Geography* 9, no. 3: 161–81.

Knight, Alan, and Wil Pansters, eds. 2006. *Caciquismo in Twentieth-Century Mexico*. Chapel Hill, NC: Institute for the Study of the Americas.

McNeish, John-Andrew, and Owen Logan, eds. 2012. *Flammable Societies: Studies on the Socio-economics of Oil and Gas*. London: Pluto.

Mitchell, Timothy. 2011. *Carbon Democracy: Political Power in the Age of Oil*. New York: Verso.

Ochoa, Enrique C. 2001. "Neoliberalism, Disorder, and Militarization in Mexico." *Latin American Perspectives* 28, no. 4: 148–59.

Sawyer, Suzana. 2004. *Crude Chronicles: Indigenous Politics, Multinational Oil, and Neoliberalism in Ecuador.* Durham, NC: Duke University Press.

Sawyer, Suzana, and Edmund Terence Gomez, eds. 2012. *The Politics of Resource Extraction: Indigenous Peoples, Multinational Corporations, and the State.* Basingstoke: Palgrave Macmillan.

Scheer, Hermann. 2004. *The Solar Economy: Renewable Energy for a Sustainable Global Future.* London: Earthscan.

World Bank. 2013. "Latin America: Pioneering Laws to Cope with Climate Change." April 12. www.worldbank.org/en/news/feature/2013/04/12/America -Latina-pionera-en-leyes-sobre-cambio-clim-225-tico.

....

Cymene Howe is an associate professor of anthropology at Rice University. She is the author of *Intimate Activism* (2013) and *Ecologics: Wind and Power in the Anthropocene* (forthcoming) — a collaborative, multimedia duograph that analyzes the contingent social and material formations of renewable energy. Her theoretical interests center on the overlapping conversations between feminist and queer theory, materialisms, multispecies ethnography, ethics, and imaginaries of the future in the Anthropocene.

Dominic Boyer is a professor of anthropology at Rice University and founding director of the Center for Energy and Environmental Research in the Human Sciences. His most recent books are *The Life Informatic* (2013) and the coedited volume *Theory Can Be More Than It Used to Be* (2015). His next book project, a collaborative multimedia duograph with Cymene Howe, explores the energopolitical complexities of wind power development in southern Mexico.

The Indicator Species:
Tracking Ecosystem Collapse
in Arid California

Andrew Lakoff

"**W**e should be standing on five feet of snow," declared California governor Jerry Brown in April 2015, as he announced the state's first-ever mandatory restrictions on urban water use. The governor was standing on a dry, brown field high in the Sierra Nevada, ninety miles east of Sacramento at Phillips Station, site of the state's annual snowpack survey, which revealed that the water content of the Sierra Nevada snowpack was at its lowest level in recorded history. Four years into a historic drought, the announcement intensified an already growing sense of crisis in California and put a national spotlight on the question of the sustainability of the state's highly engineered system of water provision. The site of Brown's speech was well chosen to provoke such reflection: without Sierra snowmelt, there would be little water to circulate through the massive complex of reservoirs, pumps, canals, and aqueducts that constitute the state's hydrological system—a system that has enabled the arid Central Valley to become the source of one-third of the United States' agricultural produce and Southern California to sustain a still-growing population of over 22 million. Beyond indicating the insufficiency of the coming year's water supply, the snowpack survey was also a portent of the longer-term future. Projections of the impact of climate change on precipitation in the Sierra Nevada indicated that over a fifty-year horizon, the snowpack levels upon which the state's water circulation system depended were likely to decline precipitously.[1]

1. Climate models indicated that future precipitation in the Sierra Nevada would increasingly come in the form of rain rather than snow. The California Climate Adaptation Strategy (2009) estimated that the snowpack would be reduced from its mid-twentieth-century average by 25–40 percent by 2050.

Public Culture 28:2   DOI 10.1215/08992363-3427439

Declining flows of water from the mountains not only threatened urban and agricultural users to the south. Just two weeks earlier, a less publicized survey was conducted in the region where the Sierra snowmelt flows, the San Francisco Bay-Delta. It held equally grim news. The California Department of Fish and Wildlife's annual Kodiak trawl survey, which measures the abundance and distribution of delta smelt by capturing them as they aggregate to spawn, caught only six of the once abundant, but now endangered, fish. The delta smelt was one of several species, also including the Sacramento River winter-run chinook salmon, the Central Valley steelhead, and the green sturgeon, whose numbers were collapsing despite preservation efforts, as state and federal water project operators continued to divert massive amounts of freshwater from the delta to Central Valley farms and Southern California cities during the drought. For many observers, the decrease in freshwater flows through the delta, due to both drought and diversion, was a key source of the steep decline in native fish populations.

"We need to be planning for delta smelt extinction," commented fisheries biologist Peter Moyle (2015), a longtime observer of fish species native to the delta, "and, perhaps, its resurrection." Moyle's reference to resurrection alluded to a captive population of the fish that was being maintained by the University of California, Davis, with the support of the Federal Bureau of Reclamation, the agency that manages one of the two major projects that pump water from the delta to arid southern regions of the state. According to the bureau, the "genetically managed refugial population" served as a "critical safeguard against species extinction in the event that the natural population continues its decline" (UC Davis 2015). Even if wild smelt ceased to exist in their current delta habitat, the captive population held out the possibility of a future reintroduction in a restored ecosystem.

At one level, the apparent demise of the delta smelt was a relatively minor event in an age of human-caused extinctions (see Kolbert 2014). The species is hardly charismatic: a two- to three-inch-long translucent fish that lives for one year in open water, it is a poor swimmer, survives on phytoplankton, and serves as prey for larger fish (see fig. 1). Had it disappeared a few decades earlier (as another native to the delta, the thicktail chub, did in the 1950s) it might never have become an object of scientific and political interest. And indeed, the delta smelt's extinction was unlikely to be mourned by those whose water supplies were threatened by its precarious position. But this modest creature had nonetheless taken on an iconic status due to its centrality to political and technical debates over water in the state over the prior two decades. Debates over how to deal with dwindling future water supplies were shaped by a long-running legal and regulatory struggle over the relative prioritization of human and nonhuman needs.

Figure 1 The endangered delta smelt. Wikimedia Commons

The smelt's significance had less to do with its intrinsic qualities than with what its disappearance might portend. For advocates of smelt protection, the continued existence of the fish was important beyond the value of preserving a unique species: the fish was an "indicator" of the health of the delta region as a whole—and its apparent demise was a tragic sign of the delta's ongoing ecological collapse. For its detractors, efforts to protect the smelt—which had led to restrictions on state and federal water project diversions—involved an irrational prioritization of fish over people. More broadly, the debate over whether and how to preserve the threatened species pointed to tensions around whether the demands of the human-built systems upon which the state's population depended could be aligned with the norms of the ecological systems they necessarily transform. And as we will see, the projected effects of climate change on future water supplies in California only exacerbated these tensions.

This essay tracks the two-decade-long struggle, conducted by an alliance of fishery biologists, sport fishermen, and environmental advocacy groups, to protect the delta smelt and other native fish populations. Through the case of the smelt, it asks how the goal of species preservation, enshrined in the 1973 Endangered Species Act, is integrated into contemporary governmental practice. What values are at play in efforts to sustain the existence of nonhuman life in a setting of intense competition over a diminishing and essential resource? What forms of knowledge are developed to gauge the health of threatened species, and what techniques are used to regulate the provision of water in the name of species protection?

The essay suggests that smelt protection efforts are guided by two temporally distinct value orientations. The first is past-oriented, emphasizing the preservation of existing species as a good in itself. This value is at the heart of the legislation that structures species protection efforts in the United States, the Endangered Species Act. The second is future-oriented, focused on staving off an approaching ecological collapse whose onset is signaled by the smelt population's decline. Here the threatened species is not valued for its own sake but rather serves as a proxy in a struggle against a broader catastrophe: it is an indicator of a more general ecological condition. From this latter perspective, the Endangered Species Act provides potentially powerful regulatory tools for limiting or redirecting human incursions into fragile ecological systems, but the impact of such regulation is limited by the act's narrow focus on species protection.

The regulatory methods adopted to redirect water toward nonhuman needs depend upon which of these value orientations is embraced. As the essay will show, while supporters of smelt protection are mainly guided by a desire to stave off the collapse of the delta ecosystem, their capacity to intervene in the water system is constrained by the legal means at their disposal. Endangered species legislation provides them with a powerful tool to counter entrenched economic and political interests, but it demands an emphasis on the preservation of particular species. Due to the smelt's threatened status, water operators have been required to closely monitor its living conditions and calibrate their pumping activities in response. It is not clear, however, whether such regulation has improved the species' long-term prospects and even less whether it has contributed to improving the health of the ecosystem.

The Management of Flows

The Bay-Delta region, which extends westward from the meeting point of the Sacramento and San Joaquin Rivers to the San Francisco Bay, is the West Coast's largest estuary, the source of much of the state's urban and agricultural water, and a refuge for dozens of native species of birds and fish. A century and a half of Euro-American habitation has transformed the region from a tidal marshland of variable salinity and regular flooding into a stable, mostly freshwater lake and river system of dredged channels, earthen levees, small islands, and irrigated farms. Beginning in the second half of the nineteenth century, settlers in the American West drained its marshes, logged its forests, and built dikes to control flooding and stabilize its course. An extensive but fragile system of canals and levees was constructed in the early twentieth century to make the land more amenable to farming. However, the most significant transformations to the delta took place from the 1930s to the 1960s, as massive federal and state water projects were built to generate hydroelectric power, control seasonal flooding, irrigate the Central Valley, and, later, provide water to consumers in the growing cities of Southern California (see fig. 2). Water circulation through the delta is so carefully managed that it is often described as the state's "plumbing system."

The engineering of California's major water systems is typical of large-scale infrastructure development in the mid-twentieth-century United States. The construction of the Central Valley Project by the New Deal–era Federal Bureau of Reclamation began in the 1930s. The project treated Sierra snowmelt

Figure 2 California's water circulation system. Wikimedia Commons

and watershed runoff as a natural resource to be exploited for agricultural production and hydroelectricity and as a flood risk to be managed. The question of whether the diversion of freshwater from the delta might have unintended ecological consequences was not part of the planning calculation. At the intersection of the two major river systems of California, the Sacramento River and the San Joaquin River, the Central Valley Project stores water in reservoirs in the Sierra foothills and releases it in controlled flows through a series of pipes and canals into the delta. From there the water either continues westward through the delta into the San Francisco Bay or is pumped southward along the eastern side of the San Joaquin Valley through multiple canals, aqueducts, and pump plants.

Another major water storage and delivery system, the State Water Project, was built in the 1960s, funded by state water bonds and managed by the California Department of Water Resources. Like the Central Valley Project, it uses massive pumps located in the southern delta to transport water south—in this case, along the western side of the San Joaquin Valley and to the urban agglomerations of Southern California. The nation's largest government-built water system, the

241

State Water Project includes thirty-four reservoirs, twenty pumping plants, five power plants, and seven hundred miles of canals and pipelines. It supplies water to 750,000 acres of farmland and 25 million residents through water contractors such as the Westlands Water District of central California and the Metropolitan Water District of Southern California.

Following the mid-twentieth-century paradigm of state-based infrastructure development, both projects conceptualized watershed flow as a natural resource to be exploited for the purpose of agricultural and urban development (see Collier and Lakoff 2015). As President John F. Kennedy put it in dedicating a portion of the Central Valley Project in 1963: "The flows of two watersheds can now be regulated for the benefit of the farms and cities of the lower valley." In turn, allowing the water to run through the delta into the sea would be a waste: "For too long, this water ran unused to the sea" (quoted in Shigley 2012). These vast engineering projects were crucial to the growth of the Central Valley agricultural industry and Southern Californian cities in the second half of the twentieth century. Today federal and state project operators continue to supervise the timing and amount of water sent from reservoirs in the mountains into the delta and then from the delta to water contractors and utility agencies in the central and southern parts of the state. Before the current period of water restrictions—due both to environmental regulations and water scarcity—the two water projects diverted an average of 6 million of the delta's 23 million acre-feet of annual freshwater flow.[2]

This model of government-managed resource extraction and circulation via big infrastructure projects came into question in California and elsewhere by the late 1970s, with the rise of the environmental movement and increasing public concern about the unintended ecological consequences of such projects (see Beck 1995). In the case of California water politics, new alliances arose to challenge the technocratic authority of water managers focused on the goals of increased agricultural production and urban growth. The ecological health of the delta was at the center of these struggles, which consolidated in the early 1980s protest of a proposed "peripheral canal" to be built at the eastern end of the delta. The proposed canal was meant to connect the Sacramento River directly to the State Water Project aqueduct to keep saltwater from the San Francisco Bay from intruding into the delta as its freshwater was pumped southward. Initially envisioned as the final element in the State Water Project, the peripheral canal project was challenged both by delta-area farmers and fishermen and by environmentalists who feared that

2. Additional in-stream and upstream diversions amount to approximately 5 million acre-feet per year. The percentage of water diverted becomes much higher during drought years. See Layzer 2008.

siphoning off more water from the Sacramento River would lead to the collapse of the entire delta ecosystem. The defeat of the canal proposal by California voters in 1982 marked a new era in the state's technopolitics, in which major infrastructure projects would face challenges from new and unexpected alliances.

In the ensuing years, tension has only increased between the continually expanding water needs of the arid parts of the state and ever more dire forecasts of the delta's ecological collapse. On the one hand, the federal and state projects have had difficulty meeting contractual obligations to local water districts, especially in drought years. On the other hand, environmental regulations have begun to restrict water operations as populations of native fish species have crashed. It is in this context—of increasing shortfalls in water delivery and intensifying environmental crisis—that the prominence of the delta smelt both as an endangered species in need of protection and as an indicator of impending ecological collapse must be understood.

An Indicator Species

The Endangered Species Act of 1973 has served as the legal basis for smelt protections and, more generally, for efforts to restore the delta habitat so that native fish populations can be sustained. There are three key regulatory steps in endangered species protection, according to the law. First, one of the federal wildlife agencies officially lists the species as threatened or endangered in response to a public request; such a listing prohibits any act that may harm the species or degrade its critical habitat. The second step is the official designation of the species' critical habitat—that area whose protection is deemed crucial to the recovery of the species. The third is the development of a recovery plan, which typically involves a strategy to restore and enhance the species' critical habitat (Benson 2012).

As noted above, efforts to protect the smelt, unlike movements to prevent the extinction of more charismatic fauna such as the red wolf or the desert tortoise, are not driven by an affective connection with the endangered animal. Rather, one finds articulated in discussions of the fate of the smelt a more general sense of endangerment: that the smelt's decline is symptomatic of a broader, unfolding tragedy of ecosystem collapse.[3] It is an event in which humans are implicated both as its cause and as one of the affected species. Thus smelt advocates commonly use the concept of the "indicator species." An indicator, as Theodore M. Porter (2015) notes, is a device used to point to something—such as the economy—that

---

3. For a historical analysis of the affect of endangerment, see Vidal and Dias 2015.

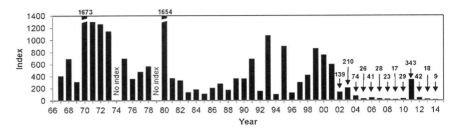

Figure 3 Results of the annual survey of delta smelt abundance. Source: State of California, Department of Fish and Game, memorandum, "Fall Midwater Trawl 2014 Annual Fish Abundance Summary," January 7, 2015

cannot be easily grasped through direct measurement. In place of the thing of interest, the indicator measures something whose movements show a consistent relationship to that thing.

In this case, annual surveys indicating rapid declines in native fish populations such as the smelt point to the possible onset of an event that is difficult to directly perceive or measure: the collapse of an ecosystem (see fig. 3). Here the indicator species function as a sentinel device—alerting us to the approach of an uncertain but catastrophic threat (see Keck and Lakoff 2013).[4] The construction of sentinel devices is designed to spur intensive action to mitigate such threats. In this sense, the sentinel device is part of a precautionary apparatus: an alert that tells us we must take action, even in the face of uncertainty, to avert disaster (Chateauraynaud and Torny 2005). By the time we are certain about the accuracy of the sentinel's warning it will be too late. However, such signals of warning face challenges in spurring intervention. When the stakes of intervention are high—when precautionary measures are costly—the validity of the sentinel's warning, or its relation to an imagined future, is often contested.[5] While a sentinel device makes it possible to perceive the onset of a possible future catastrophe, it does not by itself ward off the impending danger. In the case of the threatened delta ecosystem, this is where the Endangered Species Act proved potentially useful.

4. Historical examples of nonhuman sentinels include the use of lichen distribution to detect air pollution in nineteenth-century Paris and the use of fish to study river pollution in Germany in the early twentieth century.

5. One may think of the role of bee colony collapse in debates over pesticide use or of coral reef degradation in discussions of the effects of climate change. See Keck and Lakoff 2013.

The Smelt as Proxy

The delta smelt, an open-water species endemic to the San Francisco Bay-Delta, was once among the delta's most abundant fish. In the late 1980s, fishery biologists led by Moyle of the University of California, Davis, began to notice a sharp decline in native fish populations, including chinook salmon, steelhead trout, and delta smelt. Based on observations in Suisan Marsh, Moyle estimated that the fish's population had plummeted by 90 percent since the late 1970s. Further evidence of the fish's decline came from the California Department of Fish and Game's Summer Townet Survey, conducted annually since 1959. The survey involves a series of ten-minute-long trawls using a standard-size net to gather fish at thirty-two sampling stations in the delta. Surveyors then enumerate all of the fish caught in these trawls. The survey was initially conducted to understand the impact of the Central Valley Project on striped bass populations (an introduced species) and thus on sportfishing, but smelt and other species were also captured in the trawl and counted.[6] Using archival data from the Townet survey, fisheries biologists developed the "delta smelt index" in 1990, which generated a useful retrospective record of historical changes in smelt abundance. This index would become increasingly significant over the next two decades as a means of tracking the decline in the smelt population and, more generally, in gauging the health of the delta. According to the California Department of Fish and Wildlife (2015), "Delta smelt abundance trend data was used as supporting evidence for their listing as threatened in 1992 under the Federal and State Endangered Species Acts."

On the basis of these findings, sport and commercial fishing associations along with fisheries biologists pressed state and federal wildlife services to list the delta smelt as a threatened species under the Endangered Species Act. The proposal was immediately controversial, as state water managers and local water contractors understood that Endangered Species Act protection of the smelt's habitat—the entire delta—would likely imperil regular water deliveries to the south. For instance, it might be necessary to turn the pumps off when the smelt spawned in the late winter and early spring, typically a period of intensive water diversion. An official from the Metropolitan Water District, which supplied water to 15 million users in Southern California, estimated that pumping restrictions could lead to 25 percent shortages in water availability. To stave off such arrangements, water

---

6. The California Department of Fish and Wildlife (2015) explains that the Summer Townet Survey "began in response to the development of Central Valley Project pumping plants exporting water from the south Delta. These exports created a need for information regarding distribution of young striped bass relative to the south Delta diversions."

contractors argued that the cause of the smelt's population decline was unclear and requested further study.[7] Meanwhile, environmental activists who saw freshwater exports as destroying the San Francisco Bay and Delta ecosystem advocated an endangered species listing. As a member of the Bay Institute said, "If we can use the delta smelt to document [damage to the delta], we will" (quoted in Morain 1991). Thus even before it was officially listed as threatened, the smelt was a proxy in a larger statewide struggle over water provision.

After several years of analysis and debate, in the spring of 1993 the US Fish and Wildlife Service officially listed the delta smelt as "threatened" under the Endangered Species Act, and California's Department of Fish and Wildlife followed suit shortly thereafter. In 1994 the US Fish and Wildlife Service designated the entire San Francisco Bay-Delta as a "critical habitat" for the smelt, and in 1996, the agency released its recovery plan for delta native fisheries. These were critical steps: the listing of the species as threatened and the designation of its critical habitat meant that any action in any part of the delta that could imperil the lives of smelt was subject to sanction under the Endangered Species Act prohibition of "taking."

In its listing announcement, the Fish and Wildlife Service followed fisheries biologists and environmental activists in claiming that the smelt's significance extended beyond the species itself: its demise "may be indicative of the relative health" of the delta as a whole (Murphy 1993). The sentinel vision was already part of the rationale for preservation efforts. As a biologist with the Fish and Wildlife Service put it, "If that species gets wiped out, it is really saying the delta is going to the dogs" (quoted in ibid.). Similarly, Moyle argued that listing the species as threatened under the Endangered Species Act "tells people the delta system is in serious trouble and needs to be fixed" (quoted in ibid.). He sought to link the species-oriented values embedded in the Endangered Species Act to the problematic of ecosystem health: "The bottom line for me is that we don't have the right to eliminate a species. It is a moral issue, especially when we know keeping it around will mean a healthier ecosystem" (ibid.).

The smelt was able to take on this role of an indicator species due to its particular sensitivity to environmental change. It is dependent for its survival on the characteristics of the ecosystem in which it evolved, such as the brackish zone of low salinity where freshwater inflows meet the Bay's tidal currents, and on the availability of an abundance of phytoplankton in the food web. Smelt do not swim

7. Dick Clemmer, the Metropolitan Water District's manager of Bay-Delta affairs, said in 1991: "We are going to try to influence the decision. We firmly believe there isn't enough information to call for a listing" (quoted in Morain 1991).

well, but tend to ride along the river's currents. If these currents are redirected to deadly pumping stations, the smelt are passively "entrained" in vast numbers. The smelt population's decline was, for ecologically minded observers, intimately linked to long-term damage to its habitat. As the delta was channeled and diked, as its flows were managed and its freshwater diverted, and as it was contaminated with pesticide residue and sewage treatment runoff, it had become more hospitable to invasive plant and animal species and less so to natives like the smelt, whose die-off was the signal of an ecosystem in crisis.

For many activists and environmental scientists, the main source of this crisis was a significant decrease in freshwater flows through the delta, especially in the wake of the State Water Project's completion in the late 1960s. From this perspective, insofar as Endangered Species Act regulations might help restrict freshwater diversion, efforts to protect the smelt held the potential to achieve broader aims of ecological renewal.[8] As the executive director of the Bay Institute put it, "The listing of the delta smelt could be the most important step in restoring the delta" (quoted in Murphy 1993). But there were certain risks to the strategy of tying repair of the delta to the fate of the smelt. For one, endangered species regulations could point toward narrow protection measures rather than toward a more general ecological restoration: for instance, using monitoring techniques near the water projects' pumps to ensure that smelt were not entrained, rather than increasing freshwater flow through the entire system. In addition, a focus on the individual species would allow defenders of ongoing water exports to claim that the central issue was one of "fish versus people" rather than the overall sustainability of the state's hydrological regime. Finally, if the species did become extinct despite preservation efforts, there might no longer be a legal-regulatory basis for limiting water exports.

The Pelagic Organism Decline

The 1993 listing of the delta smelt as a threatened species led to two decades' worth of regulatory negotiation and legal contestation. In a first stage, lasting roughly until 2005, the various governmental entities involved—the Environmental Protection Agency (EPA), the Bureau of Reclamation, the Fish and Wildlife Service, and the California Department of Water Resources, among

---

8. Melinda Harm Benson (2012) points more generally to the significance of the Endangered Species Act in transforming state and federal water management practices: "The ESA disrupted the trend of resource extraction within these watersheds and forced consideration of the consequences of these activities to the ecological systems at issue."

others—sought to harmonize the seemingly opposed goals of maintaining water deliveries to the south and restoring the delta smelt's habitat. In a second stage, as it became apparent that these initial efforts had failed to stem the decline of native fish populations, a more contentious legal and scientific struggle arose over the grounds for restrictions on water project operations.[9]

The first stage was a period of increasing scientific and regulatory scrutiny of the smelt population's living conditions and the initiation of experiments in managing its well-being. In 1992, in response to long-running concerns about the effects of the water projects on the water quality and ecological health of the delta, Congress passed the Central Valley Project Improvement Act, which required the Federal Bureau of Reclamation to reconfigure its project operations to "protect, restore and enhance" fish and wildlife (Pub. L. No. 102-575, title 34, 106 Stat. 4706 [1992]). This included measures such as allowing increased flows through the delta to improve fish habitat and providing water for wildlife refuges. Soon after, in 1994, a collaborative regulatory arrangement was instituted between state officials protective of water exports and federal regulators attuned to the water projects' environmental consequences. The goal of the arrangement, called the CALFED Bay-Delta Program, was to balance among the various competing interests to provide sufficient freshwater flows to the delta to protect endangered fish populations.

CALFED's objective was not to restore a damaged ecosystem but rather to ensure that urban-agricultural water supplies were not disrupted while providing enough water to meet legal requirements for the fish (Layzer 2008). For our purposes, the arrangement is of interest as a setting in which new techniques and knowledge practices were invented to adjudicate between ecological needs and consumer demands. One of CALFED's innovations was the Environmental Water Account program, which aimed "to facilitate real-time adjustments in water project operations to prevent the deaths of migratory and estuarine species at state and federal water pumps" (Layzer 2008: 137–38). The water account sought to provide water operators with flexibility so that they could slow or shut down the pumps when the smelt were nearby. The water thus "spent" on fish protection would—in principle—be paid back through the environmental water account. However, the account remained underendowed, and so the wildlife agencies were not able to provide enough water to protect the smelt from entrainment in the pumps at the southern edge of the delta.

After a brief period in the late 1990s in which it looked as though native fish

9. For the details of this history, see Alagona 2013.

populations might rebound, there was another crash beginning in 2002, which environmental scientists termed the "pelagic organism decline" (Sommer, Breuer, and Mueller-Solger 2007). The sharpness of the decline in native fish populations was startling to scientists. Following the results of a 2005 survey, EPA fisheries biologist Bruce Herbold said: "I'm not much of an alarmist, but I'm starting to look at it that way. I'm starting to look at it as the sky is falling" (quoted in Taugher 2005). Numerous native species showed steep drop-offs in surveyed populations. Herbold reflected on the significance of declining numbers of threadfin shad, a previously common baitfish: "To have it going from really abundant to scarce, it's scary. Something is really, really wrong. It is not just the sensitive fish. The cockroaches are dying off" (ibid.). The slow, steady practice of trawling for native fish, year after year, had now generated a piercing alarm.

The delta smelt population, tracked carefully due to its threatened status, was measured in 2005 at its lowest level ever. As historian Peter S. Alagona (2013: 216) notes, the smelt's decline came to stand in for the delta's "slow-motion ecological collapse." According to Herbold, the EPA scientist, either delta conditions had now degraded past a "pivot point" and were in a state of general collapse or some other unknown factor had changed (quoted in Taugher 2005). A biologist from the California Department of Fish and Game indicated scientists' uncertainty about the cause of the rapid and sudden decline. "We're going to put everything on the table, from toxics to water operations to [invasive] species to even toxic algae," he said. "Everyone is pretty clear in that there's something going on out there. The only question is what it is and what is going to be done about it" (quoted in ibid.). Many scientists continued to suspect that the state and federal water projects' increasing diversions of freshwater from the delta were playing a large part.

Reasonable and Prudent Alternatives

At this moment of perceived crisis, the legal-regulatory regime governing management of the delta's water shifted. Here it is necessary to briefly describe the provisions of section 7 of the Endangered Species Act, which regulates federal agency actions that may affect a listed species. Section 7 requires any agency that plans such an action to consult in advance with one of the wildlife agencies. In turn, the wildlife agency generates a "biological opinion," which determines whether the proposed action is likely either to "jeopardize the continued existence of the species" or to result in "destruction or adverse modification" of the species' critical habit. If so, the biological opinion then seeks to identify a set of "reasonable and prudent alternatives" that can mitigate the threat to the species and at the same time allow the action agency to go ahead with its proposed activity (US Fish and Wildlife Service and National Marine Fisheries Service 1998: xi, xvii). It is in the details of these alternatives—which function as regulations—that the goal of species preservation is integrated into the techno-administrative procedures of resource management. As we will see, the biological opinion is the crucial document in the legal determination of how water-pumping operations must be managed in order to protect a threatened species.

In 2004, as part of the CALFED process, the Federal Bureau of Reclamation released a proposed operational plan for its coordinated Central Valley Project and State Water Project water management activities. A year later, the Fish and Wildlife Service issued its biological opinion on the bureau's plan, which concluded that the bureau's ongoing pumping activities would have no adverse effect on the recovery of the delta smelt or on its critical habitat. Diversion could go forth as planned.

In response, the Natural Resources Defense Council filed suit in federal court, challenging the biological opinion as "arbitrary and capricious" (Alagona 2013: 218). The case was assigned to the federal district court in Fresno, presided over by Judge Oliver Wanger, a conservative appointee of President George H. W. Bush. Two years later, in December 2007, the judge issued what became known as the "Wanger decision," which would become an ongoing source of consternation among water contractors in California. Wanger ruled that the project operators' pumping activities posed an unacceptable risk to the survival of the delta smelt. He grounded this decision on his understanding that the Endangered Species Act mandated the prioritization of listed species over any other competing interests.

Wanger ordered the water projects to reduce their pumping operations to avoid entraining smelt in their pumps at the southern end of the delta. Specifically, he required project operators to lower the speed at which the water projects were reversing the flow of the rivers and thereby dragging smelt into their pumping machinery (San Luis & Delta-Mendota Water Authority v. Jewell [9th Cir. 2014]: 62). For environmentalists, the ruling demonstrated the potential of using the Endangered Species Act to pursue broad aims such as habitat conservation and stream-flow restoration, whereas for the water contractors, it came as an unpleasant surprise: a small group of fisheries biologists and environmental lawyers had managed to alter the schedule of pumping activity that supplied water to over 20 million people and millions of acres of farmland (Alagona 2013). From this latter perspective, an obscure, two-inch-long fish now threatened the future reliability of the state's water supply.

Wanger also ordered the Fish and Wildlife Service to generate a revised biological opinion. The new document, released in December 2008, was over four hundred pages long and was the most complex biological opinion the agency had ever produced. It was also the most controversial. In it, the Fish and Wildlife Service reversed its prior assessment: the revised opinion found that the state and federal water projects' planned pumping operations were "likely to jeopardize the continued existence of the delta smelt" and "to adversely modify delta smelt critical habitat" (US Department of the Interior 2008: 276, 277). According to the document, the increase in water diversions due to pumping operations had led to entrainment of the smelt, reduced its habitat, and altered outflows to the delta, changing the location of the zone of low salinity in which the fish tend to live. Moreover, delta smelt were now at their lowest level of abundance since monitoring began in 1967. To recover, according to the document, the smelt would need an increased habitat and a reduction of pollutants, invasive species, and entrainment by the water project's pumps.

The biological opinion then listed the "reasonable and prudent alternatives" the Bureau of Reclamation would have to undertake for its proposed pumping operations to be approved. These regulations were notable for the careful attention to the living conditions of the smelt that would be required of project operators. For example, operators would be required to track the physical proximity of smelt to the huge pumps in the south delta that were blamed for significant fish mortality, as measured by the "daily salvage index." If the salvage index reached a certain threshold, operators would have to reduce diversions for two weeks to limit the reverse flow toward the pumps. Another example concerned the flow of freshwater through the delta out into San Francisco Bay: based on computerized models of smelt behavior, the biological opinion required project operators to adjust the rate of freshwater flows to maintain "X2," the zone of ideal salinity for young smelt, in a part of the delta that increased the smelt's suitable habitat. Thus operators would be required to engage in close supervision of several aspects of smelt existence and regulate water flows in response to these cues. The state's hydrological system would have to be adjusted in near real time in relation to the smelt's movements and to the drift of its brackish habitat.

State water managers estimated that the resulting pumping restrictions would reduce water project deliveries by 20–30 percent and challenged the scientific basis of the biological opinion (Boxall 2008). The director of the California Water Resources Board argued that the federal regulations placed too much blame for smelt decline on the water projects' pumps, noting that chemical contamination, invasive species, power plant operations, and drought conditions were all harming the delta.[10] Meanwhile, over the course of the following year, a national media campaign led by Central Valley agricultural interests attacked the federal government for its prioritization of fish over people. Farmers held public rallies to denounce the "federally mandated drought." Fox News host Sean Hannity, in his enthusiastic coverage of the protests, told his audience that the Obama administration's Interior Department had decided that "the farmers come second and the delta smelt comes first" (Hannity 2009).

Southern California and Central Valley water districts joined in legal action seeking to overturn the regulations contained in the revised biological opinion. The case again came before Wanger's court. In his December 2010 decision, the judge reversed his prior position, writing that the revised biological opinion was "arbitrary, capricious and unlawful." The decision focused on several technical areas in which, the judge argued, the Fish and Wildlife Service had not used "the best available science" as required in determining reasonable and prudent alternatives (US District Court for the Eastern District of California. 2010. *The Consolidated Delta Smelt Cases*, 225, 219). For instance, he pointed to problems in the wildlife service's method for using smelt mortality rates to limit the allowable rate of reverse river flow: required limits were based on increases in the number of smelt salvaged, but these numbers were not adjusted in relation to the overall smelt population. Wanger also criticized the service's use of two different modeling techniques to determine the optimal location of X2, the ideal habitat for young smelt: the models had not been calibrated, he argued, introducing significant bias to the analysis (ibid., 125). The judge justified his close scrutiny of the service's technical practices through reference to the high stakes of the biological opinion. As he wrote, "The practical result of the X2 Action is to allow large volumes of Project water to escape into the ocean" (Uhlman 2011). This reference to the "escape" of water assumed the hydrological engineers' view of the delta's freshwater as a resource that had been captured by engineers for the public benefit and that must be exploited for human use. From the perspective of ecosystem advocates, of course, water flowing through the delta to the ocean was not a resource being wasted but rather a critical ingredient of the estuary's health.

In later comments, Wanger lambasted the government scientists who had testified in the case as "deceitful zealots." He was especially incensed by the

10. In a *San Francisco Chronicle* op-ed, two attorneys for Central Valley water districts made a similar argument: "Myriad factors negatively affect the well-being of the delta smelt. These include, but are not limited to, a low food supply, presence of predatory fish and a toxic water habitat for the smelt" (Manson and Middleton 2009).

testimony of a Fish and Wildlife Service scientist on the need to increase freshwater outflows to maintain the ideal salinity zone (X2) for young smelt in a specific part of the delta: "The suggestion by Dr. [Jennifer M.] Norris that the failure to implement X2 at 74 kilometers [east of the Golden Gate Bridge], that that's going to end the delta smelt existence on the face of our planet is false. It is outrageous" (quoted in Barringer 2011). Meanwhile, the judge criticized the Fish and Wildlife Service for its failure to do cost-benefit analysis—to weigh the requirements for protecting a threatened species of fish against the resource demands of humans. In its biological opinion, he argued, the agency had "shown no inclination to fully and honestly address water supply needs beyond the species," even as it "interdict[ed] the water supply for domestic human consumption and agricultural use for over twenty million people who depend on the projects for their water supply" (Bailey 2014). In contrast to his earlier opinion, the judge was now unwilling to defend the antiutilitarian principles embodied in the Endangered Species Act.

The legal back-and-forth continued for several more years, as environmental groups appealed the 2010 ruling to a higher court. In March 2014, the Ninth Circuit Court of Appeals reversed Wanger's decision by a 2–1 verdict, upholding the earlier findings of the Fish and Wildlife Service in its revised biological opinion. The appellate court argued that the wildlife agency should be given considerable deference in evaluating its use and interpretation of scientific evidence and faulted Wanger for attempting to intervene in the scientific discussion by staging a "battle of the experts" (San Luis v. Jewell, US Court of Appeals, 9th Circuit, March 13, 2014 at 47). The judiciary, in other words, should not be a "forum for debating the merits" of the biological opinion (ibid. at 48).

Meanwhile, the appellate majority defended the wildlife service's technical practices in generating its list of reasonable and prudent alternatives. On the question of whether rates of smelt mortality as detected by salvage screens could be used to regulate water flows, the court acknowledged the high stakes of the question: limiting the rate of the rivers' reverse flow "has great practical significance . . . as it represents the ultimate limit on the amount of water available to sustain California's millions of urban and agricultural users." But the court held that the wildlife service "did not act arbitrarily or capriciously in choosing an analytical tool that resulted in greater protections for the imperiled smelt population" (ibid. at 62). And with respect to the service's method for determining the optimal location for the low salinity zone where young smelt congregate (X2), the court outlined the significance of the issue: "Because the location of X2 directly affects how much water can be exported to southern California for agricultural and domestic purposes, the determination of where X2 is located was critical to the parties" (ibid. at 75). But, again ceding authority to the Fish and Wildlife Service, the majority decision emphasized that it was up to the agency's reasoned judgment to decide on the appropriate method for making this determination.

Finally, the court strongly disagreed with Wanger's admonition that the wildlife service should have weighed the benefits of smelt protection measures against the costs such measures imposed on human water users. Alluding to a 1977 Supreme Court decision concerning the endangered snail darter, the court wrote: "The law prohibits us from making 'such fine utilitarian calculations' to balance the smelt's interests against the interests of the citizens of California" (quoted in Bailey 2014).[11] According to the Endangered Species Act, the value of the existence of a species was "incalculable" and so could not be brought into relation with economic costs. Thus "the FWS [Fish and Wildlife Service] is not responsible for balancing the life of the delta smelt against the impact of restrictions on CVP/SWP [Central Valley Project / and State Water Project] operations" (San Luis v. Jewell at 117). Rather, the duty of the agency, the court argued, quoting the 1977 Supreme Court opinion, is to "halt and reverse the trend toward species extinction, *whatever the cost*" (ibid. at 117).

The following year, the US Supreme Court declined to hear the water agencies' appeal of the Ninth Circuit Court's judgment. At last, it seemed that the legal wrangling over the 2008 biological opinion had come to an end. While advocates of smelt protection could take heart at the support the fish had received from the courts, their judicial triumph was dampened by the data coming in from native fish population surveys in the delta. Over the intervening years, especially given the dire drought in California, restrictions on pumping prescribed by the 2008 biological opinion had not significantly increased freshwater flow into the delta—indeed, in 2014 and 2015 these restrictions were waived in response to the drought emergency. The many possible factors leading to native fish decline remained pervasive: alongside a lack of freshwater flow and entrainment at the pumps, there were other factors, such as invasive species, pesticide residues and sewage runoff, and an interrupted food web. The Endangered Species Act listing process as a tool for intervening in human practices in the name of species survival was limited in the kinds of questions it could pose: How to prevent the entrainment of adult fish?

11. The quotation in the opinion comes from the 1977 US Supreme Court majority opinion in *Tennessee Valley Authority v. Hill*, in which the preservation of an obscure fish—the snail darter—threatened to derail a costly dam project: "[Although] the burden on the public through the loss of millions of unrecoverable dollars would [seem to] greatly outweigh the loss of the snail darter . . . neither the Endangered Species Act nor Article III of the Constitution provides federal courts with authority to make such fine utilitarian calculations" (437 US 153 [1978] at 187).

Where should the brackish, low salinity zone be located? It could not address the warning carried by the smelt as sentinel of ecological collapse: that without a more significant transformation in the state's hydrological system, the delta would cease to function as a habitat for its native species, and the only remaining refuge for the smelt population would be in the Bureau of Reclamation–funded Fish Conservation and Culture Laboratory.

Coda: Infrastructural Transformation and Climate Uncertainty

As smelt protections began to impede water deliveries in the years after 2007, state resource managers and major water contractors sought a way to stabilize flows to urban and agricultural users. One approach was to bypass the problems of the delta and its pumps, to link the mountain snowmelt and watershed runoff from the Sacramento River directly to the aqueducts to the south. It was a solution that had been proposed—and rejected—twenty-five years earlier with the peripheral canal. This time, however, the water conveyors were able to negotiate a provisional settlement with a number of environmental groups.

The resulting proposal, known as the Bay Delta Conservation Plan, was to construct two thirty-mile-long and forty-foot-wide tunnels to carry the Sacramento River's water beneath the delta, at an estimated cost of $25 billion. This massive infrastructural transformation would not actually ship more water to the south, but it would deliver water more reliably, over a time horizon of fifty years. The key to ensuring reliable deliveries was that, if the plan were adopted, project operators would no longer be subject to lawsuits on the grounds of section 7 of the Endangered Species Act. Instead, the modified conveyance system would now be regulated according to a 1982 amendment to the Endangered Species Act, section 10, which emphasized habitat restoration rather than the absolute protection of particular species. Section 10 required water managers to develop a habitat conservation plan in collaboration with the Fish and Wildlife Service and environmental scientists. If a plan could be agreed upon that promised to restore the habitat of threatened species, project operators would be exempted from the section 7 prohibition on "taking" environmental species.[12]

The initial proposal thus comprised two parts: the construction of the two massive tunnels under the delta, alongside a plan to restore one hundred thousand acres

12. The hope, as one board member of the Metropolitan Water District put it, was that the tunnels could "make the Wanger decision inoperable because there won't be as much reverse flow just because you're pulling from north Delta and maybe the rivers will be flowing more naturally and therefore that decision might fall off the face of the earth" (quoted in Maven 2015b).

of delta habitat. This latter piece of the plan helped it gain support from a number of environmental groups, as well as from environmental scientists committed to restoration of the delta. Critical to the proposed plan's success in garnering support from both water resource managers and environmental advocacy groups was the premise that over the fifty-year planning horizon, habitat restoration would be under way and, meanwhile, the water operators would be able to deliver a predictable amount of water to contractors in the central and southern parts of California.

But in the fall of 2014, the plan began to fall apart as wildlife agency administrators and environmental scientists scrutinized the Bay Delta Conservation Plan's environmental impact report. A critical issue involved the plan's claims to be able to model the successful future results of its habitat restoration efforts. Scientists argued that, given uncertainties over what climate change would do to the Sierra snowpack, the salinity levels of the delta, and the capacity of certain species to survive in altered circumstances, it was impossible to project the results of habitat restoration fifty years ahead. On these grounds, federal regulators refused to grant a section 10 permit to the State Water Resources Board.[13] The compromise with environmental groups broke down, since there was no longer a regulatory rationale for water contractors to support large-scale habitat restoration efforts. In an age of mounting climate uncertainty, the planning horizon of infrastructure managers could not be aligned with the modeled future of threatened species.

Moyle, the fisheries biologist who initially recognized the threat to delta smelt existence posed by water diversion, once pointed out that the smelt was "extraordinarily well-adapted for the system the way it was" and, for that very reason, was unable to adjust to the massive transformations the delta had undergone (quoted in Boxall 2011). In parallel fashion, we might say that the federal and state water projects were designed for a mid-twentieth-century climate, in which snow accumulated in the mountains over the winter and could then be stored, as it melted in the spring, for the dry summer ahead.[14] As the breakdown of the Bay Delta Conservation Plan indicated, it would likely prove difficult to adjust this fixed system of water circulation to a rapidly changing climate.

13. As the general manager of the Metropolitan Water District reported to a meeting of the district's special committee on the Bay-Delta: "The conversations we've had with Cal Fish & Wildlife is that their concern really has to do with scientific uncertainty. The idea that we would be projecting how everything would be operating 50 years from now has just widened the uncertainty to such a range that they believe the modeling and the documents doesn't lead to a functional permit at that point" (quoted in Maven 2015a).

14. "The whole water system that we have in California was designed for the old climate," as one climate scientist put it. "The water system wasn't built for the climate that we have now" (quoted in Gillis 2015).

References

Alagona, Peter S. 2013. *After the Grizzly: Endangered Species and the Politics of Place in California*. Berkeley: University of California Press.

Bailey, Lorraine. 2014. "Big Win for Little Fish in Ninth Circuit." Courthouse News Service, March 13. www.courthousenews.com/2014/03/13/66124.htm.

Barringer, Felicity. 2011. "More Interior Scientists Are Taking Heat." *Green* (blog), *New York Times*, September 21. green.blogs.nytimes.com/2011/09/21/more-interior-scientists-are-taking-heat.

Beck, Ulrich. 1995. *Ecological Politics in an Age of Risk*. Translated by Amos Weisz. Cambridge, UK: Polity.

Benson, Melinda Harm. 2012. "Intelligent Tinkering: The Endangered Species Act and Resilience." *Ecology and Society* 17, no. 4. doi:10.5751/ES-05116-170428.

Boxall, Bettina. 2008. "U.S. Tightens Tap on Water from N. Calif." *Los Angeles Times*, December 16.

———. 2011. "A Small Fish Caught in a Big Fuss." *Los Angeles Times*, February 2.

California Department of Fish and Wildlife. 2015. "Summer Townet Survey: Project Overview." www.wildlife.ca.gov/Conservation/Delta/Townet-Survey (accessed September 8, 2015).

Chateauraynaud, Francis, and Didier Torny. 2005. "Mobiliser autour d'un risque: Des lanceurs aux porteurs d'alerte" ("To Rally around a Risk: From Whistleblower to Whistlebearer"). In *Risques et crises alimentaires* (*Food Risks and Crises*), edited by Cécile Lahellec, 329–39. Paris: Lavoisier.

Collier, Stephen J., and Andrew Lakoff. 2015. "Vital Systems Security: Reflexive Biopolitics and the Government of Emergency." *Theory, Culture and Society* 32, no. 2: 19–51.

Gillis, Justin. 2015. "California Drought Is Made Worse by Global Warming, Scientists Say." *New York Times*, August 20.

Hannity, Sean. 2009. "The Valley Hope Forgot: California Farmers at Obama's Mercy." FoxNews.com, September 18. www.foxnews.com/story/2009/09/18/valley-hope-forgot-california-farmers-at-obama-mercy.html.

Keck, Frédéric, and Andrew Lakoff. 2013. "Sentinel Devices." *Limn*, no. 3. www.limn.it/issue/03.

Kolbert, Elizabeth. 2014. *The Sixth Extinction: An Unnatural History*. New York: Holt.

Layzer, Judith. 2008. "Averting Ecological Collapse in California's Bay-Delta." In *Natural Experiments: Ecosystem-Based Management and the Environment*, 137–71. Cambridge, MA: MIT Press.

Manson, Craig, and Brandon Middleton. 2009. "Shutting off the Water Pumps to Save Delta Smelt Unwarranted." *San Francisco Chronicle*, January 8.

Maven [Chris Austin]. 2015a. "Bay Delta Conservation Plan Update: A Comparison of Regulatory Approaches." *Maven's Notebook* (blog), April 30. mavensnote book.com/2015/04/30/bay-delta-conservation-plan-update-a-comparison-of -regulatory-approaches.

———. 2015b. "Metropolitan's Special Committee on the Bay Delta Hears an Overview of the Cal Water Fix Documents and an Update on Drought Operations in the Delta." *Maven's Notebook* (blog), August 5. mavensnotebook .com/2015/08/05/metropolitans-special-committee-on-the-bay-delta-gets-an -overview-of-the-cal-water-fix-documents-and-an-update-on-drought-operations -in-the-delta.

Morain, Dan. 1991. "Plight of Delta Smelt Could Curb Water Flow." *Los Angeles Times*, June 10.

Moyle, Peter. 2015. "Prepare for Extinction of the Delta Smelt." *California Water-Blog*, March 18. californiawaterblog.com/2015/03/18/prepare-for-extinction -of-delta-smelt/.

Murphy, Dean E. 1993. "Delta Smelt Designated as Threatened Species." *Los Angeles Times*, March 5.

Porter, Theodore M. 2015. "The Flight of the Indicator." In *The World of Indicators: The Making of Governmental Knowledge through Quantification*, edited by Richard Rottenberg et al., 34–55. Cambridge: Cambridge University Press.

Shigley, Paul. 2012. "The Devil Is in the Delta." *Planning*, January. www.planning .org/planning/2012/jan/waterwarriorsside1.htm.

Sommer, Ted, Rich Breuer, and Anke Mueller-Solger. 2007. "The Pelagic Organism Decline (POD) in the Upper San Francisco Estuary and Implications for the Sacramento River Watershed." *Waterways: Sacramento River Watershed Program* 22 (February): 1–2.

Taugher, Mike. 2005. "Environmental Sirens in Delta Are Screaming." *Contra Costa Times*, May 1.

UC Davis. 2015. "'Refuge' for the Endangered Delta Smelt — Newly Funded." *News and Information*, March 25. news.ucdavis.edu/search/news_detail.lasso?id =11182.

Uhlman, Lisa. 2011. "California Water Groups Force Hold on Smelt Protection Plan." *Law 360*, August 31. www.law360.com/articles/268798/calif-water -groups-force-hold-on-smelt-protection-plan.

US Department of the Interior, Fish and Wildlife Service. 2008. "Formal Endangered Species Act Consultation on the Proposed Coordinated Operations of the Central Valley Project (CVP) and State Water Project (SWP)." December. Sacramento: US Department of the Interior, Fish and Wildlife Service, California and Nevada Region.

US Fish and Wildlife Service and National Marine Fisheries Service. 1998. *Endangered Species Consultation Handbook: Procedures for Conducting Consultation and Conference Activities under Section 7 of the Endangered Species Act* (March).

Vidal, Fernando, and Nélia Dias. 2015. "Introduction: The Endangerment Sensibility." In *Endangerment, Biodiversity, and Culture*, edited by Fernando Vidal and Nélia Dias, 1–38. New York: Routledge.

Andrew Lakoff is an associate professor of sociology and communication at the University of Southern California. He is the author of *Pharmaceutical Reason: Knowledge and Value in Global Psychiatry* (2006) and coeditor of *Global Pharmaceuticals: Ethics, Markets, Practices* (2006) and *Biosecurity Interventions: Global Health and Security in Question* (2008).

The Rationed City:
The Politics of Water, Housing,
and Land Use in Drought-Parched
São Paulo

Daniel Aldana Cohen

Specters of rationing haunt metro São Paulo. Drinking water supplies have plunged to historic and dangerous lows. Overall water use has been slashed by a fifth. But the region's largest and third-largest supply systems still verge on collapse. Water shortages have caused repeated school closures; proliferating uncovered rainwater containers have helped triple the rate of dengue infections; water contamination due to pressure reductions has caused a spike in dysentery; and the army is preparing for a collapse in supplies and has war gamed a daylong takeover of a utility station in central São Paulo.

In the vicious political debate that has engulfed the crisis, the idea of rationing has become a flashpoint. The state's center-right governor, Geraldo Alckmin, has insisted since early 2014 that rationing would be avoided at all costs, stating, "There is not any possibility of rationing, even amidst the greatest drought in the past 84 years" (Pimentel 2014). And if rationing did occur, it would be cata-

For reading and providing comments on earlier versions of this article and for helping me think through its conceptual apparatus, I thank Hillary Angelo, Gianpaolo Baiocchi, Neil Brenner, Craig Calhoun, Eric Klinenberg, Liz Koslov, Tom Malleson, Jeff Manza, Nate Millington, David Wachsmuth, and the two anonymous reviewers. Mistakes and misconceptions are mine alone. I also thank those in São Paulo who assisted in my research on housing, land use, and environmental politics, including Angela Alonso, Renata Bichir, Ruy Braga, Mariana Fix, Eduardo Marques (and the staff at the Centro de Estudos da Metropole), Daniel Sanfelici, Paula Santoro, and João Seitte Whitaker. I thank the Social Sciences and Humanities Research Council and the Institute for Public Knowledge at New York University for funding this research. Last, and most important, I thank all those I have interviewed or followed around for their time and generosity.

All translations from Portuguese-language sources are by the author.

Public Culture 28:2 DOI 10.1215/08992363-3427451

strophic, with residents going two days with water and five days without. Alckmin and the Companhia de Saneamento Básico do Estado de São Paulo (SABESP), the state's water utility, have issued financial bonuses and penalties to encourage conservation; they have imposed daily reductions in water pressure that dry taps for hours on end, disproportionately hurting the poor.[1] They have also insisted that these measures do not constitute rationing.

Alckmin's critics have meanwhile accused the governor and SABESP of an undeclared and unequal rationing that is punishing the poor. The issue of whether there is a de facto rationing of water (which the evidence supports), or whether SABESP should ration more equitably and transparently, concentrates the drought's fundamental questions: How is a suddenly scarce necessity being shared? How should it be?

It is not shocking that the government has resisted the stigma and operational risks associated with outright rationing. But at certain moments, high-level officials have suggested that rationing was just weeks away. São Paulo came within days of implementing rationing during the 2003 drought. Some cities in São Paulo's metro region, like Mauá and Guarulhos, not directly served by SABESP, have undergone outright rationing, with water service regularly shut off for days at a time. So have dozens of cities in the country's northeast, and so has Puerto Rico's San Juan.[2] Rationing is politically problematic, but it is plausible.

My aim here is not to explain why São Paulo's water is not being rationed equitably. Instead, I use an analysis of the historic and contemporary underpinnings of the present crisis, of the state and SABESP's de facto, passive rationing, and of the reaction and alternative proposals from several civil society groups, to propose a new approach to ecological scarcity. To understand the rationed city—whether the rationing is transparent and equitable or opaque and unequal—I argue that we should revitalize, in a socioecological and crisis-sensitive form, Manuel Castells's (1977, 1983, 2002) concept of collective consumption politics: namely, contests over how states provide, or facilitate, the goods and services that sustain urban living, with struggles over any one element implicating several others.

More specifically, I argue that in São Paulo the politics of water rationing doubly fuse with those of housing and land use—physically and politically. And more broadly, I contend that in large, segregated cities in a warming world, the politics of extreme weather are the politics of collective consumption. The question is how

1. SABESP directly serves most, but not all, of the state's water consumers, including the city of São Paulo and most neighboring municipalities.
2. Rationing of outdoor water use is more common worldwide, but is less intrusive than wholesale shutoffs.

acute crises and long-standing socioecological struggles interact, from above and below.

Collective Consumption and the Rationed City

The most vibrant accounts of urban water politics come from the field of urban political ecology, for which water has served as a leading case of the co-constitution of nature, urbanization, and modernity (Gandy 2014; Heynen, Kaika, and Swyngedouw 2006; Kaika 2005; Keil 2005; Swyngedouw 2004). The field has paid increasing attention to urban regions of the global South, especially water's entwinement with a broad array of messy urban processes, where the problems of unequal housing and land use often play a central role (Amin 2014; Anand 2011; Bakker and Kooy 2010; Barnes 2014; Kane 2012; Meehan 2013; Rademacher 2011). A crucial dilemma, to which the field keeps returning, is how to place water struggles in relation to overlapping, meso-level politics in volatile moments.

For many, the answer lies outside the familiar domains of water governance and their institutions. Karen Bakker (2010) argues that the levers of sociopolitical power needed to democratize water governance will be found in "right to the city" struggles. Patrick Bond (2012) develops that idea, locating water struggles in a broader South African "right to the city" movement, showing how these are connected, and analogous, to other battles around the decommodification of basic necessities, like housing and antiretroviral treatments for AIDS. Meanwhile, Erik Swyngedouw (2009: 228) expresses frustration that, most often, a "post-political environmental consensus . . . forestalls the articulation of divergent, conflicting and alternative trajectories of future socio-environmental possibilities."

The "right to the city," or the genuinely "political," serves as a helpful category for naming what broad coalitions fight for or for distinguishing struggle from co-optation. But how should we characterize the viscera of a socioecological politics still in motion?

The issue with rationing is that in a city of "splintered infrastructure networks" (Graham and Marvin 2001), there can be no clean one-to-one relationship between a logic of distribution, infrastructural practices, physical topography, and the related patterns of land use and housing. There is no one button anyone can press to guarantee that each resident receives the same quantity of liquid. For physical and political reasons, the politics of water implicates both the substance of other issues and the rules of state rule.

Here a revitalized socioecological notion of collective consumption, made sensitive to political volatility, proves helpful. Castells (1977, 2002) first developed the concept to specify what he viewed as the distinctive function of the urban, namely, the state-facilitated reproduction of labor—in other words, keeping workers alive and productive. This required goods and services, like housing and health care, that it would be inefficient for the market to provide. (Or so it seemed in 1970s Paris.) As the Fordist state crumbled, Castells (1983) adopted a less structuralist position, reformulating collective consumption politics in conjoined material and cultural terms and taking the internal dynamics of movements more seriously. Collective consumption goods and services were still facilitated by the state, but now Castells viewed the quality and extent of the state's activities more as the result of social movement struggle than of the functional requirements of capital.[3] Throughout, key threads of continuity are the emphasis on the state's role in facilitating these goods and services and the emphasis on their unequal provision as the contested crux of urban inequality.

Parsing the debates spurred by the concept is beyond this article's scope. Instead, I redeploy it here to emphasize political struggle from below and above where water is but one of several, interconnected, state-facilitated socioecological goods and services whose caliber and distribution are crucial to the quality of urban life. Paying attention to political volatility, where prevailing schemas and resources can be reconfigured (Sewell 2005), tightens our focus on the question of political contagion, which is pursued by social movements, and containment, which is typically pursued from above.[4]

Returning to São Paulo's water crisis, I argue that two of these classic collective consumption issues, housing and land use, possess priority. In unequal megacities like São Paulo, housing and land use are already key arenas for the accumulation of capital and for popular struggles to assert citizenship (Holston 2008; Roy 2009). Housing and land use are also central to a long-term sustainability and climate adaptation agenda. The construction of dense, affordable housing in well-serviced areas will be necessary for cities to lower their carbon emissions, a root cause of extreme weather (Cohen, forthcoming; Seto et al. 2014). And expanding affordable housing stock in well-serviced areas, and improving it in peripheral ones, would relieve pressure on urban areas' ecologically delicate edges—often favored sites for informal construction—while reducing people's vulnerability and facilitating the universalization of clean water and sanitation systems.

3. In São Paulo, social movement scholar Lúcio Kowarick (2000) has used Castells's concept and traced a similar path, from a narrower focus on housing movements' material interests to a closer engagement with their subjectivity.

4. For a prior example in the context of ecological crisis, see Cohen and Liboiron 2014 and Superstorm Research Lab 2013.

In May 2015, I conducted three weeks of interviews and participant observation in São Paulo, building on twelve prior months of fieldwork in the city on housing and ecological politics and using a relational approach consistent with the collective consumption concept. Relational fieldwork "gives ontological primacy, not to groups or places, but to configurations of relations . . . [and hence focus on] dynamics that emerge between groups or agencies qualitatively different from, yet oriented toward and enmeshed with, one another" (Desmond 2014: 554; see also Emirbayer 1997).

I have focused in particular on a range of actors seeking to transform the city's housing, transit, climate, and water politics. I have interviewed nearly sixty green policy elites, housing movement actors, and city planners and policy makers. I have attended their meetings and events, from rowdy housing protests and quiet gatherings in occupied buildings to city officials' public meetings about a new master plan to environmental seminars and green business networking events. And I have assembled and studied government documents, gray policy studies, and media reports.

The argument that follows reflects this cumulative research engagement, during which I have witnessed both mutual estrangement and, now, tentative cooperation between the city's housing and environmental movements. I write in the midst of São Paulo's dry season. Water managers have averted a collapse in supplies, but the city's reservoirs sit emptier than one year ago. The advantage of informed, snapshot research in the midst of a crisis is that the moment's possible futures are viscerally present.

I begin my account of São Paulo's water crisis by briefly summarizing the historic entwinement of São Paulo's water, housing, and land-use politics, and then trace the more contemporary socioecological contours of the crisis. Then I explore how the state and SABESP have pursued de facto rationing, while environmentalists and housing movements have advocated more sweeping and democratic programs of sharing scarce water.

Toward Mutual Estrangement

It was no accident that São Paulo became a "city of walls" (Caldeira 2000). The explosive growth of São Paulo's poor peripheries was first sparked by city elites' expelling the working class from a once compacted, mixed-income, streetcar-linked downtown, in an effort to homogenize central urban spaces (Holston 2008). Subsequent federal housing policies exacerbated the trend of sprawling peripheral development (Santoro, Ferrara, and Whately 2008), although the resulting areas were always socially varied; segregation has operated at a finer grain than the core-periphery opposition suggests (Caldeira 2000; Holston 2008).

The peripheries' expansion coincided with transformations of the city's river and road systems. Twentieth-century governments paved over the city's countless rivers and streams to create a vast network of freeways to facilitate the movement of people and goods (Jacobi et al. 2015). The city's biggest rivers, Tietê and Pinheiros, and the larger of its two great southern reservoirs, Billings, were badly polluted by raw sewage and industrial waste. Neglect became the norm. When Pedro Jacobi and Camila Giorgetti (2009) surveyed residents of a peripheral, riverside neighborhood subject to flooding, more residents hoped that the adjacent stream would be paved over than the number who wanted it ecologically restored as a site for leisure.

Another crucial development was a 1977 environmental law that restricted legal land occupation along the edges of the southern zone's massive reservoirs and their watersheds. As land prices in the newly restricted areas collapsed, and a broader economic slowdown increased poverty, hundreds of thousands, perhaps a million, people moved into these and other precarious waterside areas (Jacobi 2006; Santoro, Ferrara, and Whately 2008). Many of the resulting informal communities lack decent infrastructure, are vulnerable to flash floods and mudslides, and dump sewage into waterways. Poor communities are not the only actors contributing to the degradation of the urban region's surface waters, but capturing and treating their sewage would help.[5]

There have been waves of contradictory policy efforts aimed at urbanizing or removing these communities, including a program to build "linear parks" along rivers. These efforts have seen some success but moved slowly. Throughout, a core problem has been that those settled in vulnerable areas often resist efforts to displace them, even temporarily, usually because of residents' dissatisfaction with proposed resettlement offers or suspicion of formal authorities. As efforts to recuperate the city's waters have been pursued more vigorously by environmentalists since the 1990s, this dynamic has caused increasing tensions between two camps: on the one hand, residents of these areas (typically termed "invaders"), housing movements, and allies in the city's Workers' Party; on the other, the city's environmental advocates and policy makers. Over and over, housing movement leaders have told me that these struggles alienated them from the city's environmental movement.

5. In fact, while access to clean water is very good in São Paulo's formal neighborhoods, sanitation coverage is, for various reasons, much worse. It is likely that just over half the city's sewage is treated.

Political ecologists of São Paulo's water governance have grappled with these tensions. Prominent scholars have chronicled the segregated city's shifting historical relationship to local and regional waters (Abers and Keck 2013; Jacobi 2009; Jacobi et al. 2013; Jacobi, Fracalanza, and Silva-Sánchez 2015; Ribeiro 2011). But the authors' repeated calls for participatory processes rarely mention really existing housing movements. Yet those groups, in recent decades, have become the city's most consequential and vibrant activists (Earle 2012; Hirata and Oliveira 2012; Kowarick 1994). An excellent synthesis of the current water crisis never mentions the city's housing movements (Jacobi et al. 2015). Neither do Ana Paula Fracalanza, Amanda Martins Jacob, and Rodrigo Furtado Eça et al. (2013), even in their argument for a more egalitarian approach to water governance, which they frame in terms of environmental justice, but without reference to the "right to the city" concept, which is enshrined in Brazilian federal law, or to the broad urban reform movement.[6]

It is true that most of the city's consolidated housing groups are focused on gaining access to vacant properties in the city center. But their urban reform agenda remains closely linked to the issue of ecological areas. The urbanist Maria Luisa Refinetti Martins (2011: 64), a rare housing scholar who engages ecological debates, argues that movements' housing agenda should be "observed as belonging to the same environmental perspective" as discussions of "urban expansion in environmentally fragile areas." The current Workers' Party mayor's new master plan for the city takes this basic approach. And its development has drawn cautious praise from environmentalists and housing activists. But it is a long way from being implemented.

In sum, clashing claims on the state, framed in terms of housing and economic justice, on the one hand, and environmental terms, on the other, have established a political culture that has pitted against each other two mobilized groups of advocates for more democratic, higher-quality collective consumption. It is difficult to imagine a democratization of the urban region's water governance if these two camps cannot find some common ground. But as we shall see, the state and SABESP's actions during the current crisis are facilitating a tentative rapprochement.

---

6. To be sure, the city's more politicized housing movements have historically focused on the city center, with the exception of the Homeless Workers' Movement (MTST). Many other ad hoc groups are widely accused of being led by opportunists who hope to profit from eventual resettlement incentives and who mislead and coerce vulnerable followers desperate for somewhere to set up a shack.

Contours of the Crisis

Rainfall levels in 2013 and 2014 were the lowest in the region's recorded history, as the governor and SABESP have repeatedly emphasized. But rainfall was nearly as low in 1953. Moreover, experts and government bodies have long warned that the city's water supply system was not keeping up with the region's growing population and consumption and that it could "enter into collapse in the short term" (Ribeiro 2011: 130; see also Estado de São Paulo—Secretaría do Meio Ambiente 2009). Indeed, São Paulo's metro region is notoriously water stressed and therefore highly dependent on distant watersheds.

The governor and others have argued that the current drought was unforeseeable and have blamed its severity on anthropogenic climate change. But the best science expects global warming to increase rainfall (and flash floods) in São Paulo, not dry it out (C. Nobre 2010). There is, however, some evidence that human-driven climatic factors are aggravating the low rainfall—but these are regional, not planetary, and linked to Brazil's agro-industrial sectors.

In the University of São Paulo's Institute for Biosciences, I met the postdoctoral scholar Leandro Tambosi, whose research shows that some of São Paulo state's new vegetation is actually drying the Cantareira water system. As the price of raising cattle rises, pasture land is being planted with eucalyptus to supply cellulose for making paper. But the eucalyptus trees suck great quantities of water out of the ground; when that water is evapotranspirated into the air, prevailing winds blow it away. The news is not all bad. Scholars in the state's environmental ministry tell me that they will soon publish results showing that São Paulo state's reforestation—largely eucalyptus-driven—means that the region's forests, for the first time in years, are net absorbers of carbon.

Farther afield, there is another story of the agro-ecological degradation of São Paulo's water supplies. The Amazon scholar Antonio Nobre (2014: 17–18) released a high-profile, much-discussed research synthesis in late 2014 that drew attention to the theory of flying rivers. The theory states that Amazonian trees evaporate massive amounts of water into enormous streams of vapor. These transport water high aboveground to southeastern Brazil, where it falls as rain. This explains the relative humidity of the regions around Rio de Janeiro and São Paulo, while most of the globe, at that latitude, is desert dry.

But as A. Nobre has argued repeatedly in the Brazilian press, the Amazon's progressive deforestation, historically driven by the cattle and soya industries, is shrinking those flying rivers. The model implies that one region is exporting the other's water—not piped directly into clear plastic bottles but indirectly embedded in legumes and flesh. In both São Paulo state and farther afield, the latest science suggests, land-use decisions implicating booming export sectors are shaping the city's water supply.

I now turn to the narrower question of the water system's fortunes and management. Governor Alckmin is familiar with São Paulo's water stress. He was also in office in 2003, when water levels in the Cantareira system dropped below 5 percent of capacity, excluding the system's "dead volume." Reviewing press coverage from the era, I found several weeks when the implementation of rationing was thought to be days away, each time averted at the last minute by sudden rainfall. The following year, when SABESP renewed its contract for managing the region's water system, it agreed to a series of infrastructural projects to increase water supplies. Most were never started, but they have reappeared during the current crisis as emergency measures to be rushed.

With this drought, rationing has returned to the headlines. By late 2013, it was clear that the state could be facing an unprecedented crisis. But in 2014, Alckmin was running for reelection. The state and SABESP forswore rationing, instead moving in February 2014 to reduce the water pressure in the pipes, announce a discount on water bills for those who cut consumption, link up several water systems to reduce dependence on the Cantareira, and, for the first time, draw water from that system's dead volume. The state government would also pursue a series of emergency infrastructural fixes to pull more water, both from the metro region and from other watersheds, into the city's supply system. To pay for all this, SABESP has hiked water rates and cut its spending on its sewage system in half. It has emerged, however, that at the dawn of the crisis, SABESP's workers in fact planned to ration.

In an internal document prepared in January 2014, technicians laid out a detailed rationing plan that addressed both technical challenges and community outreach. It urged careful work to keep the population informed of looming water cuts, asserting that it was "vital that there be a week before the public announcement of a water rotation [*rodízio*] and its actual initiation" and detailing the need for daily and monthly informational updates on all aspects of the rationing and broader water situation (SABESP 2014: 14, 23–24). In the operational core of a public-private utility, bureaucrats had articulated a plan oriented toward community needs.

The plan was not implemented, and the Cantareira system bore the immediate brunt of the historic drought. Operated by SABESP, the Cantareira has been the focus of analysis and media commentary for good reason: the system supplies nearly half the drinking water of metro São Paulo, including 9 million residential customers (Ribeiro 2011). The system is "a complex network of canals and pumping stations owned by the state and federal governments that divert[s] 31 cubic meters of water per second from tributaries of the Piracicaba River to provide water for the residents of São Paulo, less than 100 miles to the southeast" (Abers and Keck 2013: 146). At the time of writing, water withdrawals had been reduced by over seventeen cubic meters per second, down from thirty-two, in early 2014.

Even so, the Cantareira's water is being drawn from "technical reserves," better known as its dead volumes. These are three layers of water that until the current crisis had never been tapped; the water lies beneath dams' existing floodgates and is disproportionately polluted. Indeed, until 2014, the quantity of the dead volume, which makes up nearly a fifth of the system's overall capacity, was not included in measures of available water supply.[7]

In mid-2014, SABESP resorted to the Cantareira's dead volume with little publicity, spending tens of millions of dollars to deploy new pipes and floating water pumps to extract the water. In October 2014, Alckmin said on television, "There is no water shortage in São Paulo. There will be no water shortage in São Paulo." In fact, resorting to the Cantareira's dead volume as SABESP had done months earlier would expose and dry much of its ground soil, breaking the system's seal. It could take a decade to recover completely.

Were the timid water restraint measures of 2014 a mere question of political interference? Many critics do not think so, arguing persuasively that the utility's negligence was consistent with its status as a for-profit public-private utility. While the state owns a slender majority of the stocks, the rest have been listed on the São Paulo and New York exchanges since 2004. Federal and state public prosecutors have argued that, with support from the state government, SABESP prioritized easy profits over long-term investment and prudent management, even running up profits in 2012 and 2013 as the historic drought developed (Ministério Público Federal and Ministério Público do Estado de São Paulo 2014). Since SABESP's income depends on selling water, the allegation runs, it is biased against taking measures to reduce water consumption.

In truth, it is difficult to trace the width and path of each line of authority in the state's complex water governance system, which includes a wide range of actors and agencies. But it remains the case that SABESP is by far the largest

7. Critics, including the state's public ministry, have argued that SABESP is misleading the public and should report reserves on its website and in public releases as a *negative* percentage, to accurately reflect the unprecedented use of the dead volume and facilitate comparisons with historic water levels. SABESP has retorted that negative percentages are mathematically incoherent and that, in fact, water in the dead volume is of almost equal quality to normal reserves.

and wealthiest of the water institutions and that Alckmin directly or indirectly chooses the heads of the major water institutions These are the two key actors in the crisis, and this is why I focus on them. Moreover, SABESP has always implemented Alckmin's top priority in the crisis—to downplay its severity and to rule out rationing—even when utility leaders differed in opinion.

For instance, in late 2014, its leadership grew gravely concerned with public complacency, as revealed by a recording of a top-level meeting on October 20, 2014, leaked to the newspaper *Folha de São Paulo*. One director describes the situation as "agonizing," saying that he did not know what to do if the 2014–15 rainy season was as sparse as in 2013–14. SABESP's president said: "I think that because of guidance from above, SABESP has been in the media very little. I think it's a mistake. We needed to be in the media more . . . all of us [utility leaders] on the same theme: conserve water. . . . This needed to be reiterated in the media, but we had to follow guidance. We have superiors" (Boghossian and Gama 2014). Whether this was a reference to Alckmin's office or to SABESP's board of directors (the majority appointed by Alckmin) was unclear.

In sum, the water crisis has implicated a range of contentious political issues, from agro-industrial land use beyond city limits to the actions of, and the relationship between, a governor's office and a profit-driven utility. In each case, Alckmin and SABESP have sought to contain the crisis by taking the minimum outward measures to curb water consumption or publicize the crisis. One result was the resort to the Cantareira's dead volume; state and city depleted the urban region's most important supply system more than necessary. Still, reductions from the Cantareira were nearly halved through 2014 and further cut in 2015. How?

Rationing the City

The rationing debate in São Paulo turns on two words that are often, but not always, used interchangeably. *Rodízio* literally means "rotation" (like the alternation of water service on and off) but is often used in the more abstract sense of "rationing." *Racionamento* means "rationing" in the English sense—namely, it refers to fixed allocations and implies (but does not require) that these are equitable.

Nobody really contests the fact that SABESP's systematic reductions in water pressure, lasting several hours per day, lead taps to run dry (although the governor has said that no one has "lacked for" water). Water will only flow from the faucet during off-hours if enough of it has been stored in a tank. Meanwhile, government entities and SABESP are pressing clients to reduce water use with financial incentives—bonuses for significant cutbacks since February 2014, and fines for using more water than in the previous year, since February 2015. But Alckmin has repeatedly argued that only switching neighborhood taps on and off would constitute actual rationing.

SABESP's official plan for 2015 (released only in May) doubles down on this argument in its opening pages, arguing that the utility has instead pursued only *voluntary* measures to curb consumption (nowhere in the report does the word *racionamento* appear). The report frames the water pressure reductions not in terms of curbing consumption but exclusively as a strategy to reduce leakage from pipes (through which a quarter to a third of the utility's water is lost). The report insists that rotation proper, in the sense of switching neighborhood water mains on and off, must be avoided: first, because this would be unduly coercive and, second, because leaky pipes left empty for extended periods would expose the population to contamination, since soil and sewage could enter into depressurized pipes (SABESP 2015a: 13–14). Of course, reduced pressure also allows contaminants into pipes.

Fundamentally, the debate hinges on the issue of whether pressure reductions constitute a compulsory reduction of consumption and, if so, whose consumption is most forcibly reduced. The report strangely states that "it would be imperious to emphasize that pressure reductions have been the most effective measure in confronting the water crisis, being responsible for reducing water drawn from the Cantareira system by only 7.3 m^3/s [cubic meters per second]" (ibid.: 20). But it is clear from the quantitative data presented pages later that pressure reduction *was* the measure responsible for the greatest reduction in the use of the Cantareira's water. Pressure reductions cut consumption by more than twice as much as voluntary reductions, the next most important measure, according to SABESP's own calculations (ibid.: 24–25).

It may not shock readers to learn that the poor have suffered the most from these reductions, but discovering *how* is crucial to understanding the role of housing and land use.[8] The clearest evidence for pressure reduction's unequal burden comes from polls by Datafolha. In October 2014 and February 2015, it asked respondents if they had experienced a disruption in water service. Each time it found that twice as many poor households as rich households reported dry taps, 65 percent to 32 percent in October and 50 percent to 25 percent in February (Datafolha 2014: 36; 2015: 35).

Why the disjuncture? Poor neighborhoods and favelas are often farthest from transfer stations and on the highest ground. The poorest homes lack water tanks

---

8. The report never addresses the issue of the potential inequality of water provision.

to store water if it does reach them, which means that their homes cannot accumulate water if and when it runs. SABESP (2015b: 1) has argued since January that even half-day reductions in water pressure would "not be noticed" by anyone living in a building with sufficiently large water tanks, pointing out (somewhat passive-aggressively) that "the National Institute of Technical Norms dictates that the client should possess water storage capacity to last a minimum of twenty-four hours." The October 2014 Datafolha poll found that house dwellers were nearly three times as likely as apartment dwellers to go without water.

In recognition of this issue, the state government, in January 2015, announced that it would distribute twenty-five thousand water tanks to homes in the periphery by June; in early May, only 20 percent had been delivered (Lobel 2015). There is also the question of elevation. In February, SABESP's president conceded in testimony before São Paulo's city council that the utility was not, despite earlier promises, maintaining water pressure at the threshold required by the National Institute of Technical Norms to ensure that water would reach elevated areas (Pinho 2015). Indeed, journalists have found several poor, peripheral neighborhoods where no water has run for days at a time.

In brief, when the total water supply is zero-sum and declining, tanks are a technology of systematically unequal distribution, not just individual convenience. Topography plays a supporting role. If the poor are getting less, then that leaves more water for the rest, and vice versa.

Meanwhile, there are reports that, in fact, SABESP technicians *are* switching taps for whole neighborhoods on and off. Journalists (Garcia and Sorano 2015) secretly recorded utility workers saying that they do exactly this every day (and are thus not merely reducing pressure); a high-level SABESP source told the *Estado de São Paulo* newspaper that up to 40 percent of the metro region's neighborhoods were daily having their water toggled on and off (Leite 2015). Such reports are impossible to verify, but they are easy to believe for those who track the city's politics.

A lawsuit filed against the state's water management by São Paulo's municipal Workers' Party calls the water pressure reductions "an undeclared rotation [*rodízio*], as various neighborhoods in the city's periphery report that for nearly a year they have gone without water for days" (Cardoso and Fiorilo 2015: 20). When I raised the issue of rationing to a member of the Homeless Workers' Movement (Movimento dos Trabalhadores Sem Teto, or MTST) who lives in the city's southern zone, she replied, "Maybe there's no rotation [*rodízio*] for the governor, but here there's rotation every day." She said that her neighborhood had gone up to five full days without water, making it impossible to send her child to school (which also sometimes closed when its taps ran dry) and that the situation caused delays in getting medical care. During other long stretches, she said, water only flowed from after midnight to the late morning. The woman's companions also spoke of water running dark and smelly and causing weeklong spells of diarrhea. Epidemiologists have found that a spike in dysentery in 2014 was associated with water pressure reductions (Martin 2015).

Finally, I note the existence, widely denounced by many in civil society, of contracts with SABESP that charge companies a discounted water fee, reducing clients' economic incentive to save water. Five hundred thirty-seven such contracts were obtained and analyzed by independent media groups, Pública and Artigo 19, in May 2015. Until 2014, the contracts stipulated a minimum level of water consumption that companies had to pay for, and they forbade investment in alternative sources or water recycling. In 2014 SABESP struck these two conditions, but it still signed thirty-six new fixed-price contracts. Clients included banks, auto companies, sport clubs, and supermarkets (Arteta et al. 2015).

In May the utility and government returned to arguing that if emergency works to add water to the reservoir system are not completed, and there is a profound emergency, there would need to be a rotation of five days without water, two days with water. SABESP held a seminar with regional army commanders, where the director of SABESP warned of total social breakdown as early as July unless emergency works to add water to the utility's supply system are completed, saying: "There will be terror. There will be no food, no electricity . . . like a scene from the end of the world. . . . But I hope that will not happen" (quoted in Rodrigues 2015). Two weeks later, an army division war gamed the takeover of a SABESP building in a leafy, central neighborhood.

The positive case for transparent, equitable rationing is that it amounts to a difficult but ultimately open, democratic, and fair method of distributing scarce resources (Cox 2013). By late May 2015, the state government and SABESP had reframed rationing as a proto-apocalyptic last resort, the final gasp of a collapsing water system with the army looming behind dry taps. What is occluded by this harsh rhetoric is the notion that rationing need not be achieved by pipes and taps alone, but could instead be realized through a combination of top-down, state-led action and grassroots governance from below. In other words, one could agree with SABESP's view that large-scale rotation is impractical but still support egalitarian rationing. But if this vision of collective consumption were to be implemented for water, why should it end there? And what would this imply for the rules of state rule?

Below I show that in the self-conscious politics of housing and environmental movement organizers, the relationship of housing and land use to water is front of mind. But demands for more democratic water governance also draw on, and spill into, other domains of collective consumption struggle.

The "June Days" of 2013 are a crucial precedent to the present crisis. In late June of that year, hundreds of thousands took to the streets of São Paulo and other major cities to protest a R$0.20 hike to bus fare (Maricato 2013). They were the largest demonstrations in two decades. Fare hikes were repealed across the country. Protesters represented Brazil's full class and race spectrum, fostering unexpected encounters and alliances. And there was a kind of issue contagion from the R$0.20 transit fare hike to a gamut of collective consumption concerns. Complaints quickly encompassed health and education services, government corruption, and wasted spending on the World Cup. Less obvious in the moment was that this brief eruption lingered and expanded in São Paulo's peripheries, where housing anchored a range of "right to the city" demands.[9]

In December 2013, as I sat in on a meeting of the MTST in a movement occupation that members called the Gaza Strip, an organizer told me, "We're harvesting the fruits of June." Also in December, the city government's district administrator of a peripheral neighborhood in the city's southern zone would tell me, albeit less enthusiastically, that the number of vacant land occupations by housing movements in her district had exploded.

Figure 1　Jussara Basso of the MTST in the New Palestine encampment in São Paulo's southwestern zone. Photograph by the author

In May 2015, in the MTST encampment called New Palestine at the city's southwestern edge (see fig. 1), the organizer Jussara Basso argued that nearly two years after the June Days, the MTST was still growing thanks to its aftermath. Basso said that while canceling the bus fare hike stemmed the downtown protests, it also showed workers in the periphery that political action had immediate effects.

9. Indeed, the housing movement's political partner, the group Periferia Ativa (Active Periphery) (2013a, 2013b), was already making this argument in its newsletter in June and July 2013.

"By the end of 2013," she said, "there were fifty-four housing occupations just in São Paulo, many of them spontaneous." They were housing occupations—not bus protests. With the MTST seizing leadership of the new energy in the housing movement, its most visible leader, Guilherme Boulos, was offered a column in the mainstream *Folha de São Paulo*. The most boisterous protest against the state's handling of the water crisis was led by the MTST, drawing fifteen thousand people into downtown streets in February 2015.

I note the June Days' precedent because as the state and SABESP focus primarily on water infrastructure, and the mainstream media provides only intermittent coverage of the crisis, the visible, public politics of São Paulo's water shortage have largely been driven by sectors of civil society (broadly conceived) experimenting with cooperation and alliance—especially the housing movements mobilizing the poor and the environmental groups with an audience in the city's middle class. The broad-based, unruly, unpredictable social eruption of June 2013 threatens to reappear here, extending the egalitarian logic of rationing water into broader demands.

I met a leading member of the environmental movement in one of the city's first community gardens in Pinheiros, a wealthy neighborhood a world away from New Palestine. Claudia Visoni, an activist with the Alliance for Water, told me that "São Paulo is the most humid desert in the world." The city draws its drinking water largely from the city's hinterlands, ignoring long-polluted sources closer to home. As I help Visoni haul sap-sticky wood from her station wagon's trunk to the garden to fortify a bridge over a wrinkle in the ground, she tells me how her fellow gardeners found a tiny water source, just beneath the ground surface. They dug out around it and are now using it to irrigate fruits, vegetables, and flowers. The city is full of such small springs, but environmental activists have only recently taken an interest. One group, called Ruas e Ríos (Roads and Rivers), produced a widely viewed online video reminding residents that almost every major avenue was paved over a river just decades ago.

In fact, both environmentalists and housing movement leaders have called for the state government to help community groups test, store, and find uses for springwater and well water. And they blame SABESP's business model—selling water as a product—for the state's and the utility's reluctance to help people get water elsewhere, actions that would empower citizens and break SABESP's monopoly on the provision of water. The focus on taking better care of local sources resonates with a desire, increasingly widespread across civil society, for government to go further in peeling back the city's ubiquitous concrete and planting more vegetation. Doing so would help stave off heat waves and flash floods, each projected to worsen with global warming. The architect Milton Braga has even called for a massive campaign to build rooftop and sidewalk gardens as a system of "micro-drainage." "Think about a salad spinner," he told me. "You see how much water comes out when you dry the leaves?"

In its more elaborate form, the alternative paradigm with broad support from environmentalists is to reduce dependence on distant water sources and instead focus on reducing consumption and on retaining rainwater and storm water, treating all of the city's sewage, cleaning the water in the city's rivers and reservoirs, and expanding and revitalizing local watersheds. Its message is, what's clean enough to drink, drink; what's not, use for anything else.

This alternative paradigm resonates with urban projects around the world that are seeking to "climate proof" their water supplies by ramping up sewage recycling, building desalination plants, or dramatically reducing unnecessary (frequently outdoor) water use. But these are typically the projects of prosperous cities, which have the luxury of taking already decent, and universal, drinking and sewage networks for granted. São Paulo, like other southern metropolises, faces a more encompassing set of challenges related to its patterns of housing and land use. A succession of the city's municipal governments, although not directly responsible for providing clean water or sewage, have facilitated coordinated housing and sanitation plans that, in theory, project the urbanization of all the city's favelas, and the universalization of the sanitation system, by 2025. But the plans are languishing behind schedule and are underfunded, in need of more federal support.

None of this rules out an immediate, if slow and low-tech, shift to the alternative paradigm. Part of the problem, argues Marussia Whately of the Alliance for Water, is that the government's emergency measures are entrenching an already broken model: seeking water from farther away (especially the already stressed Paraíba do Sul river), ignoring untreated water close by, slashing investment in sewage treatment, and refusing to lead a sustained and attractive campaign for water conservation. Green groups are pushing back, though with limited resources. Visoni is active with Cisterns Now!, an organization that has been running workshops to teach residents how to make cheap cisterns with plastic barrels and polyvinyl chloride (PVC) tubing, to capture and safely store rainwater for watering plants and washing homes, vehicles, and sidewalks. The group is building a diverse constituency.

In São Mateus, a poor neighborhood in the city's peripheral eastern reaches, I visited Terezinha Silva, a long-standing housing movement activist with the Movement to Defend the Favelado, the organizer of a cooperative of woman cooks and artisans, and now a key figure in the Urban Program, an initiative of two housing movements, the British charity the Catholic Agency for Overseas Development (CAFOD), and European development funding. The program aims to integrate sustainability and housing politics. Silva had learned to make cisterns thanks to Cisterns Now! And she won mainstream media attention for building and brightly painting her own and then leading dozens of workshops in the favelas of her neighborhood, where she helped others in the housing movement build theirs. In her own backyard, Silva uses a network of three cisterns, one with the slogan Responsible Consumption painted on it, to store rainwater to use in her garden. The cisterns cut her water bills by two-thirds, she told me, even as rates have increased. But when I asked her if the system allowed her to escape, in part, from the water crisis, she bristled. "The state is politically responsible for providing water," she insisted.

But this was a message she would have to repeat. AJ+, an online branch of Al Jazeera that films short videos, had also found Silva and produced a seventy-second video, with English subtitles, of Silva talking about her cistern work in her garden. The American site Upworthy then picked it up. On Facebook alone, the video had amassed over 650,000 views. Silva shared the link—but strained to articulate her basic message (AJ+ 2015). Unusually writing in all caps, she pointed out: "We each have to do our part! And not let the state off the hook for fulfilling its duties; the water crisis is not the people's fault. It's the state's fault." In fact, the vision that Silva's housing movement has pressed is neither self-help nor state reliance, but a more challenging campaign that links greater grassroots autonomy to increased state accountability (on this vision of democracy, see Baiocchi, Heller, and Silva 2011). In this vein, the movements affiliated with the Urban Program have occupied vacant buildings and terrains to highlight the state's responsibility, enshrined in law, to promote the "social function" of property. This campaign has merged social, economic, and environmental demands for a decent quality of life and pursued these with confrontational vigor.

Back in São Mateus, other housing activists were emphatic about the historic entwinement of multiple collective consumption demands. In a cramped, dark garage, Silva helped another family build its own cistern, while a longtime housing organizer told me of the thirty years it had taken her neighborhood movement to get the city government—with federal financial help—to pave the roads in their informal community, regularize their land titles, and build new, safer housing to protect inhabitants from floods (see fig. 2). The cisterns would help. But it had taken decades just to get a decent connection to SABESP's network of pipes. Their latest triumph was a local day care center. For these activists, there was

a sharper division between government neglect and mobilized democracy than between decent housing, supported by public services, and a SABESP utility bill. This is a politics of collective consumption, where symbols and services, social and ecological goods, are knotted together and anchored by housing.

Basso, the MTST housing organizer, made this argument to me even more directly at the New Palestine encampment. "The issue with raising the housing banner," Basso said, "is that housing is the foundation. If you don't have an address, you can't get work, you can't get your child into a day care, you can't get into a school, you can't get public health care, you need to show proof of residence to be hired by a company. . . . It's the foundation of human dignity." But not just any housing, even if subsidized by the state. Here she echoed a broad housing movement discourse, saying, "Normal construction companies [that receive state subsidies] will buy the cheapest land, with the least public transit, the fewest schools, to make apartments with the worst materials they can find," using public

Figure 2 A housing project built near the São Mateus neighborhood in São Paulo after years of community advocacy led by the Movement to Defend the Favelado. Photograph by the author

subsidies. When the MTST secured federal housing for its members via its strategy of occupations, she said, "We have the vision of dignity, quality of life, which is a right."

Basso added that she had been surprised at the potential for new alliance building during the drought. "Some dumb environmentalists still blame us for polluting the water by occupying places like this [near waterways]," she said. She would not name individuals, but said that a number of environmentalists had approached the MTST to discuss cooperation. And she said the MTST was demanding, among other things, that the state support community efforts at using rainwater and local sources by distributing filters and other water capture and treatment tools, echoing the demands raised by conventional environmentalist groups like the Alliance for Water and its allies. Indeed, in August 2015, activists from Cisterns Now! visited New Palestine and pledged to help install cisterns to capture rainwater for the occupation's gardens and for cleaning its kitchens.

The MTST's demands echoed the vision of responsible, equitable rationing laid out by Marzeni Pereira, a SABESP technician and respected authority on the current crisis, who was fired for challenging utility policies. After a meeting of the Water Yes, Profits No collective that he helped to organize, Pereira presented a rare, comprehensive defense of water rationing. "Better than a water rotation [*rodízio*] in my point of view is rationing [*racionamento*]," he said. "Rationing means that you guarantee supply for every person, that every person has a minimal quota. . . . It's better than a rotation, because with a rotation, if you don't have a water tank, or you have a small water tank and a big family, you go without water."

I asked Pereira about the problems with SABESP's infrastructure. He said that in every home, there was a water meter that could establish how much each household received. "You can send water in trucks, and open wells and treat the water, for areas [SABESP's] network doesn't reach. You do a program to collect and use rainwater, with government support to guarantee that the water is minimally treated for uses besides drinking." Rationing, he continued, was a social and collective solution. "Rationing requires a big awareness program, the involvement of neighbors, the community. It gives a whole other vision. Similarly—" and here he paused. "We defend—it doesn't make sense for one person to have four cars, while another takes the bus. It's necessary to ration resources." Soon he was talking about solar panels and quantifying the export of water, embodied in agricultural goods, from the Amazon region and citing the theory of the Amazon's flying rivers.

Overall, the comments presented a holistic vision of rationing that resembled Silva's and her housing group's. It combined state resources, community-oriented technicians, and grassroots groups, emphasizing the joint role of a more accountable state and confrontational social movements. But it was precisely this joining impulse, and its underpinning analysis, that makes the vision threatening. If water, why not cars? If a public utility, why not a fully democratic one?

How else would a broad coalition operate? I attended the second meeting of the State Assembly of Water, a daylong event that manifested some of the June 2013 eruption's other key qualities—a multiracial, multiclass assemblage and strong representation from the city's peripheries. By day's end, the agreed demands included calls for SABESP to be renationalized and then subjected to "democratic control." But the masses were missing. In the building of the metro workers' union, whose central area was a colorful indoor soccer pitch-cum-amphitheater, the number of participants peaked near 130. The contrast between the breadth of speakers—drawn from several housing movements, community groups, unions, socialist parties, and middle-class environmental groups—and the overall size of the gathering struck me as ominous. Political contagion requires not just networking at the level of groups' leaders but also existing and expanding memberships.[10]

In everyday life and in the media, as I experienced them in May 2015, the water crisis was a nuisance and a source of anxiety, but it had lost the sting of an acute, imminent crisis. Or perhaps more importantly, Governor Alckmin's political vulnerability has been moderated by the even deeper crisis facing his natural rival, the Workers' Party, in São Paulo and throughout Brazil. In the summer of 2015, President Dilma Rousseff polled below 10 percent support as she bore the brunt of the country's most damaging corruption crisis in decades, which is coinciding with a painful recession. Crises are fickle. At present, it is impossible to predict what will happen to the city's water supplies—whether emergency waterworks will be completed, whether rains will return to more normal levels, or how federal politics will influence those of the state and urban region. The mobilizing capacity of the emerging civil society alliances will depend on all those factors. Paradoxically, both Alckmin's efforts to contain the water crisis and a range of social movements' efforts to explode it may succeed for some time.

Between Unequal and Democratic Ecologies

In the wake of the June 2013 protests, with their rapid spread of discontent from a R$0.20 bus ticket increase to health and education and corruption, the prospect of a broad, angry alliance anchored in water and housing protest remains a real possibility. As the MTST's Basso put it to me: "Everyone is asking themselves

10. But as a lead organizer of the Free Fare movement that sparked the June Days told me in 2013, in the weeks before that explosion of those protests, only forty people attended organizing meetings.

now, what's the new R$0.20 going to be?" Meanwhile, the leftist activists of the Water Yes, Profits No collective search for a way to make water into what they term an "intersectional" issue, binding a whole series of struggles together. But if the city's water supplies hold until the rainy season, and rains fall at typical levels, the moment will pass. Ecological suffering will again be governed by the pace of "slow violence," unspectacular environmental injustice that is so difficult to combat (Auyero and Swistun 2009; Nixon 2011).

I want to conclude here, then, in the midst of crisis, by seeking to clarify how two projects to shift the city's politics of collective consumption express two of this event's emergent logics (Sewell 2005): one reinforcing unequal ecologies, one in pursuit of democratic ecologies; the first seeking to contain the crisis, the second to explode it.

For governing elites, the path of least resistance is to preserve the status quo: adjust the pressure to keep the present regime of collective consumption going, however fitfully. Muddling along with patch-ups while leaving untouched most of the privileges of the elite and the middle class means reinforcing unequal ecologies while trying to downplay the suffering of the poor. In São Paulo, this drift has resulted from the state and its water utility doubling down on existing lines of authority and implementing opaque, unequal, and de facto rationing through water pressure reductions. If water shortages continue, or emergency waterworks are again delayed, the costs of this approach will rise. For the already prosperous liable to choose or support this path, it looks less like an endorsement of a long-term strategy for confronting concatenating ecological crises than it does a perpetual preference for what, step-by-step, feels closest to the familiar present, while containing unpredictable political contagion among social movements. Unequal ecologies result from elites'—and their supporters'—political loss aversion.

The alternative path is one of democratic ecologies, where goods accepted as essential are furnished and distributed by the state and its community partners with a nonmarket logic, with leadership and autonomy from below, alliance with experts, and the financial support of public institutions. But such a program is constitutively vague (see Bakker 2010). How can a newly democratic arrangement be coherently specified in advance? Where would the line be drawn between basic services beyond the pale of the market and other consumption goods? If access to water is guaranteed, why not housing? If housing, why not secondary education, why not top universities? Why not a basic minimum income? And what exactly would the novel institutional configurations that share power look like? These questions, of course, presume success. More modest questions might be asked of a situation like São Paulo's, where democratic ecologies are more likely to be a lasting project pursued at the margins than they are an immediate achievement. How can environmentalists and housing movements, so long at odds, keep cooperating once the shock of crisis fades? How might popular movements work to expand contacts with sympathetic professional class experts, who recognize the issues but whose everyday life occurs in other social realms?

If the perpetuation of unequal ecologies defers political uncertainty, the pursuit of democratic ecologies begins with them.

For most of the world, the era of cheap and plentiful drinking water has passed. For water, and likely other resources besides, the twenty-first-century city will be rationed. The question is how. Compared to rationing medicine, which entails the refusal of potentially lifesaving treatment to certain patients (Scheunemann and White 2011), sharing water fairly and transparently would seem to be simple and obvious. But in sociospatially segregated urban regions, whose politics of land use and housing are fused with water infrastructures, and whose dynamics structure core economic and political logics, the question of water is a question of power (Swyngedouw 2004). In the rationed city, sharing the first requires sharing the second.

References

Abers, Rebecca Neaera, and Margaret E. Keck. 2013. *Practical Authority: Agency and Institutional Change in Brazilian Water Politics*. New York: Oxford University Press.

AJ+. 2015. "Favela Water Crisis: How to Collect Rainwater in a Drought." *Al Jazeera English*, February 5.

Amin, Ash. 2014. "Lively Infrastructure." *Theory, Culture and Society* 31, nos. 7–8: 137–61.

Anand, Nikhil. 2011. "Pressure: The PoliTechnics of Water Supply in Mumbai." *Cultural Anthropology* 26, no. 4: 542–64.

Arteta, Carolina, Marcelo Grava, Marina Dias, Maurício Moraes, and Natalia Viana. 2015. "Finalmente, os contratos de demanda firme" ("Finally, the Fixed-Demand Contracts"). *Pública*, May 22. apublica.org/2015/05/finalmente -os-contratos-de-demanda-firme/.

Auyero, Javier, and Débora Alejandra Swistun. 2009. *Flammable: Environmental Suffering in an Argentine Shantytown*. New York: Oxford University Press.

Baiocchi, Gianpaolo, Patrick Heller, and Marcelo Silva. 2011. *Bootstrapping Democracy: Transforming Local Governance and Civil Society in Brazil*. Stanford, CA: Stanford University Press.

Bakker, Karen. 2010. *Privatizing Water: Governance Failure and the World's Urban Water Crisis*. Ithaca, NY: Cornell University Press.

Bakker, Karen, and Michelle Kooy. 2010. "Citizens without a City: The Techno-Politics of Urban Water Governance." In Bakker, *Privatizing Water*, 108–32.

Barnes, Jessica. 2014. *Cultivating the Nile: The Everyday Politics of Water in Egypt*. Durham, NC: Duke University Press.

Boghossian, Bruno, and Paulo Gama. 2014. "'Orientação superior' impediu alerta maior sobre crise, diz presidente da Sabesp" ("'Superior Direction' Impeded Greater Warning of the Crisis, Says President of SABESP"). *Folha de São Paulo*, October 24. www1.folha.uol.com.br/cotidiano/2014/10/1537493 -orientacao-superior-impediu-alerta-sobre-crise-diz-presidente-da-sabesp .shtml.

Bond, Patrick. 2012. *Politics of Climate Justice: Paralysis Above, Movement Below*. Durban: University of KwaZulu-Natal Press.

Caldeira, Teresa P. R. 2000. *City of Walls: Crime, Segregation, and Citizenship in São Paulo*. Berkeley: University of California Press.

Cardoso, Juliana, and Paulo Roberto Fiorilo. 2015. *Untitled [Request to the Public Ministry of São Paulo for a Civic Inquiry]*. São Paulo: São Paulo City Council Workers' Party Caucus.

Castells, Manuel. 1977. *The Urban Question: A Marxist Approach*. Translated by Alan Sheridan. Cambridge, MA: MIT Press.

———. 1983. *The City and the Grassroots: A Cross-Cultural Theory of Urban Social Movements*. London: Edward Arnold.

———. 2002. "Collective Consumption and Urban Contradictions in Advanced Capitalism." In *The Castells Reader on Cities and Social Theory*, edited by Ida Susser. London: Wiley, 107–29.

Cohen, Daniel Aldana. Forthcoming. "The Other Low-Carbon Protagonists: Poor People's Movements and Climate Politics in a Global City." In *The City Is the Factory*, edited by Miriam Greenberg and Penny Lewis. Ithaca, NY: Cornell University Press.

Cohen, Daniel Aldana, and Max Liboiron. 2014. "New York's Two Sandys." *Metropolitics*, October 30. www.metropolitiques.eu/New-York-s-Two-Sandys .html.

Datafolha. 2014. "Termômetro paulistano: Crise da água em São Paulo" ("Thermometer of São Paulo: Water Crisis in São Paulo"). October 17.

———. 2015. "Avaliação do Governador Geraldo Alckmin (Principal problema do estado, crise hídrica)" ("Evaluation of the Governor Geraldo Alckmin (Prin-

cipal Problem of the State, Water Crisis"). February 9. media.folha.uol.com.br
/datafolha/2015/02/09/arquivo-estado-de-sp.pdf.

Desmond, Matthew. 2014. "Relational Ethnography." *Theory and Society* 43, no.
5: 547–79.

Earle, Lucy. 2012. "From Insurgent to Transgressive Citizenship: Housing, Social
Movements and the Politics of Rights in São Paulo." *Journal of Latin American Studies* 44, no. 1: 97–126.

Emirbayer, Mustafa. 1997. "Manifesto for a Relational Sociology." *American
Journal of Sociology* 103, no. 2: 281–317.

Estado de São Paulo—Secretaría do Meio Ambiente. 2009. *Cenários ambientais
2020 (Environmental Scenarios 2020)*. São Paulo.

Fracalanza, Ana Paula, Martins Jacob Amanda, and Rodrigo Furtado Eça.
2013. "Justiça ambiental e práticas de governança da água: (Re)introduzindo
questões de igualdade na agenda" ("Environmental Justice and Water Governance Practices: Re-introducing Questions of Equality into the Agenda").
Ambiente & Sociedade 26, no. 1: 19–38.

Gandy, Matthew. 2014. *The Fabric of Space: Water, Modernity, and the Urban
Imagination*. Cambridge, MA: MIT Press.

Garcia, Carolina, and Vitor Sorano. 2015. "SABESP corta água em SP e não
só reduz pressão, denunciam técnicos da empresa" ("SABESP Cuts Water in
São Paulo and Does Not Just Reduce Pressure, Allege Utility Technicians").
IG São Paulo, February 6. ultimosegundo.ig.com.br/brasil/seca/2015-02-06
/sabesp-corta-agua-em-sp-e-nao-so-reduz-pressao-denunciam-tecnicos-da
-empresa.html.

Graham, Stephen, and Simon Marvin. 2001. *Splintering Urbanism: Networked
Infrastructures, Technological Mobilities, and the Urban Condition*. New
York: Routledge.

Heynen, Nik, Maria Kaika, and Erik Swyngedouw, eds. 2006. *In the Nature of
Cities: Urban Political Ecology and the Politics of Urban Metabolism*. New
York: Routledge.

Hirata, Francini, and Nathalia C. Oliveira. 2012. "Os movimentos mos sem-teto
em São Paulo no contexto neoliberal" ("Housing Movements in São Paulo in
the Neoliberal Context"). In *Política e clases sociais no Brasil dos anos 2000
(Politics and Social Classes in Brazil in the 2000s)*, edited by Armando Boito
Jr. and Andréia Galvão, 367–400. São Paulo: Alameda.

Holston, James. 2008. *Insurgent Citizenship: Disjunctions of Democracy and
Modernity in Brazil*. Princeton, NJ: Princeton University Press.

Jacobi, Pedro Roberto, ed. 2009. *Governança da agua no Estado de São Paulo* (*Water Governance in São Paulo State*). São Paulo: Annablume.

Jacobi, Pedro R. 2006. *Cidade e meio ambiente: Percepções e práticas em São Paulo* (*City and Environment: Perceptions and Practices in São Paulo*). 2nd ed. São Paulo: Annablume.

Jacobi, Pedro Roberto, Ana Paula Fracalanza, and Solange Silva-Sánchez. 2015. "Governança da água e inovação na política de recuperação de recursos hídricos na Cidade de São Paulo" ("Water Governance and Innovation in Water Resource Restoration Policies in the City of São Paulo"). *Cadernos Metrópole* 17, no. 33: 61–81.

Jacobi, Pedro Roberto, and Camila Giorgetti. 2009. "Os moradores e a água na bacia do rio Pirajuçara na Região Metropolitana de São Paulo: Percepções e atitudes num contexto crítico de degradação de fonte hídricas" ("Residents and Water in the Watershed of the Pirajucara River in the Metropolitan Region of São Paulo: Perceptions and Attitudes in the Critical Context of the Degradation of Water Sources"). In *Atores e processos na governança da água no Estado de São Paulo*, edited by Pedro Roberto Jacobi, 87–108. São Paulo: Annablume.

Kaika, Maria. 2005. *City of Flows: Modernity, Nature, and the City*. New York: Routledge.

Kane, Stephanie C. 2012. *Where Rivers Meet the Sea: The Political Ecology of Water*. Philadelphia: Temple University Press.

Keil, Roger. 2005. "Progress Report—Urban Political Ecology." *Urban Geography* 26, no. 7: 640–51.

Kowarick, Lúcio, ed. 1994. *Social Struggles and the City: The Case of São Paulo*. New York: Monthly Review Press.

———. 2000. *Escritos urbanos* (*Urban Writings*). Translated by Tomás Rezende. São Paulo: Editora 34.

Leite, Fabio. 2015. "Sem redutores de pressão, SABESP já corta água durante o dia de 40% da rede" ("Without Pressure Reduction, SABESP Is Already Cutting Water during the Day in 40% of the Network"). *Estado de São Paulo*, February 7. sao-paulo.estadao.com.br/noticias/geral,sem-redutores-de-pressao -sabesp-ja-corta-agua-durante-o-dia-de-40-da-rede,1630881.

Lobel, Fábricio. 2015. "Promessa de caixas-d'água para a periferia trava em São Paulo" ("Promise of Water Tanks for the Periphery Delayed in São Paulo"). *Folha de São Paulo*, May 9. www1.folha.uol.com.br/cotidiano/2015/05 /1626838-promessa-de-caixas-dagua-para-a-periferia-trava-em-sao-paulo .shtml?cmpid=twfolha.

Maricato, Ermínia. 2013. *Cidades rebeldes: Passe livre e as manifestações que tomaram as ruas do Brasil* (*Rebel Cities: Free Fare and the Demonstrations That Took the Streets of Brazil*). São Paulo: Boitempo.

Martín, María. 2015. "Durante a crise hídrica, casos de diarreia se multiplicam em São Paulo" ("During the Water Crisis, Cases of Diarrhoea Multiplied in São Paulo"). *El País Brasil*, July 16. brasil.elpais.com/brasil/2015/07/10/politica /1436557827_946009.html.

Martins, Maria Lucia Refinetti. 2011. "São Paulo, centro e periferia: A retórica ambiental e os limites da política urbana" ("São Paulo, Center and Periphery: Environmental Rhetoric and the Limits of Urban Policy"). *Estudos avançados* 25, no. 71: 59–72.

Meehan, Katharine. 2013. "Disciplining De Facto Development: Water Theft and Hydrosocial Order in Tijuana." *Environment and Planning D: Society and Space* 31, no. 2: 319–36.

Ministério Público Federal and Ministério Público do Estado de São Paulo. 2014. *Public Suit*. São Paulo. www.mpsp.mp.br/portal/page/portal/cao_urbanismo _e_meio_ambiente/GTEaguas/GTEaguas_AcoesCivPubl/ACP_VOLUME _MORTO_PETICAO_INICIAL_com_bookmarks.pdf.

Nixon, Rob. 2011. *Slow Violence and the Environmentalism of the Poor*. Cambridge, MA: Harvard University Press.

Nobre, Antonio. 2014. *O futuro climático da Amazônia* (*The Future Climate of Amazonia*). São José dos Campos, Brazil: Articulación Regional Amazónica.

Nobre, Carlos. 2010. *Vulnerabilidades das megacidades brasileiras às mudanças climáticas: Região Metropolitana de São Paulo; Sumário executivo* (*Vulnerabilities of Brazilian Megacities to Climate Change: Metropolitan Region of São Paulo; Executive Summary*). São Paulo: Centro de Ciência do Sistema Terrestre do Instituto Nacional de Pesquisas Espaciais.

Periferia Ativa. 2013a. "Mãos ao alto, 3,20 é um assalto: Por que estamos nas ruas?" ("Hands Up, 3.20 [Brazilian reales] Is an Assault: Why Are We in the Streets?"). Newsletter, June: 5.

———. 2013b. "A Periferia Parou" ("The Periphery Shut Down"). Newsletter, July: 4.

Pimentel, Jéssica. 2014. "Governador de São Paulo volta a descartar racionamento de água" ("Governor of São Paulo Returns to Rejecting Water Rationing"). *G1*, February 26. g1.globo.com/sao-paulo/sorocaba-jundiai/noticia/2014/02 /governador-de-sao-paulo-volta-descartar-racionamento-de-agua.html.

Pinho, Márcio. 2015. "SABESP admite ter reduzido pressão d'água além do indicado pela ABNT" ("SABESP Admits Having Reduced Water Pressure beyond the Level Indicated by the ABNT"). *G1*, February 25. g1.globo.com /sao-paulo/noticia/2015/02/sabesp-admite-ter-reduzido-pressao-dagua-alem -do-indicado-pela-abnt.html.

Rademacher, Anne M. 2011. *Reigning the River: Urban Ecologies and the Political Transformation in Kathmandu*. Durham, NC: Duke University Press.

Ribeiro, Wagner Costa. 2011. "Oferta e estresse hídrico na região Metropolitana de São Paulo" ("Water Supply and Water Stress in the Metropolitan Region of São Paulo"). *Estudos avançados* 25, no. 71: 119–33.

Rodrigues, Lúcia. 2015. "Chance de caos social por falta d'água mobiliza exército" ("Possibility of Social Chaos Because of Lack of Water Mobilizes Army"). *CartaCapital*, May 6. www.cartacapital.com.br/sociedade/possibilidade-de -caos-social-por-falta-de-agua-em-sp-mobiliza-comando-do-exercito-2589 .html.

Roy, Ananya. 2009. "The 21st Century Metropolis: New Geographies of Theory." *Regional Studies* 43, no. 6: 819–30.

SABESP (Companhia de Saneamento Básico do Estado de São Paulo). 2014. *Rodízio do sistema Cantareira 2014: Versão síntese* (*Rotation in the Cantareira System 2014: Synthesis Report*). São Paulo: SABESP. January.

———. 2015a. *Crise hídrica, estratégia, e soluções da SABESP para a região Metropolitana de São Paulo* (*Water Crisis, Strategy, and Solutions from SABESP for the Metropolitan Region of São Paulo*). São Paulo: SABESP.

———. 2015b. *Deliberação ARSESP 545/15—Artigo 8* (*Deliberation ARSESP 545/15—Article 8*). São Paulo: SABESP.

Santoro, Paula Freire, Luciana Nicolau Ferrara, and Marussia Whately, eds. 2008. *Mananciais: Diagnóstico e políticas habitacionais* (*Reservoirs: Diagnostic and Housing Policies*). São Paulo: Instituto Socioambiental (ISA).

Scheunemann, Leslie P., and Douglas B. White. 2011. "The Ethics and Reality of Rationing in Medicine." *Chest* 140, no. 6: 1625–32.

Seto, Karen C., et al. 2014. "Human Settlements, Infrastructure, and Spatial Planning." In *Climate Change 2014: Mitigation of Climate Change; Working Group III Contribution to the Fifth Assessment Report of the Intergovernmental Panel on Climate Change*. Cambridge: Cambridge University Press.

Sewell, William H., Jr. 2005. "A Theory of the Event: Marshall Sahlins's 'Possible Theory of History.'" In *Logics of History: Social Theory and Social Transformation*, 197–224. Chicago: University of Chicago Press.

Superstorm Research Lab. 2013. *A Tale of Two Sandys*. White paper. New York: Superstorm Research Lab. superstormresearchlab.files.wordpress.com/2013 /10/srl-a-tale-of-two-sandys.pdf.

Swyngedouw, Erik. 2009. "The Antinomies of the Postpolitical City: In Search of a Democratic Politics of Environmental Production." *International Journal of Urban and Regional Research* 33, no. 3: 601–20.

———. 2014. *Social Power and the Urbanization of Water—Flows of Power.* New York: Oxford University Press.

....

Daniel Aldana Cohen is a PhD candidate in sociology at New York University and a founding member of the Superstorm Research Lab. He studies social movements and the politics of climate change in New York and São Paulo.

The Infinity of Water: Climate Change Adaptation in the Arabian Peninsula

Gökçe Günel

If climate change mitigation is about energy, adaptation is about water. While mitigation efforts attend to the main drivers of climate change, specifically by limiting emissions through innovation in renewable energy and clean technology, adaptation work concentrates on managing the already observed impacts of climate change as well as those predicted to happen with a high degree of certainty, such as water scarcity. Accordingly, the Intergovernmental Panel on Climate Change (IPCC 2015), the transnational body responsible for climate change governance, defines adaptation as "adjustments in ecological, social, or economic systems in response to actual or expected climatic stimuli and their effects or impacts" and adds that "it refers to changes in processes, practices, and structures to moderate potential damages or to benefit from opportunities associated with climate change."

In the Arabian Peninsula, adaptation takes a slightly more nuanced form. Drawing on seventeen months of fieldwork on climate change governance in the United Arab Emirates (UAE), ethnographic research at climate change summits in Durban (COP17) and Doha (COP18), and recent interviews with climate change consultants, this article analyzes how the definition of climate change adaptation becomes negotiated and reinterpreted in the region in ways that shape how

I am indebted to Eric Klinenberg for his engagement with various versions of this piece and to Stephen Twilley and Tim Neff for their editorial assistance. Sarah El-Kazaz, Bridget Guarasci, and Sophia Stamatopoulou-Robbins read an earlier draft and made helpful comments. Wenner Gren Foundation, Cornell University, Rice University, and the ACLS Foundation provided funding for research. Finally, I thank my interlocutors in Abu Dhabi and elsewhere for taking the time to share their perspectives on climate change.

Public Culture 28:2 DOI 10.1215/08992363-3427463

oil-rich nations articulate and act upon environmental problems.[1] I argue that climate change adaptation projects in the Arabian Peninsula are often attempts at reframing water-related challenges that are already present, regardless of the effects of climate change; for instance, the groundwater sources in the UAE will be destroyed not necessarily due to the predicted impacts of climate change but because they will soon be sucked dry. These challenges are born of not just environmental but also social, political, and economic conditions, such as high levels of per capita water consumption or increasing population, which receive less attention from policy makers. In other words, in the Arabian Peninsula climate change adaptation is about water, while water is not necessarily about climate change adaptation.

In this article, I show how the UAE government advances a view that I call the "infinity of water," by relying on technological solutions, particularly desalination, the process of removing salt and other minerals from seawater. The UAE (along with Kuwait, Libya, Saudi Arabia, Jordan, and Singapore) suffers from absolute water scarcity, which means that it has an annual renewable water capacity of less than five hundred cubic meters per capita, a rate that worsens every year due to increasing population levels (Baba et al. 2011: 39).[2] However, the renewable sources are supplemented by nonrenewable nonconventional desalinated water. The "man-made" quality of water—where more can be generated through desalination whenever necessary—allows the actors in the area to envision and embrace its infinity, regardless of existing water scarcity. Such attempts at imagining the infinity of water deny and efface the "natural" characteristics of this resource. In the UAE, water has become a product of sophisticated technical procedures, social relations, and historical trajectories that can be manipulated and governed.

The imaginary of "infinite water" mirrors what happens in the energy sector. Timothy Mitchell (2012) argues that conceptions of endless oil supplies enabled progress to be conceived as infinitely expandable, without any material constraints. In the mid-twentieth century, the cost of energy did not present a limit to economic growth, as oil prices continuously declined. Given how simple it was to ship oil across the world, this resource could easily be treated as inexhaustible. This belief in the infinity of oil also played a key role in producing the "economy"

1. COP17 and COP18 stand for the 17th and 18th sessions of the Conference of the Parties to the United Nations Framework Convention on Climate Change (UNFCCC). Recent works in history, anthropology, and political science that share this focus include Jones 2010, Limbert 2010, Luomi 2012, and Mitchell 2012.

2. For an inquiry into the production of water scarcity in Egypt, see Barnes 2014: 35–71.

as an object, which could expand without any limits. In Abu Dhabi, the imagined infinity of wealth engenders an illusory capacity to construct water infrastructures whenever necessary. Through its ever-expanding oil economy, the Emirates can perhaps manage its water.

We now know that the age of abundant fossil fuel supplies is ending, but we seem unable to abandon the ways of living and thinking that fossil fuels made possible. In preparing for a future without abundant oil, the Arabian Gulf, and especially the Abu Dhabi government, attempts new strategies of resource management, hoping to generate a new type of infinity through what I call "technical adjustments": imaginative responses to environmental problems and energy scarcity that open up certain interventions (such as extending technological complexity), while foreclosing others (such as asking larger-scale questions regarding how to live).[3] Such adjustments provide a means for vaulting into a future where humans will continue to enjoy abundance without interrogating existing social, political, and economic relations.

Next, I demonstrate how the complexities of water pricing inform a strategy for regulating water consumption for the climate change consultants working in the region. Climate change consultants come to the UAE from all over the world for professional purposes and assist in the production of national and international climate change policy, serving as key players in the climate debate.[4] The consultants I met in the UAE worked for state-funded organizations such as the Directorate of Energy and Climate Change at the Ministry of Foreign Affairs and Masdar and pursued opportunities in intergovernmental institutions such as the International Renewable Energy Agency (IRENA) and the United Nations Framework Convention on Climate Change (UNFCCC) as well as consulting companies, namely, Ernst and Young, Deloitte, KPMG, and PricewaterhouseCoopers. The climate consultants attended climate change summits, followed the debates related to various aspects of climate change governance, drafted reports for internal use and for the development of low-carbon technologies in other countries, and contributed

3. For a lengthier discussion, see Günel, forthcoming.

4. During my fieldwork in the UAE, I worked at Masdar's climate change consultancy unit, Masdar Carbon, which was responsible for preparing a policy submission to the United Nations Framework Convention on Climate Change about carbon capture and storage, a controversial climate change mitigation technology. In 2011 and 2012 I followed the process of composing this submission in Abu Dhabi, tracked the submission to Bonn, and subsequently observed the final stages of decision making at climate summits in Durban and Doha. Generally speaking, my experience with climate change consultants related to the making of carbon capture and storage policy. In this article, I not only draw on my experiences in 2010–12 but also rely on recent conversations with some of these professionals, focused on climate change adaptation.

to the policy production and implementation landscape at the intergovernmental level. Given their global experiences, they changed jobs, moved between organizations, and often left the UAE for positions elsewhere some years after their arrival. The climate consultants I met did not necessarily identify as "environmentalists"; rather, in the words of one consultant, they believed that "the environment is a sexy part of the economy." Accordingly, in the UAE they attempted to employ market mechanisms such as water pricing to change human behavior regarding consumption. In providing an overview of the climate change adaptation process, this article draws on recent conversations with climate change consultants on adaptation strategies, in addition to reports and scientific assessments on climate change dynamics in the region.

Finally, I analyze the impact that debates on climate change and energy scarcity have on the establishment of research organizations in the region. By exploring water-related research at the Masdar Institute and the King Abdullah University of Science and Technology (KAUST)—two institutions that have been put together to form the foundations of a knowledge-based economy in the Arabian Peninsula—I seek to demonstrate how these research centers participate in the making of technical adjustments that enable the extension of fossil fuel–based lifestyles.[5] At the same time, however, these emergent institutions have the potential to serve as spaces where the existing modes of living will be interrogated, eliciting new imaginaries that do not rely solely on such technical adjustments.

Water in the Arabian Peninsula

Toby Craig Jones (2010) starts his book *Desert Kingdom* with a story about the efforts to tow a 100-million-ton iceberg from Antarctica to the Red Sea. In 1976 Mohammed al-Faisal, a nephew of the Saudi king, invested millions of dollars to establish Iceberg Transport International, a company whose only purpose was to haul icebergs to the water-poor regions of the world. The goal was to complete the 5,000-mile voyage in six months to a year for a cost of around $100 million. For a combination of reasons, the project never came to be realized and the company went bankrupt.

The irony of the attempt to transport icebergs is not in its ambition, however, but in the fact that al-Faisal abandoned desalination projects to implement this

---

5. The Masdar Institute is part of Abu Dhabi's flagship renewable energy and clean technology company, Masdar. It was established in 2009 and began to occupy an ecofriendly building inside Masdar City in September 2010. In 2014 the institute employed 91 faculty from thirty countries and 491 students from sixty-six countries around the world.

seemingly less plausible idea. While icebergs never became popular or feasible water infrastructures (since it was unclear how they would be utilized once they reached the coast or how they would be integrated with the existing water pipelines), desalination now constitutes one of the foremost sources of water in the region. Saudi Arabia alone currently produces about 18 percent of the desalinated water in the world.[6]

In the Arabian Peninsula, most of the natural water supply comes from groundwater and shallow or deep aquifers—resources that are exploited at a rate far outpacing their natural replenishment. Increasing population, rapid urbanization, agricultural production, and the construction of infrastructures and energy-heavy industries have intensified demand for already stressed resources, especially in the past three decades. The shift is perhaps most vivid in Saudi Arabia and the UAE, two countries that have attracted larger populations and related urbanization efforts.[7]

In this context, desalination has become vital to the provision of cities and industries in the region with supplies of potable water. Bahrain and Kuwait were the first to make use of desalination plants, in the mid-twentieth century, but the technology quickly spread across the Gulf. Out of approximately 17,500 desalination plants in the world today, Saudi Arabia, Oman, the UAE, Kuwait, Bahrain, and Qatar (otherwise known as the Gulf Cooperation Council, or GCC countries) host 7,500—roughly 43 percent of the share. The global desalination capacity of these plants is approximately 94,500,000 cubic meters per day—from which 62,340,000 cubic meters per day come from Saudi Arabia, Oman, the UAE, Kuwait, Bahrain, and Qatar, with a share of almost 70 percent (al-Hashemi et al. 2014).

Despite the challenges of producing potable water, the average daily per capita water use in the UAE, a country with a population of about 9 million people, is estimated to be 360 liters. In Abu Dhabi, the wealthiest of the emirates, this number is as high as 550 liters a day, two to three times the world average of 180–200 liters (Solomon 2010). In some ways, these high levels of consumption are related to an environmental imaginary rooted in a colonial sensibility of the environment

6. For a review of these figures, see al-Suhaimy 2013.

7. Climate change adaptation protocols throughout the Arabian Peninsula share some tendencies in terms of technical adjustments. However, it is important to keep in mind that population dynamics and economic policies in the region differ drastically. For instance, while the UAE and Qatar seek to provide comfortable living conditions to all of their citizens, this is not the case for countries with larger income disparities such as Bahrain and Saudi Arabia, where such lifestyles are available to a select few.

in the Arabian Gulf that places Abu Dhabi's arid saline landscape outside the possible normalcy of European geographies. As Diana K. Davis (2011: 4) writes, "Much of the early Western representation of the Middle East and North Africa environment, in fact, might be interpreted as a form of environmental orientalism in that the environment was narrated by those who became the imperial powers, primarily Britain and France, as a 'strange and defective' environment compared to Europe's 'normal and productive' environment." In this context, Davis continues, "the perceived extreme aridity and the constraints that this was seen to place on 'normal' agricultural production fueled an intense interest in hydraulic management by the British and the French." The ability to manufacture and consume water at these excessive rates thereby becomes a symptom of successful hydraulic management, this time by the Emirati government. The presumably successful management of its environment helps the state increase its legitimacy and power.

Desalination, an energy-intensive process, costs the UAE about $18 million each day. The UAE, which is the second-biggest producer of desalinated water after Saudi Arabia, desalinates the equivalent of 9 million cubic meters of water, roughly the size of 3.6 million Olympic pools, in exchange for this $18 million. The desalination capacity of Abu Dhabi in particular increased by over 360 percent between 1998 and 2007 (EAD 2009). These practices attract businesses, immigrants, and tourism to the Arabian Gulf, while at the same time contributing to the production of sovereignty, where the seemingly reckless expenditure generates social standing and prestige. The prevalent use of technical adjustments such as desalination enables and facilitates the imaginary that current social, political, and economic relations can be extended indefinitely.

Ben, a British expatriate who lives in the UAE and has been an active participant in climate change governance for the past twenty years, working for think tanks and nongovernmental organizations as well as national governments, tells me about an unforeseen consequence of the imagined infinity of water:

> In Abu Dhabi, if you drive around, you still see people hosing down their driveways to get rid of the dust. In some of the areas around Abu Dhabi, because a lot of the rocky ground here has a lot of salt, people have been watering their gardens so much that it dissolves the rock, so people get these pitholes under their houses. You know, essentially, you have this area where, for a million years, there has been one day of rain a year, and now suddenly somebody is watering their garden every day. So it dissolves the salt.

The materiality of water—as a costly man-made product with low levels of salinity—leads to geological transformations in the area and operates in a way that the Abu Dhabi residents or policy makers cannot predict.

Landscaping also appears to be a way of performing the infinity of water, generated by technically sophisticated water infrastructures. For about thirty miles, the road from Abu Dhabi to Dubai is ornamented with date palms, green grass, and, at times, wildflowers. While there are no clear estimates of how much water is required for these landscaping practices, many suggest that the Abu Dhabi government expends an extraordinary amount of resources to keep these roads verdant, second only to military expenses, using desalinated water to take care of the imported plants. As we chat, Ben points out that people in the UAE "are starting to move away from this idea that everywhere needs a green, grassy lawn like it's the South of England. But at the same time, of course, people are doing a lot of golf courses and all that." And yet he does not expect consistency and welcomes the rock gardens and cacti arrangements that are beginning to replace the expansive landscaping work.

Through these discussions and practices, water ceases to be a "natural" entity; instead, it emerges as an assemblage of complex technical procedures, social relations, and historical trajectories. As Jessica Barnes (2014) argues in the case of Egypt, water in the Arabian Gulf is not a given. Rather, it is created by and through various groups of experts, technologies, policies, and users who formulate decisions based on a variety of factors, making water the outcome of a social, political, and economic process. As Ben Orlove and Steven C. Caton (2010: 401) suggest, it is necessary to examine "the multiple, often conflicting knowledge systems through which actors understand water." To understand these "multiple, often conflicting systems," it is essential to investigate the specific technologies of water management and desalination, which give rise to multiple, often unexpected concerns, such as rising levels of salinity and algal blooming.

Most of the desalination in the UAE, and more generally in the Gulf, relies on multistage flash (MSF) technology. Here the MSF distillation plants, especially large ones, are paired with power plants in a configuration where they cogenerate water and electricity. Waste heat from the power plant is used to heat seawater; at the same time, seawater provides cooling for the power plant. This reduces the energy needed and drastically alters the costs of running the plant, since energy is the largest operating cost of MSF desalination plants. However, this arrangement also has disadvantages, because it renders water production dependent on electricity generation. For instance, while the demand for electricity varies greatly between winter and summer, given the higher need for air-conditioning in the summer months, water needs remain roughly consistent. As a consequence, in the summer months the MSF plants produce much more water than necessary.

Faced with this imbalance in seasonal production and consumption levels, the UAE started a pilot activity in which it collects the excess water and injects it into groundwater aquifers, creating strategic reserves rather than dumping it back into the Gulf, a practice that has received criticism. The location of the reserve remains secret, to prevent people from digging wells around the area and extracting water for private use. In the case of a possible disruption in desalination infrastructures, these reserves might become the UAE's lifelines.

As the Gulf countries increasingly rely on desalination for their water supply, the associated energy costs and environmental consequences become ever more incontrovertible. The *Abu Dhabi Water Resources Master Plan* (EAD 2009: 19) notes that "overall fossil fuel use in the cogeneration plants is around 21 million tons equivalent of CO_2 per year and the share attributed to water production and use lies between 20 and 45%." "Thus water use probably contributes between 4 and 9 million tons of CO_2 equivalent per year" and promotes ways of thinking past these issues, such as research and development of newer, less resource-intensive desalination technologies. Reverse osmosis desalination technology, which delinks the practices of electricity generation and water generation, has been one way of avoiding the problems associated with MSF. Mimicking cellular processes, reverse osmosis involves pumping water under pressure through a series of membranes. Since it eliminates the need to heat the water, reverse osmosis requires lower capital investments and less energy. In some parts of the region, reverse osmosis plants are expected to rely on solar energy, an effort currently spearheaded by the Japanese conglomerate Hitachi and supported by Masdar.[8]

But there are problems with desalination that membrane technologies cannot solve, including rising levels of salinity in the sea. As a result of increased desalination activities, the Arabian Gulf's salinity levels have risen to forty-seven thousand parts per million, from thirty-two thousand about thirty years ago (Alderman 2010). The rivers that used to flow into the Gulf, such as the Tigris and the Euphrates, have long been dammed, decreasing the yearly freshwater input. Nor are the precipitation levels high enough to keep salinity levels under control. This results in conditions that threaten the already stressed marine ecosystems in the Gulf, generating future risks for the coral reefs, the mudflats, the seagrass beds, and

8. For some examples, see Hitachi 2015. For an overview of Masdar's proposed program, see Masdar 2015.

the mangrove swamps (Naser 2014). "Never mind peak oil, or even peak water," one article in the English-language UAE newspaper *The National* starts: "Some experts are pondering the possibility of the UAE's development being limited by 'peak salt'—the notional point at which the Arabian Gulf becomes so salty that relying on it for fresh water stops being economically feasible" (Todorova 2009).

Another problem with desalination is the risk of harmful algal blooming, more commonly known as red tide (although the symptoms of algal blooming are not always red). Red tide takes place in the Gulf as a result of increasing seawater temperatures, low current movement, and high nutrient content, especially nitrogen and phosphorus. The algal blooms increase the levels of toxicity and absorb the oxygen in the ocean, suffocating the fish. The blooms also have adverse effects on desalination infrastructures, forcing the plants to close, mainly to prevent the clogging of intake filters. To avoid these circumstances, researchers and policy makers in the Gulf have stressed the need to control pollution and reduce nutrients in coastal waters. Red tide motivates the policy makers in the region to examine the human activity that indissolubly binds together land and sea (see also Helmreich 2011).

It is also important to keep in mind the materiality of the water and to trace its multiple ways of being in the Arabian Gulf. Through its salinity, toxicity, or mere availability on or under the ground, water as a material directly affects the livelihoods of humans and nonhumans in the region and influences decision-making practices. The emergence of increasing salinity levels and algal blooming as significant problems in the region also proves that environmental governance is elusive. Despite the efforts to contain and manage the environment through new business models and emergent technological advancements, there is always a remainder that refuses and escapes control.[9] Not even the more ecologically benign technical adjustments, such as solar-powered desalination techniques, can adequately restrain and subdue this remainder.

Environmental problems have done little to limit expectations for future population growth in the region. Due to an increasing expatriate labor force, the UAE's

9. Like all modern state builders, the governments of the Arabian Peninsula perceive their power over the environment as being instrumental to having power over their constituencies as well as their brand image abroad. Through environmental governance, the UAE manages to attract profitable business enterprises and large numbers of tourists to the region, in addition to generating prestige. However, as many scholars have already shown, the practices of environmental management remain an impossibility, always leading to unintended consequences and unexpected results that challenge these practices of state building and the related claims to power. For a fitting example of this scholarship, see Scott 1998.

population has grown dramatically, from under three hundred thousand people in 1971 to about 9 million today. "By 2030, Abu Dhabi's population is expected to more than triple," states a key report on the economic development of Abu Dhabi (Government of Abu Dhabi 2015). Another report predicts that the UAE's population will exceed 12 million people in 2060 (UNDESA 2015). This surge in population will happen in a context of increasing environmental stress, water scarcity, and climatic transformation, leading to risks and uncertainties regarding how to inhabit the cities of the Gulf.

The Price of Water

While there are a variety of technical adjustments under way in the Gulf that aim at resolving the problem of water scarcity, there is little emphasis on transforming the human relationship with water. As Mohamed Daoud, of the state-run Environment Agency–Abu Dhabi (EAD), explains: "We need to convince [people] that water here isn't a free resource. It's not even a natural resource, it's manmade. It is costly, and it has a big environmental impact" (quoted in Solomon 2010). However, this expectation does not match the luxurious lifestyle that the UAE promotes on an everyday basis, with amenities such as water parks, indoor ski slopes, golf courses, and large water fountains, all supplied by desalination plants.

Emergent water infrastructures in the Gulf are typically not directed at changing or regulating human behavior, as some demand-based systems in other parts of the world are. For instance, in the case of South Africa, Antina von Schnitzler (2013) shows how prepaid electric and water meters (enacted as part of a "save water" campaign) emerge as political terrains and sites of negotiation, motivating consumers to use fewer resources and to pay on time and thereby creating new forms of citizenship and community belonging. In the Arabian Gulf, however, emergent water infrastructures, such as new desalination plants, confront water scarcity from the supply side and help residents sustain their everyday habits of consumption, therefore performing a political feat and signifying that the state will be able to maintain carbon-intensive lifestyles in the years to come.

Climate change consultants who live and work in the region argue that human behavior needs to be transformed and offer demand-related strategies to achieve just that. They propose market-based mechanisms as means of emphasizing water conservation and, at times, push for unprecedented changes. For instance, in January 2015, Emirati nationals began to pay for water for the first time, between AED 1.70 and 1.89 (about US$0.46–$0.51) for one thousand liters (roughly 264 gallons). The new water pricing mechanism also calls for additional price increases for the expatriates, raising the rate from AED 2.20 per one thousand liters to between AED 5.95 and 9.90. The price of water will vary based on consumption benchmarks and will take into account whether the consumer occupies an apartment or a villa.

Abu Dhabi's water supply had been set up in the 1960s, when the Emirate was under British control and provided water to all residents of the city free of charge. Slowly, pricing mechanisms started being implemented. The first transformation was the flat rate, where expatriates began to pay AED 50 (about US$14) regardless of the amount of monthly consumption. In 1997 water meters were installed in buildings for the first time, and non-Emirati residents began being charged AED 2.2 for one thousand liters. The 2015 price increase, which introduced tiered rates for both Emiratis and non-Emiratis, is presumably the first hike in utility prices since 1997. In its current configuration, the UAE is among the Gulf countries where water is relatively more expensive. In contrast, Saudi Arabia has the cheapest water rates in the region (Wasmi 2014).

Celebrating this transition, climate change consultants and researchers perceive water pricing as a tool that will generate awareness and have an immediate impact on overall consumption patterns. Some propose that increased water prices should be able to partially cover the costs of desalination, an undertaking that is heavily subsidized by the government, while promoting water conservation. In some ways, the consultants I met in Abu Dhabi and at climate change summits in Durban and Doha aspire for what Andrea Ballestero (2015: 265), writing about Costa Rica, calls a "calculation grammar," a process that "governs the relative weights and proportions of the elements that constitute a price, infusing those numeric propositions with distinct meanings." In this way, water price would account for the ethical and environmental aspects of water scarcity while satisfying the population's everyday consumption needs.

Charging for water became a popular conservation strategy and policy tool in many parts of the world in the 1990s, prompting debates on whether water should be conceptualized as an economic good, for sale to the highest bidder, or a social good, available to everyone.[10] One side of this debate argues that consumers do not have any incentives to save water when it is free or underpriced. Yet if water were to be sold at the full price of production, then consumers would behave more carefully and conserve water. Others claim that, however scarce it is, water

10. This debate is a result of two contradictory protocols: the 1992 Fourth Dublin Principle and the 1992 First Rio Principle. While the Dublin principle asserted that water is an economic good, the Rio principle underlined how safe water was a social good that had to be available to everyone. For more information on this debate, see Dinar, Pochat, and Albiac-Murillo 2015 and Page 2005.

should not be commodified in this manner, because privatization dispossesses local populations from a basic resource that was once freely accessible while also generating a dependency on global water companies.[11] In India, for instance, there have been struggles to keep out the companies that are there to bottle the groundwater (Aiyer 2007).

The commodification of water in the Arabian Gulf has its own particular set of connotations. Given that freshwater in the Arabian Gulf is synthetic and already expensive, many climate change consultants advocate that charging for water is the only plausible way to control consumption. According to the consultants I spoke with, the fact that water is close to being free for the Emirati nationals makes it harder for consumption patterns to change. Although water production costs billions of dollars, this cost never surfaces in everyday calculations. For these professionals, pricing the water and formulating it as a commodity is a first step toward showing people in the region that they may soon run out.

In some ways, this debate is reminiscent of the pricing of water use in California. Many advocates of water conservation push for creative water pricing systems there, where drought has led to mandatory reductions of use, with heavy fees for overuse. Despite growing discussions about water pricing, a court decision dated April 2015 rejected the proposal for a tiered-rate structure for water in the Orange County city of San Juan Capistrano. According to the tiered-rate structure proposal, all users would pay a relatively small amount per unit for their basic needs, but as their usage increased they would pay not just for more gallons but more per gallon, giving them an increased incentive to make do with less. However, the court ruled that water price could not be increased purely for the sake of conservation. The state, which sought to implement the tiered-rate price increase, would have to prove that it costs it more to deliver the hundredth gallon of water than the first, because the state constitution bars the government from charging more for a service than it costs to provide.[12] Yet tiered-rate pricing has been adopted in other areas of the United States, such as in Santa Fe (Schwartz 2015). Little by little, water pricing has emerged as a go-to conservation mechanism in various water-scarce parts of the world.

One major difference between the Arabian Gulf and California is that the for-

---

11. For good examples of these discussions, see Shiva 2002 and Goldman 2005.

12. However, there are other policies that have proved more effective in California. For instance, researchers found that public information campaigns decreased household water consumption by 8 percent, retrofit subsidies by 9 percent, water rationing by 19 percent, and water restrictions (which prohibit certain water-intensive practices, like watering lawns) by 29 percent (Renwick and Green 2000).

mer does not significantly rely on rainwater or groundwater supplies for everyday domestic consumption needs. Instead, the water resources can be produced whenever necessary, through desalination. At the same time, the lack of a calculative grammar through which actors discuss water price prohibits climate change consultants from demonstrating that water is a technical product, whose production depends on a combination of factors and which may become inaccessible to many in the near future.

In the case of the Arabian Gulf, water infrastructures produce an added layer of sovereignty for the authorities who demonstrate an ability to control such natural flows.[13] The infinity of water—its consistent waste, its possible end, its future destruction—translates into a particular type of exuberance and related value, which grants further legitimacy to the authorities in the region. The production of water infrastructure is not only a technical but also a political accomplishment. Managing hydraulic infrastructures in a famously arid climate not only performs a mark of progress for the Gulf countries at the international scale but also generates domestic legitimacy (see also Luomi 2012), ensuring that life will be infinitely available to those who seek to reside there.

Climate Change Adaptation

Despite the lack of needed engagement with water scarcity in the Emirates in particular and in the Gulf in general, research on climate change adaptation processes in the region suggests that there are real, emerging constraints. For instance, the 2011 United Nations report on climate change adaptation and water vulnerability in the Arab world states: "Climate change and climate variability can increase the risks and the costs of water resources management, impact the quantity and quality of water resources, and generate secondary effects that influence socio-economic vulnerability and environmental sustainability." It also proposes further research in regard to the social impacts of such environmental transformations (UN-ESCWA 2011). The environmental conditions of the region have been examined in several Arab Human Development Reports (AHDRs) as well, leading to further proposals about sea level rise, coastal infrastructures, and water scarcity. While the reports' authors strive to contribute to the making of climate change policy in the Middle East and North Africa, their social and political impacts have been minimal (see also Spiess 2008).

In June 2015, Said, a Jordanian citizen who had worked on the United Nations report cited above, told me how climate change adaptation discourses and prac-

---

13. For a similar argument, see Jones 2010.

tices influenced the existing conditions of water usage in the Arabian Peninsula. Said had spent more than a decade working on climate change adaptation and water scarcity in the Gulf and had contributed to academic and governmental research on this issue. He held a PhD in water resources engineering and had been utilizing his training in various institutions around the Middle East and North Africa for the past twenty years. Said insisted that climate change adaptation and mitigation were marginal political issues in the region. He complained that nobody cared, mostly because people had trouble imagining climate change or responding to environmental problems unless they experienced them firsthand. Said thought that the profligate production and usage of water gave elites in the region a feeling of immunity from ecological reality and environmental responsibility.

When I asked Ben, the British climate change consultant living in the UAE, how he felt about the impact of the climate change adaptation discourse and practice, he gave me a rather similar response. He told me that the EAD had been conducting studies looking at the potential impact of climate change on Abu Dhabi: "Conveniently for them, they've concluded that there won't be much." This finding was partly the result of the model the EAD was using, which did not include much in terms of global glacial melt. In this case, the sea level rise that the model postulated was small. However, the implications of higher levels of sea level rise for this region are drastic. For instance, coastal zones in the UAE, home to approximately 85 percent of the population, over 90 percent of the infrastructure, many sensitive ecological subsystems, and important cultural heritage sites, are highly vulnerable to such impacts of climate change. As a report on the impact of sea level rise in the Arab region illustrates, even a one-meter rise in sea levels will lead to the inundation of 1,155 square kilometers of land in the UAE (el-Raey 2010).

There are factors other than sea level rise that may affect the UAE in particular and the Arabian Peninsula in general. For instance, the IPCC reports that temperatures in the Arabian Peninsula region could increase by 1°C–2°C by the 2030–50 period and that precipitation levels could significantly decline. Ben explained, however, that the region was already equipped to deal with the higher temperatures that might arise from climate change. He imagined that a research project by the EAD could have been useful to promote the production of sturdy coastal infrastructures, which would become imperative in the next fifty-year period. Ben's comment showed that despite the financial resources, physical capacity, and breadth of institutions, there was not adequate monitoring of climate change–related transformations in the UAE.

In a critical article on climate change adaptation in the Arabian Gulf, Andy Spiess (2008) touches upon this lack and explains how the implementation of climate change adaptation strategies requires strong institutions, transparent decision-making systems, formal and informal networks that promote collective action, human skills and knowledge, and financial capital and natural resources. Nevertheless, he writes, in confronting climate change "the GCC member states still believe that their financial resources will be sufficient to buy solutions" whenever they are necessary. In some ways this is understandable, because fulfilling Spiess's requirements would challenge and perhaps subvert the political system of the UAE in its entirety. In this context, technical adjustments such as desalination or low-carbon technologies that will be bought by or manufactured inside institutions such as the Masdar Institute and KAUST emerge as tools to manage the existing and impending problems of climate change and energy scarcity, without challenging the social, economic, and political landscape.

At the same time, conversations with climate change consultants show that the idea of water as infinite—and the efforts to realize this idea through technical adjustments—was not uniform in the UAE in particular or the Arabian Peninsula in general. Professionals like Ben and Said participated in the production of knowledge, technology, and governance regarding energy and climate change, but also understood the problems associated with their innovations, and tried to explain why technological solutions or business models may not resolve the climate change problem.

"Now they are rich, but who knows what the conditions are going to be in 2030?" Said wondered at the end of our conversation. "Will the economic power of oil continue, especially now with renewable energies stations being produced at such accessible prices?" According to him, climate change could affect the Arabian Gulf in an unexpected way, initiating investments in renewable energy and clean technology and negatively influencing the significance of oil as a fuel and a commodity. By asking whether oil will still be valuable in 2030, Said pointed to an anxiety that persists among policy makers in the Gulf. In confronting the possibility of a future with less oil, the UAE aims to boost the non-oil share of the economy to more than 60 percent of the gross domestic product, from just over 40 percent today (Government of Abu Dhabi 2015). Like other oil-producing countries, such as Saudi Arabia, the UAE seeks to improve its capacities of innovation and invention through investing in the growth and sustenance of technical and cultural institutions, leading to more "technical adjustments" in the region.

Knowledge-Based Economy

Faced with concerns regarding the future of the oil economy, some governments in the region have been promoting institutions of higher education to build up local expertise, diversify the economy, and transform the countries into global centers of innovation in science and technology. In this model of economic development, which marks a transition from the fossil fuel–based models of development, research centers are expected to function as test beds from which new, exportable ideas and goods will emerge. The guiding premise is that knowledge will constitute a resource in its own right (Callon 2007), with the underlying assumption that innovative intellectual products and services may be exported for a high-value return, eventually triggering the expansion of a high-tech industry, similar to Silicon Valley or Boston 128.

Knowledge production is one of the most prominent ways in which the UAE handles climate change mitigation as well as adaptation, investing in the construction of hubs that will implement technical adjustments in the coming decades. Emergent institutions of knowledge production in the Gulf, such as the Masdar Institute in Abu Dhabi and KAUST in Saudi Arabia, are notable players in climate change debates, because they are expected to engender developments in science and technology that respond to future energy and climate challenges by collaborating with partners inside and outside the region.[14] The Masdar Institute was established and is supervised by the Technology and Development Program at the Massachusetts Institute of Technology, while KAUST receives research support from institutions including but not limited to Stanford University; the University of California, Berkeley; and Cambridge University. Diverging from the branch campus model prevalent in the region (New York University [NYU] Abu Dhabi, the Sorbonne Abu Dhabi, etc.), these hubs propose alternative models for building global universities.[15] Thanks to the aesthetic value of their campuses and their extensive research contracts with third parties, these research centers are expected to operate as networking platforms, creating a buzz outside their walls and drawing attention to the growing landscape of science and technology in the Arabian Peninsula.

These hubs are also expected to form the foundations for research and develop-

14. For a commentary on KAUST and its political and economic significance in Saudi Arabia, see Jones 2010.

15. The founders of NYU Abu Dhabi and Sorbonne Abu Dhabi have at times claimed theirs are stand-alone institutions, with unique intellectual makeups, and challenge the notion of a branch campus. For an analysis of the global university, see Looser 2012 and Günel, forthcoming.

ment in water management. For instance, as the Masdar Institute website (2015a) argues, "water has been one of Masdar Institute's key focus areas since inception, with diverse research looking to address challenges in desalination, water treatment, preservation and monitoring." The website (ibid.) continues, "Serving as a key pillar of innovation and human capital, Masdar Institute remains fundamental to Masdar's core objectives of developing Abu Dhabi's knowledge economy and finding solutions to humanity's toughest challenges such as climate change." Accordingly, the Institute Center for Water and Environment (iWater) at the Masdar Institute (2015b), on the one hand, seeks to become "a regionally focused but globally recognized university research center that produces knowledge and technologies that address the clean water production and management, climate change and the environment, and water resource challenges faced by the UAE and the region." On the other hand, the center features projects that fill research gaps regarding regional climatic dynamics. For instance, one of the research projects in the center concentrates on improving the accuracy of future water availability scenarios in the Middle East, specifically by analyzing large-scale atmospheric models, expected precipitation levels, and land surface processes. In particular, the center aspires to deliver research on water technologies, water resource management, and environmental conservation.

In Saudi Arabia, KAUST promotes a similar message. The Water Desalination and Reuse Center at KAUST focuses its activities on the optimization of current technologies and development of new ones and argues for exporting its findings in other parts of the world that suffer from water challenges. "This mandate will serve the Kingdom of Saudi Arabia (KSA), deprived of sufficient fresh water supplies and already heavily involved in desalination, as well as the proximate region spanning the Arabian Gulf/Peninsula, the Middle East, Northern/Eastern Africa, and South Asia," its mission statement notes (KAUST 2015a). "The Center will help thrust the KSA to the global forefront of desalination and reuse technology research, development, adaptation, and dissemination" (ibid.).[16] In addition to conceptualizing knowledge production as an economic development strategy, these hubs assemble innovations from across different geographies and promote them regionally.

What separates these institutions from their counterparts in other wealthy economies is not only that they are brand-new but also that they aim to train local citizens for the workforce, contributing to the Emiratization movement (and, in

16. For more specific information on the research activities at KAUST, see the "Publications" page in KAUST 2015b.

the case of Saudi Arabia, Saudization). Of the 9 million people who live and work in the UAE, almost 8 million are not Emirati citizens. These immigrants come to the UAE on temporary renewable work contracts sponsored by their employers, a system known as *kafala*. Although work contracts can be renewed indefinitely, many immigrants know that eventually their visas will expire and they will have to leave the country. The temporary nature of these contracts impedes immigrants from forming communities or feeling a sense of belonging in the UAE and underscores how they will remain perpetual outsiders, without the prospect of cultural assimilation or naturalization as Emirati citizens.[17] Some of these immigrants hold white-collar jobs in tourism, finance, and construction; many others are low-wage male workers from South Asia. The UAE's violations of workers' rights, especially on construction sites, are well documented by international institutions as well as the media.[18]

As Christopher M. Davidson (2009) notes, since the founding of the UAE in 1971, Emirati nationals have been consistently provided with the material benefits of the oil-extraction economy, thereby depriving them of motivation to participate in a competitive labor market. While there are no reliable statistics on the issue, Davidson (ibid.: 149–52) suggests that the nationals constitute about 9 percent of the workforce. In resolving this problem, he argues, "the only long-term solution is improved education at all levels," through which Emirati citizens will acquire the necessary skills to compete with the large number of expatriates living in the UAE. Studying the history of the education sector, Davidson finds that the major problem leading to a lack of education among Emiratis has been, rather shockingly, a "lack of funding." He writes, "Although the federal budget allocation for education now exceeds $2 billion, this is only a third of the allocation for military expenditure and, in relative terms, is about a quarter of the educational expenditure of some other Arab states." Accordingly, Davidson understands the new emphasis put on education, as seen in the founding of the NYU Abu Dhabi, the Masdar Institute, or the Sorbonne Abu Dhabi, to be positive, both in terms of training more qualified Emirati youths and of making the education sector more high profile within domestic politics.

In this economic vision, knowledge—in both the technical and cultural spheres (the latter promoted in particular via museums, art fairs, and biennales)—becomes a direct agent in the UAE's transformation into a "more elite" country, powered

17. For an analysis of how these policies affect migrant communities in the UAE, see Vora 2013. For an exposé of the types of exploitation that the *kafala* system facilitates, see Human Rights Watch 2014.

18. For a good example, see Human Rights Watch 2015.

by a knowledge-based economy.[19] In this vision, categories of the technical and the cultural merge seamlessly, both serving as products and generators of innovation. The two types of knowledge share an emphasis on products: the technical knowledge infrastructure is expected to incubate new technologically advanced artifacts, while the cultural sector will facilitate investments in the art market. Knowledge is a method for producing profitable innovation strategies, which may create marginal differences that allow these countries to succeed in the world economy. Through these knowledge infrastructures, some of the countries in the region seek to reengineer and refashion themselves for a future that relies less on oil export revenues.

The timeline of the knowledge-based economy emerges as a significant problem in the implementation of research infrastructures in the UAE in particular and in the Arabian Gulf in general. On the one hand, the decision makers in the region, such as university presidents, warn the authorities that it will take time to build the social context that facilitates knowledge hubs with capacities to trigger technological transformation, and they stress the thought processes and socio-cultural attributes that elicit the production of knowledge.[20] On the other hand, regional authorities, including the executives at Abu Dhabi's renewable energy and clean technology company Masdar, are critical of the fact that there are not enough start-up companies in the region, despite the extensive investment in institutions of higher education. A university president I met during my fieldwork, a US-trained expatriate with considerable experience in building institutions in the UAE, explained that the Emiratis were not farmers who would know that it takes time to harvest any produce, but rather they were traders who expected quick gains from their ventures. In this way, the president tried to describe how the temporalities of knowledge did not overlap with the expected timeline of economic development in the Emirates.

While the emphasis on domestic knowledge production and the cultivation of a national (as opposed to immigrant) workforce is a significant transformation in the region, it is unclear how much of this transformation will lead to climate change adaptation or mitigation work, especially if knowledge production capacities are

19. For a critical analysis of the production of Guggenheim Abu Dhabi as well as other institutions of knowledge, see Ross 2015.

20. For instance, Wasim Maziak (2005), a Syrian scientist who published in *Science* about the production of knowledge in the Arab world, underlines how "most Arabs view science as a commodity that can be separated from the thought processes and socio-cultural attributes of its producers." While Maziak's perspective may have changed since the publication of the piece, investments in high technology continue to characterize knowledge production in Abu Dhabi. The Masdar City project is a good example of these types of investments.

perceived as ways to extend the lifestyles and thinking that fossil fuel exports make possible. At the same time, however, these emergent institutions may serve as spaces where the existing modes of living will be interrogated, leading to the cultivation of alternative futures in the region that do not rely solely on technical adjustments. By involving the local population in the production of knowledge, such alternative futures may allow for the informal and formal networks and spaces of collective action, which trigger more informed ways of engaging with climate change. The involvement of the local population may also contribute to a sense of belonging to the landscapes, the same landscapes that are under threat by climate change.

Conclusion

It is clear that the affluent oil economies of the Arabian Peninsula wield considerable influence in the production of global environmental policy and practice; nonetheless, to date, they have received little attention from scholars working on climate governance. To better understand the global workings of climate politics, however, it is useful to examine how these economies conceive and mold energy and climate futures. Perceptions of climate change mitigation and adaptation shape and become reshaped by the social context in which they are interpreted. Therefore it is necessary to complement the scientific reports on the environmental conditions of the region with *why* and *how* questions that delve into the social, political, and economic context.

While professionals like Daoud of the state-run EAD argue that stressing the man-made qualities of water will make water seem more valuable, or less of a free source, in fact these qualities have the opposite effect: the man-made character of water leads to a celebration of water's interminable abundance; more of it can always be manufactured, regardless of the environmental conditions of the region. Or, as Said argues, climate change will not have much of an impact on desalination plants. The expectation is that even under dire environmental conditions, the plants will continue to operate and provide water to their constituents.

In preparing for a future rife with energy scarcity and climate change, some countries in the Arabian Peninsula are building knowledge hubs that can prompt innovation domestically. Saudi Arabia and the UAE, to construct a post-oil economy, capitalize on the networks and wealth that their current oil production makes available. Currently, these hubs are at work to create technologies that can be exported, serving as methods of economic diversification as well as marketing and branding, making the Gulf, as one of my interlocutors put it, "more elite." These efforts are also a call to the nationals in the region to participate in the economy, to help constitute a new permanent workforce with different types of expertise. These emergent institutions of knowledge, despite their multiple problems, appear to be the most promising pieces of the climate change puzzle in the Arabian Peninsula, since they may allow for the flourishing of new ideas, new collectivities, and perhaps new forms of living.

This article grounds technical adjustments in the Arabian Peninsula; however, it is easy to observe such adjustments in other parts of the world. Electric cars, biodegradable plastic bags, and energy-efficient lightbulbs characterize contemporary methodologies of engaging with energy scarcity and climate change and provide the piecemeal means through which humans seek to extend their lifestyles into the future while at the same time tackling climate change. Perhaps here "technical adjustments" emerges as an ethnographic category, one that finds various expressions in different contexts, that guides living arrangements and shapes social possibilities in technocratic and, typically, anthropocentric manners, along the lines drawn by affluent nations. But in fact climate change and energy scarcity should propel humans to challenge such ideals of technological development and economic growth, to pay attention to the alternative futures rendered invisible by the drive for infinity, and to cultivate a new mode of inhabiting the planet.

References

Aiyer, Ananthakrishnan. 2007. "The Allure of the Transnational: Notes on Some Aspects of the Political Economy of Water in India." *Cultural Anthropology* 22, no. 4: 640–58.

Alderman, Liz. 2010. "Dubai Faces Environmental Problems after Growth." *New York Times*, October 27. www.nytimes.com/2010/10/28/business/energy-environment/28dubai.html.

Baba, Alper, et al., eds. 2011. *Climate Change and Its Effects on Water Resources: Issues of National and Global Security.* Dordrecht: Springer.

Ballestero, Andrea. 2015. "The Ethics of a Formula: Calculating a Financial-Humanitarian Price for Water." *American Ethnologist* 42, no. 2: 262–78.

Barnes, Jessica. 2014. *Cultivating the Nile: The Everyday Politics of Water in Egypt.* Durham, NC: Duke University Press.

Callon, Michel. 2007. "An Essay on the Growing Contribution of Economic Markets to the Proliferation of the Social." *Theory, Culture and Society* 24, nos. 7–8: 139–63.

Davidson, Christopher M. 2009. *Abu Dhabi: Oil and Beyond*. New York: Columbia University Press.

Davis, Diana K. 2011. "Imperialism, Orientalism, and the Environment in the Middle East: History, Policy, Power, and Practice." In *Environmental Imaginaries of the Middle East and North Africa*, edited by Diana K. Davis and Edmund Burke III, 1–23. Athens: Ohio University Press.

Dinar, Ariel, Víctor Pochat, and José Albiac-Murillo, eds. 2015. *Water Pricing Experiences and Innovations*. Dordrecht: Springer.

EAD (Environment Agency–Abu Dhabi). 2009. *Abu Dhabi Water Resources Master Plan*. Abu Dhabi: EAD. www.scribd.com/doc/224889521/Abu-Dhabi -Water-Rosources-Master-Plan.

Goldman, Michael. 2005. *Imperial Nature: The World Bank and Struggles for Social Justice in the Age of Globalization*. New Haven, CT: Yale University Press.

Government of Abu Dhabi. 2008. "The Abu Dhabi Economic Vision 2030." www.ecouncil.ae/PublicationsEn/economic-vision-2030-full-versionEn.pdf (accessed June 21, 2015).

Günel, Gökçe. Forthcoming. *Spaceship in the Desert: Energy, Climate Change, and Green Business in Abu Dhabi*. Durham, NC: Duke University Press.

Hashemi, Rahma al-, et al. 2014. "A Review of Desalination Trends in the Gulf Cooperation Council Countries." *International Interdisciplinary Journal of Scientific Research* 1, no. 2: 72–96.

Helmreich, Stefan. 2011. "Nature/Culture/Seawater." *American Anthropologist* 113, no. 1: 132–44.

Hitachi. 2015. "Hitachi Solar-Powered Desalination Plants, Abu Dhabi." www .hitachi.ae/eng/case_studies/desalination-plants (accessed June 16, 2015).

Human Rights Watch. 2014. "'I Already Bought You': Abuse and Exploitation of Female Migrant Domestic Workers in the United Arab Emirates." October 22. New York: Human Rights Watch. www.hrw.org/report/2014/10/22/i-already -bought-you/abuse-and-exploitation-female-migrant-domestic-workers-united.

———. 2015. "Migrant Workers' Rights on Saadiyat Island in the United Arab Emirates: 2015 Progress Report." February 10. New York: Human Rights Watch. www.hrw.org/report/2015/02/10/migrant-workers-rights-saadiyat -island-united-arab-emirates/2015-progress-report.

IPCC (Intergovernmental Panel on Climate Change). 2001. "Adaptation to Climate Change in the Context of Sustainable Development and Equity." Chapter 18 in *Climate Change 2001: Impacts, Adaptation, and Vulnerability*. Geneva: IPCC. www.ipcc.ch/ipccreports/tar/wg2/index.php?idp=641.

Jones, Toby Craig. 2010. *Desert Kingdom: How Oil and Water Forged Modern Saudi Arabia*. Cambridge, MA: Harvard University Press.

KAUST (King Abdullah University of Science and Technology), Water Desalination and Reuse Center. 2015a. "Center Mission." wdrc.kaust.edu.sa/Pages/VisionMission.aspx (accessed August 5, 2015).

———. 2015b. "Publications." wdrc.kaust.edu.sa/Pages/Publications.aspx (accessed August 5, 2015).

Limbert, Mandana E. 2010. *In the Time of Oil: Piety, Memory, and Social Life in an Omani Town*. Stanford, CA: Stanford University Press.

Looser, Tom. 2012. "The Global University, Area Studies, and the World Citizen: Neoliberal Geography's Redistribution of the 'World.'" *Cultural Anthropology* 27, no. 1: 97–117.

Luomi, Mari. 2012. *The Gulf Monarchies and Climate Change: Abu Dhabi and Qatar in an Era of Natural Unsustainability*. London: Hurst.

Masdar. 2015. "Masdar Launches Renewable Energy Desalination Program." masdar.ae/en/media/detail/masdar-launches-renewable-energy-desalination-program (accessed September 1, 2015).

Masdar Institute. 2015a. "Masdar Institute Revealing Desalination Nanotechnology Progress and More at World Water Forum 2015." April 12. masdar.ac.ae/media-section/news/item/6506-masdar-institute-revealing-desalination-nanotechnology-progress-and-more-at-world-water-forum-2015.

———. 2015b. "Institute Center for Water and Environment (iWater)." www.masdar.ac.ae/research/research-centers/icenters-research/iwater (accessed August 29, 2015).

Maziak, Wasim. 2005. "Science in the Arab World: Vision of Glories Beyond." *Science* 308, no. 5727: 1416–18.

Mitchell, Timothy. 2012. *Carbon Democracy: Political Power in the Age of Oil*. New York: Verso.

Naser, Humood. 2014. "Marine Ecosystem Diversity in the Gulf: Threats and Conservation." In *Biodiversity: The Dynamic Balance of the Planet*, edited by Oscar Grillo, 297–328. Rijeka, Croatia: InTech.

Orlove, Ben, and Steven C. Caton. 2010. "Water Sustainability: Anthropological Approaches and Prospects." *Annual Review of Anthropology* 39: 401–15.

Page, Ben. 2005. "Paying for Water and the Geography of Commodities." *Transactions of the Institute of British Geographers* 30, no. 3: 293–306.

Raey, Mohamed el-. 2010. "Impact of Sea-Level Rise on the Arab Region." New York: Arab Climate Change Initiative, United Nations Development Pro-

gramme. www.arabclimateinitiative.org/Countries/egypt/ElRaey_Impact_of
_Sea_Level_Rise_on_the_Arab_Region.pdf.

Renwick, Mary E., and Richard D. Green. 2000. "Do Residential Water Demand
Side Management Policies Measure Up? An Analysis of Eight California
Water Agencies." *Journal of Environmental Economics and Management* 40,
no. 1: 37–55.

Ross, Andrew. 2015. *The Gulf: High Culture / Hard Labor.* New York: OR Books.

Schnitzler, Antina von. 2013. "Traveling Technologies: Infrastructure, Ethical
Regimes, and the Materiality of Politics in South Africa." *Cultural Anthropology* 28, no. 2: 320–43.

Schwartz, Nelson D. 2015. "Water Pricing in Two Thirsty Cities: In One, Guzzlers Pay More, and Use Less." *New York Times,* May 6. www.nytimes.com
/2015/05/07/business/energy-environment/water-pricing-in-two-thirsty-cities
.html.

Scott, James C. 1998. *Seeing like a State: How Certain Schemes to Improve the
Human Condition Have Failed.* New Haven, CT: Yale University Press.

Shiva, Vandana. 2002. *Water Wars: Privatization, Pollution, and Profit.* Cambridge, MA: South End.

Solomon, Erika. 2010. "As Tiny UAE's Water Tab Grows, Resources Run Dry."
Reuters, June 21. www.reuters.com/article/2010/06/21/us-emirates-water
-feature-idUSTRE65K3MK20100621.

Spiess, Andy. 2008. "Developing Adaptive Capacity for Responding to Environmental Change in the Arab Gulf States: Uncertainties to Linking Ecosystem
Conservation, Sustainable Development, and Society in Authoritarian Rentier
Economies." *Global and Planetary Change* 64, nos. 3–4: 244–52.

Suhaimy, Ubaid al-. 2013. "Saudi Arabia: The Desalination Nation." *Asharq
al-Awsat,* July 2. www.aawsat.net/2013/07/article55308131/the-desalination
-nation.

Todorova, Vesela. 2009. "Desalination Threat to the Growing Gulf." *National* (UAE),
August 31. www.thenational.ae/news/uae-news/environment/desalination
-threat-to-the-growing-gulf.

UNDESA (United Nations Department of Economic and Social Affairs). 2015.
"World Population Prospects, the 2015 Revision." New York. esa.un.org/unpd
/wpp/Publications/Files/Key_Findings_WPP_2015.pdf.

UN-ESCWA (United Nations Economic and Social Commission for Western
Asia). 2011. "Assessing the Impact of Climate Change on Water Resources and
Socio-economic Vulnerability in the Arab Region: A Methodological Frame-

work for Pursuing an Integrated Assessment." Beirut: UN-ESCWA. www
.escwa.un.org/information/pubaction.asp?PubID=1118.

Vora, Neha. 2013. *Impossible Citizens: Dubai's Indian Diaspora*. Durham, NC:
Duke University Press.

Wasmi, Naser Al. 2014. "Abu Dhabi Residents Brace for Utility Price Hikes." *National*
(UAE), December 23. www.thenational.ae/uae/abu-dhabi-residents-brace
-for-utility-price-hikes.

Gökçe Günel is a lecturer in anthropology at Columbia University. She earned her
PhD in anthropology from Cornell University in 2012. Her forthcoming book *Spaceship
in the Desert: Energy, Climate Change, and Green Business in Abu Dhabi* focuses on the
construction of renewable energy and clean technology infrastructures in the United
Arab Emirates, specifically concentrating on the Masdar City project.

Interviews with Rebuild by Design's Working Group of Experts

Daniel Aldana Cohen

In the fall of 2014, Rebuild by Design, an initiative of President Barack Obama's Hurricane Sandy Rebuilding Task Force, convened an international working group of experts to advance a global conversation on resiliency, design, and politics. As part of that process, the researcher Daniel Aldana Cohen interviewed several members of the working group on the challenges and opportunities that cities increasingly face in a warming world, with a focus on revealing common points of interest, shared understandings, and divergent opinions.

HENK OVINK, with ERIC KLINENBERG

Principal of Rebuild by Design
and Special Envoy for International Water Affairs for the Netherlands

Background

Daniel Aldana Cohen (DAC): How did you come to work on ecological issues and resiliency? Which aspects of your earlier work shaped how you approach these issues today?

Henk Ovink (HO): I did not get to where I am now through research, but through practice. In this practice, I sought to connect transformative processes with the ways that societal developments affect multiple environments—the urban, the

Public Culture 28:2   DOI 10.1215/08992363-3451339

rural, rivers, the sea. In all these situations, one is confronted by the dysfunction and disconnect between the issues at stake and the ways that various stakeholders are used to acting. It's hard to make progress, to move forward. In part, this has to do with bureaucrats' tendency to avoid confronting complexity in a context of superficial political analysis and public opinion. So in my practice, working with schools, universities, research institutes, governments, engineers, designers, developers, and investors, the first thing I would aim for was a more sophisticated understanding of the problems—How do we do this? Can we organize a better understanding, in a different way than we used to do?—so a better understanding, a different process, and then a different type of collaboration in that process, where you would bring in the different partners, not after their negotiated positioning but before. And you engage with them in a dedicated and substantial way, through that process of understanding, and not through positioning or negotiating, turning negotiations into collaborations. I learned to use the power of design in this approach.

Now there's a ton of research out there. You can go back decades or years. Every year adds another layer of understanding to the complexity and the interdependencies between all these issues. The World Economic Forum's risk report illustrates this. They've been doing these analyses for a decade now. And what they show is the power—but also the threat—of the connectivity of risks in the social, cultural, economic, and ecological realms, a clear connectivity in both the origin and impact of these risks. In other words, exploring the pathway for mitigation and adaptation strategies. What we tended to do in the past—and I'm sorry to say, we still do—is try to split up that risk into different isolated areas: infrastructure resilience, or housing resilience, or community resilience, or social resilience. We didn't even call it "resilience," but the capacity to survive—or, in modernist terms, the capacity to be bold and future-proof.

If you look at these challenges not through modernist or engineering lenses but more through an ecological lens, then all of a sudden those interdependencies make sense. You find that it's not a matter of drawing a line on the map and saying, "This is my country or my city and I'm going to run it." You have to look underneath and on top of it. You have to say, "Hey, how does the system of social, cultural, economic, ecological interrelationships work? And how can you organize, mitigate, adapt, and thus influence and act upon this system?" For me, grasping that complexity adds to my political wish to change the world.

This is exactly what Design and Politics was about. Its aim wasn't to have an abstract debate, but instead to make politics understand this complexity and to give the design professionals an understanding of the political realm by bringing in complexity. Though I must be very honest: the professional world is very bad at understanding that complexity, too. The World Economic Forum report is not read by a lot of professionals. And professionals in the scientific, business, NGO [nongovernmental organization], design, and engineering worlds work just as fragmented as government [does]. So for me, there's a need and an opportunity for this kind of approach, despite its complexity.

DAC: Eric, you started out with your book on Chicago's heat wave (Klinenberg [2002] 2015). Could you say something about coming from a place, sociology, where bringing in nature, the shifting planetary ecology, is not at all automatic?

Eric Klinenberg (EK): Yes, I started my work in this area when I was doing a dissertation on the great heat wave in Chicago in 1995 that killed hundreds of people. I wanted to understand why mortality rates were so different across the city, even in places that looked very similar on paper, places that had similar rates of poverty and similar rates of vulnerability, places where you would have predicted really comparable outcomes. What I recognized is that most of the people who used the tool of research I was using at the time, ethnography, were using it to observe and to try to understand people. But you could learn a lot by using observational research to understand the characteristics of places. And that became very apparent when I looked at differences between neighborhoods in Chicago. I found a couple of pairs of neighborhoods that were right across the street from each other and should have had very similar outcomes during the disaster but in fact had really different outcomes. One place would be very safe, the other very dangerous. You couldn't explain that through the standard concepts or measures. During my fieldwork, I discovered the significance of what I thought of then as the social ecology of neighborhoods, what I now think of as the social infrastructure of neighborhoods—namely, the characteristics of the streets, and sidewalks, and commercial outlets, and parks, and even more rudimentary things, like stairs and lighting systems. And those things collectively can make a place feel much more comfortable and welcoming for people, or they can make a place feel more threatening.

When I looked at the numbers closely, I realized that actually the social infrastructure of those neighborhoods explained a lot more about who lived and who died than the traditional measures did. I finished that research in the early 2000s. The disaster was in 1995. Since then, the world has gotten hotter. We've seen more extreme events of great significance. And I found myself invited to participate in these big national panels on disaster planning or disaster preparedness and climate change science. And in those meetings, I would often be the only social scientist, surrounded by engineers and other people who worked on the physical environment and kind of took the social for granted. It became apparent to me that there was a real need for us to understand those social factors that play into the way that we live in cities, but that the social sciences would have to fight our way to the table. And so one of the very nice things about the Rebuild by Design competition, for me, is that I didn't have to fight my way there! I got an invitation from Henk out of nowhere. And so it turns out that the way we see things is very similar, even though we come to it from different vantage points.

Crisis and Timing

DAC: Let's talk now about the aftermath of crisis. One issue is coalition building and getting things done. But another is time and urgency. As you've both discussed, the lenses of resiliency and design are ways of recognizing complexity. But after a disaster, there's a lot of pressure to move more quickly than complex thinking and acting requires. How do you extend the time needed for design? What are the challenges that you face in this?

EK: I would say, first of all, that the reason we can't rebuild quickly after disasters is because up until now we thought so little about what it means to have good design that will be resilient for the twenty-first-century world. Had we spent more time doing careful design for the places that are vulnerable, we would have plans that could be reapplied. The problem is that, so often, we see breakdowns in systems because they were poorly designed and poorly made in the first place. So you can't just build back what was there before. That means you need to initiate a thoughtful process of reimagining what those systems and structures would look like.

There's no reason, in the abstract, that we can't be doing that work all the time, so that we're ready when the next crisis hits. But we haven't done that yet. So one of the challenges we have is to create a new cultural awareness and political will to do that. That's part of the fight we're in now. This is one of the things that are unique about Rebuild by Design, from my perspective. The competition began with a three-month research period, during which the teams were forbidden from presenting proposals; [the process was] quite the opposite. The condition of participating in the competition was that they had to experience this three-month, quite rigorous, research process in which members of the teams, who came from all over the world, traveled by foot, by bus, by rail, by boat, throughout the region. By bike as well, Henk always reminds me. Right? They had to put their soles on the terrain that they would be designing projects for. They had to spend time in often-long meetings with the people, the stakeholders who lived there, with the political officials who governed there, with members of the private sector who employed people there. It was an extraordinarily demanding process.

During that process, we also created a group of really premier scholars from several different disciplines, law and engineering, sociology and public health, to provide expert commentary or guidance. But they themselves had to learn about these places firsthand, because they knew about things at a higher level of abstraction. And so we built this kind of collaborative culture that felt uncertain as we were doing it. You know, the joke during the competition was that everyone who did it had to be willing to build the airplane while we were flying. The result was that the teams had a chance to think really seriously about the needs and the vulnerabilities but also the possibilities for all the places where they were designing things. And in some cases, I think that was tough for the people who had been seriously affected by the storm. Let's face it: their recovery from Sandy was far slower than it should have been. The rebuilding took too long. But the truth is that wasn't the fault of the Rebuild by Design competition. There were other programs that were responsible for the immediate and urgent rebuilding process. We were trying to think about how to build larger systems and larger structures that would have enduring presence in the area. I think in most cases it's completely appropriate to spend not just three months but years doing the planning for those kinds of structures.

DAC: Henk, do you agree that the design doesn't have to take a lot of time if there was already a design culture before the crisis hit? And could you say something about the kind of institutional, or noninstitutional, structure that gets set up in order to avoid the typical political pressures for speed? Rebuild by Design isn't a typical agency or an inherited program. It's a unique constellation of actors.

HO: I agree with Eric. We don't need crises to be intelligent, but sometimes we need crises to be reminded of the capacity of our intelligence. But in this case, Sandy was a necessary reminder. If you see everything that went astray during Sandy, everything that was failing in the social and physical infrastructure—I mean, this is New York, one of the best regions in the world at so many levels, but not in terms of its performance during the storm. And Sandy wasn't even a hurricane. It slowed down before it hit, and it could have been worse. Still, we had well over $60 billion in damage and a couple of hundred people killed and hundreds of thousands of houses lost and businesses lost. So we were not ready. There's a thing to the crisis part I want to address. Eric touched upon it a little. And that is that people say, "Never let a crisis go to waste." Lots of political leaders like to say that. If it's in the Philippines after Typhoon Haiyan, or in New Jersey or New York after Hurricane Sandy, or in New Orleans after Katrina, I don't think you will find anyone that agrees with that. People that lost their daughter, their house, their business, their lives, they love what they lost and they aren't interested in change. They want to go back, fast. They want to get back what they lost. So developing a better understanding is not just a scientific or policy issue. Ultimately, it's about really building relationships, engaging with the people who were affected. Rebuild by Design captured that complexity, not only the complexity of storm surges and economic distress but also the complexity of social distress. The process of engagement was totally collaborative and inclusive. In my words, the door was always open. One was never too late, which was very important for an engaged process, for better understanding among all partners, and for building capacity to capture change—so necessary, but not easy, in times of great distress.

Normally these processes are organized by businesses or scientists or governments. Most of the time, it's the professional groups that want to organize themselves first, one by one, rather than organize collaborations among professionals; only later do they engage with the public. Rebuild by Design turned it inside out and said: "We're not ready for answers; you're needed because we don't know. We have to build the plane while we're flying it. We will adjust and be flexible in the process, to be as inclusive as possible, to move faster in the end." Because there was no way anyone could predict next steps. We changed the way the steps interacted. We removed steps. We added steps. We added people. We added organizations. And in this way we built trust across government, philanthropy, businesses, professionals, academics, researchers, designers, engineers, politicians and community leaders, individuals and businesses. And that was a slow process, in a pressure cooker. That was an absolute necessity. And therefore, Rebuild by Design was an organization, but also a network and a process. We had a team of organizations, the federal government, states and local governments across the region: New York University's (NYU) IPK [Institute for Public Knowledge], headed by Eric; the Regional Plan Association; the Municipal Art Society; the Van Alen Institute; and other groups. We worked with Occupy Sandy, community groups, local mayors. All told, it was over five hundred organizations, thousands of people that were not in the teams but were in the process in every different step. That was very important for our success. It was not only an understanding of what went wrong and where interdependencies and vulnerabilities could be addressed and where the opportunities could be allocated; it was really an understanding of the culture, because it was different in the Meadowlands or Hoboken or Jersey City and different in Hunts Point than it was on Long Island, on Staten Island, or in Manhattan. And all of this raised the bar and the ambition on how comprehensive we could be.

Building Coalitions

DAC: Yes, it makes sense that ordinary people don't come into this immediately wanting to have a transformative design process, and my guess is that if you actually talked to businesses, associations, many people in government, you would find that, with the exception of design professionals and academics, not that many people are going into this wanting to have a transformative design experience. So in terms of setting up the coalition, can you talk a bit about what kinds of stakeholders, in your experience with Rebuild by Design, are relatively easy to bring on board? What were some of the challenges that other stakeholders brought to you?

HO: The interesting thing is that when you call design "innovation," all of a sudden you have more friends. So that was nice. [And] using competition also builds it into a whole new family-and-friends network. So with innovation, with competition, all of a sudden there's the opportunity to engage with a broader world than if we would only say, "Well, we're going to redesign your city, beach, or your street." And this was also not a design competition in the sense that we wanted the designs. That was part of it, but it was a cultural process to bring understanding and change and, out of that change, projects that we could actually deliver on the ambition of change. Of course, Shaun Donovan played a key role. He's not only a born-and-raised New Yorker; he's also a trained architect. And he headed the Housing and Urban Development (HUD) agency that knows about planning and design. So his professional and personal background, and his political position, were definitely key. Without him, nothing.

[In addition], there was the White House Office of Science and Technology Policy that came out of the America COMPETES Act [America Creating Opportunities to Meaningfully Promote Excellence in Technology, Education, and Science Act of 2007], an act that was initiated by the Bush administration. But the Obama administration turned it around. So there was an institutional world on the political and agency level within HUD. There was the opportunity of a task force that was chaired by Donovan, with a president who was focused on climate change, resiliency approaches, driven by innovation to a new condition of the whole United States, using Sandy as an opportunity to move his climate agenda forward. So we have a presidential buy-in, a secretary who's design-oriented, and a White House office that is focused on innovation and competition. So on the federal level, they were the partners that, although not understanding the complexity of Rebuild by Design, understood the opportunity and also the need. On the grantee levels of cities and states, you could see the same. New Jersey, New York City, New York State, Connecticut—they were all trying to figure out how this was working in the aftermath of a disaster and immediately found out it was not easy.

It was not easy to rebuild. And it was harder to rebuild in a way that was satisfactory and actually dealing with the future. That's not to say that they were out of options, but they needed new options, actually. So in the institutional part, there was a clear understanding of the lack of capacity to deal with this. That brings in [another] layer, which is philanthropy. Rebuild by Design engaged in discussions with over two dozen philanthropic organizations in this region on the idea of using a competition as an instrument to drive innovation, to move this region to where it's more resilient from a social, economic, ecological, and cultural perspective. For them, it was a clear case, much clearer than for anyone else. And then, after my first meeting with them, it became clear to me that this was not a money issue, but actually a partner issue. If they could partner with us, they could actually help understand the federal government, the opportunity of such an approach. So out of that partnership, six funders stepped up. One of them, of course, was the lead supporter, the Rockefeller Foundation. It engaged in the idea of using the competition not only to raise resiliency in the region but actually to change government. Philanthropic organizations aren't only interested in getting stuff done; [they're] also [interested] in getting decision makers to think differently, to be more impactful and effective. And they saw the whole engagement with Rebuild by Design as an opportunity to put in a couple of million dollars, to leverage a billion or even more, and to inform the federal government of a different process, in other words, actually building capacity and change within government.

So we had the institutional world, NGOs, the philanthropic organizations, and then of course the partners like NYU IPK, because they brought in the knowledge, the activism, the feet on the ground they already had. Eric's team was there right after Sandy, and not only after Sandy but working in the region with communities, trying to get that understanding. So a combination of academic and activist approaches. Then there was the Regional Plan Association with the regional scoping, and of course planning and design is in their guts. There was the Municipal Art Society, which had expertise on the social aspect, and the engagement, and the long-term history of this region. And [there was] the Van Alen Institute, with a clear design focus and expertise in competitions and innovative engagement processes around the region.

EK: Can I ask something? Could you find institutional partners like the ones we had in Rebuild by Design all over the world?

HO: Yes.

EK: It's replicable?

HO: Yes. And you will find different partners because you have different conditions in different situations. But sometimes you have to bring in a little more from the outside. But there are always local partners, always. You go to Egypt, there are local partners. You go to India, there are local partners. You go to the Philippines, there are local partners. And sometimes you have to bring in more organizing capacity, sometimes more funding capacity, sometimes more specific professional capacity. But there's always capacity on the ground.

EK: Do you hear from places that want to do something similar to Rebuild by Design now?

HO: Yes.

EK: What kinds of places?

HO: It differs a lot. Cali, places in Bangladesh and Myanmar, the Philippines, Jakarta, Singapore, Cape Town, São Paulo, Quito, Boston, Jakarta, Detroit, San Francisco.

EK: The state of Colorado.

HO: The state of Colorado. The governor of Colorado immediately approached me during Rebuild by Design. But it's not only that *places* are interested. The UN picked it up. And, of course, the UN is kind of a complex organization in itself. How could they pick it up? Because, luckily, their headquarters is here [in New York City]. And there are intelligent people working there. They read the paper and understand what's going on. So now, today, Hoboken is being named by UNISDR [the United Nations International Strategy for Disaster Reduction] as a model city for resiliency, based on the Rebuild by Design strategy. Next to that, the UN has a public/private program called the R!SE program, where public and private partners said: "We have to join forces in an even more innovative way. Let's look at Rebuild by Design as an opportunity to move ahead and find places around the world that public and private partners can invest in and see." I helped develop a resiliency challenge with the Rockefeller Foundation, USAID [United States Agency for International Development], and the Swedish government. And in the aftermath of the task force with the federal government we developed the National Disaster Resilience Competition, which started in sixty-seven places all across the United States. And I just heard they're doing other competitive approaches building on the success of Rebuild by Design.

So there's a clear interest. But I have to say, I'm cautious. Mostly, I'm very optimistic and positive in my nature, but you can't copy this. It's not that you say, "Oh, let's do a Rebuild by Design in whatchamacallit," because it doesn't work. We did not design a blueprint and execute it step-by-step. We designed an ambition together. And every step informed that ambition and changed it and loaded capacity onto it and informed the steps moving forward. If you can't be that flexible, you can't use the culture. The other part of it is that most of the time, specifically in aid structures around the world, there's a top-down approach where aid money is put into this machine and then moves around in all these different organizations that engage in different ways, and when it hits the ground, for every dollar, there's $0.10 or $0.15 left for the actual project. And the challenge that I helped develop with USAID and Rockefeller and others, based on Rebuild by Design's insight, was a process where you could bring in talent on the ground in those communities with just a little money, not the aid money, just a little money to engage locally and regionally, and come up with the great and best ideas and then, immediately, one-on-one fund those ideas. So you don't need the whole structure. So there are other ways to intervene with risks and vulnerabilities around the world. But that's not a copy-and-paste of Rebuild by Design. It's a different process, but [one] informed by the lessons learned.

EK: Henk, one more question. You said that design allows you to do things in politics that are very hard to do without design. And I wonder if you could elaborate on that and on how you see that working across these different places in very different contexts.

HO: It's also because of the politics part in the design. I'm looking for engagement. Politics gives itself more leeway, more room with a design realm. It's the interesting part. If you use innovation all of a sudden, and you use a process that feels a bit like an escape, all of a sudden freethinking is normal. And politicians are human beings, too. They want to do the best for their citizens, for the people who voted or did not vote for them. But they are also organized in the normal and limited way. So the moment you come up with an opportunity for them, for engagement and real reform and change, they will immediately say yes. Now design can help inform that appetite in that sense. And design also helps because, and I use it again, the World Economic Forum's risk report shows that these risks—the social, cultural, economic, ecological—are interdependent but also interrelated on a physical scale, an urban, regional scale. The devastating impact of that is one part, but the opportunity to engage with this interrelationship is enormous. And that means that you can actually mitigate and adapt to where those risks are or with those risks in place. And that interrelationship in a physical realm is exactly what design and planning are all about and where they can bring innovation, resilience, and change. They can bring all these relations together. And that is because, intrinsically, design is comprehensive.

So now that's why the capacity for innovation is not siloed but holistic, comprehensive. And because an ambition for innovation in a comprehensive way, engaging in this relationship, immediately interacts with these risks, right? But through design you can analyze, do research, develop scenarios of future developments, build out a strategy on a day-by-day basis that is very concrete, and then showcase those interrelationships and a way forward. And for politicians, all of this is great. They can engage with the past. They can engage with the future. They can engage with the present. Now politics can actually inform that process. So I think designers and politicians are partners, far better partners than a lot of other professionals in this world.

DAC: So people out there are wrestling with the issue of what the word *resiliency* really means. Some say it's an unnecessary word or a cover for something unsavory, for neoliberalism. Is it important to defend the word? What does it mean to you?

HO: You don't have to defend it. But *resiliency* did bring a word into our vocabulary to better understand how we, societies around the world, want to deal with our uncertain future. In my terms, I don't like the way that *resiliency* is positioned as the condition of being able to bounce back and deal with shocks and stresses of all kind. I really think it's far more progressive. There's a huge amount of learning and experience in resiliency. So I think of it more in terms of the ability of our society's political system, our institutions, to deal with shocks and stresses in a very progressive way. Otherwise, it's a condition. *Resiliency* has to mean progress. And so I do think it's a helpful term. I was once invited to a conference organized by the UN with Ban Ki-moon. And during one panel, a student asked, "What's the difference between *sustainability* and *resilience*?" And of course, those two words, they stand for different things. But at the same time, they're part of the same way forward. I think that if we can use those terms in a way that helps us better perform, make better decisions, act better, and change the way we deal with the planet's risks, then that's fine. If they become an excuse for inactivity, then they were the worst presents that we gave to ourselves.

EDGAR PIETERSE
South African Research Chair in Urban Policy and Director of the African Center for Cities

Background

Daniel Adana Cohen (DAC): You've long been an urbanist, but you've become progressively more involved in issues of sustainability, resiliency, design. How did this happen?

Edgar Pieterse (EP): It's quite hard to disentangle. First, I started off as an activist engaged in urban politics, and then a broader intellectual, academic trajectory followed. When I went to high school in the mid-1980s, in Cape Town, I was very involved in student politics. The focus, of course, was the antiapartheid struggle. And it was done in a grassroots way. We were involved with movements in black communities, mobilizing around social reproduction needs—housing, energy, services, and so on. At the end of the 1980s, when the political transition started, I was entering my undergrad years. And I was soon asked to help set up a research center to enable social movements to access academic knowledge for their campaigns. We very quickly realized there wasn't actually enough academic research that was of relevance. Meanwhile, at that point, the struggles were all around service tariffs and municipal fiscal policies.

The fiscal model at the time was that black neighborhoods cross-subsidized white municipal areas against a backdrop of official racial segregation. I know that sounds completely insane, but that's how it was. From there, it was a long series of engagements that always included practical work around things like municipal budgeting, equitable service provision models, and so on. However, these issues were unique to South Africa.

From the early 1990s onward our work considered the very different urban contexts throughout Africa. Through that engagement, a big lesson emerged and endured: in most sub-Saharan African cities, the state is absent, especially the local state. So these places are produced by people themselves, in terms of everything, basically. And there was something about how that dense sociality presents a really profound epistemic challenge to how we thought about urban theory and policy, but also from a research point of view—how do we actually know what the fuck is going on?

So I came to recognize that you've got to tread lightly as you intervene into very complex, dense social fabrics. And then it became clear that there was a real limitation to a basic needs agenda, which was the operative frame in South African struggles: that one had to think about economic inclusion and transformation and an environmental agenda. The environmental bit was very poorly developed in our own thinking. I really came to it through a confrontation that stemmed from my collaboration with Mark Swilling and Eve Annecke, who came to Cape Town in 1998 to establish something called the Sustainability Institute. They asked me to join the board from the beginning and help conceptualize what it could become.

Sustainability Politics in Cape Town

DAC: There seems to be a lot going on in Cape Town around urban climate and sustainability politics. Could you explain what's happening there?

EP: Cape Town is a very tricky situation. The context is that South Africa had its policy-development process in the mid-1990s, reflecting the neoliberal culture of that moment, intertwined with the rise of integrated development discourses. There's a lot of emphasis on integration, holism, et cetera. The end result in legal and regulatory terms was such a complex institutional system that very little changes, because you always have to address everything at once. There's no way of thinking about prioritization or sequencing. We've got elaborate environmental impact assessment legislation. We've got elaborate social impact legislation. We've got heritage legislation. We've got analysts. The list goes on. So, effectively, to do anything takes planning and also takes anywhere between five and eight years to move from need identification to plan and implementation. In this institutional context, to do something radical, profound, is almost impossible. The process is so convoluted it induces profound risk aversion in the public sector, along with a whole series of legal tangles. And Cape Town is an extreme example of this. So you've got a pretty large crew of professionals who are expert at this development discourse who do the policy drafting, the policy workshops, the process work. There's an amazing array of policy on everything you can think of, from mass transport to pedestrianization, to open space systems, to biodiversity protection. But practically, it creates an unbearable discursive weight, so much so that the metropolitan government is incapable of actually implementing much.

So you're not going to find a shortage of sophisticated, beautifully produced policies on a raft of environmental and sustainability questions on Cape Town. Whether those are actually implemented and whether they add up to structural change—in the economy of the city and questions of environmental justice—that's another story. In my reading, no. Although, on the face of it, it looks like there are a lot of things going on, and a lot of it is actually quite cutting-edge. I suppose the biggest thing in Cape Town would be the shift to bus rapid transit (BRT), namely, the development of high-speed, dedicated bus lanes where you pay your fare before boarding, and a very heavy emphasis on transit-oriented development (TOD), which calls for building up density around nodes and corridors of mass transit.

DAC: That sounds a lot like Brazil, where there's also an abundance of incredibly bright civil servants but barriers to implementation. Could you say a bit more about these barriers in Cape Town?

EP: The one obvious barrier is the intense poverty and the pressure that puts on the city. In South Africa, the urban government has a legal obligation to provide a social safety net in the form of minimum free basic services, public housing, and so on. But because unemployment is so high, perhaps up to 40 percent depending on the definition, the economy is not growing fast enough to pay for these amazing plans. So the city then focuses on fulfilling its legal obligations. And the cost of that keeps going up, along with doing the capital maintenance work to make sure the golden goose continues to lay the golden egg for the taxpayers.

DAC: The golden goose?

EP: The golden goose is the middle classes and the commercial areas that pay property tax. Property tax is nearly 60 percent of the total municipal income. One result is that, for the cool projects and ideas, there's basically no money. So they're in a perpetual piloting phase. Every cool thing has a pilot. You can scrape some money together for a pilot, but it never becomes anything else. When there's a new fashion, they'll produce a new set of policies, and there will be a new pilot. And this helps the administration feel that it is doing something profound, to communicate that it is this sustainable, dynamic city on a mission to solve big urban questions. But I don't foresee any of this stuff making a major difference in the overall trajectory of the city. At least, that's the lesson of the past twenty years.

Ecological Improvements and Displacement

DAC: Is there a parallel between Cape Town and places like New York, São Paulo, and other cities where green improvements drive up land prices, displacing those who would benefit the most? Is this happening in Cape Town?

EP: Yes, in a way. Cape Town has tried to promote urban renewal with an above-standard mix of allowing the creative industries a foothold, supporting that, relaxing zoning and other regulations, public infrastructure investments, et cetera. This has happened in the inner city in particular and then some zones that are nearby. In commercial terms, it's been very significant in the past decade. All that coincides with a kind of hipster environmentalism. So there's definitely a perception that pedestrianization, street culture, café culture connected with museums or galleries and boutiques, and so forth are tied in with environmentalism as a coherent modality of urban renewal. And as we speak, there has been an emergence of a radical critique of this in Cape Town. The city hasn't offered a coherent response to date.

Still, the underlying problem is fiscal. What are the institutional and the fiscal instruments to moderate the displacement? I don't think you can do away with it, but you can moderate it. And you can then create a new class of clemency arrangements and communal occupancy and social housing in the midst of these processes of gentrification and renewal. That debate, nobody is having. Nobody is projecting that into the public domain. But I suspect it's because the debate is relatively new.

Rescuing Resilience Discourse

DAC: And how prominent is the discourse of resilience in all of this?

EP: It's climbing the development discourse hit parade. And it's getting to the top of the charts. It has the benefit of demonstrating green credentials, being seen to be "with it" in terms of international thinking. And for deep environmentalists, it's a strategic opportunity to return to the environmental debate and hopefully make a better show of it this time around. So its circulation and its resonance are significant. And as an activist, my instinct is to use whatever is at my disposal to open up debate. And it certainly has that potential. So, absolutely, let's talk about resilience with regard to ecological systems. But when we talk about the economy or when we talk about social processes, there are more effective concepts, and let's put those distinctions in play. So I hope there is a way to rescue the ecological systems dimensions of the resilience discourse, but not transpose them to the social sphere. Otherwise, you end up with a problematic, liberal glossing over of structural inequalities and deep difference.

Politics and Design

DAC: What about design? You've talked about the ways that innovative policies are sort of trapped in the governance logic of Cape Town. What about the idea of a design process for politics as a way out of that trap?

EP: This raises a few issues, I think. One is the urban change models and focus, in deliberative democracy discussions, on discourse. I think that that has been at the expense of the visual and the tactile. So maybe the one profound significance of a design dimension is that it foregrounds visual registers, which has a potentially democratizing effect.

There are also the ideas that I explored in my book *City Futures* (Pieterse 2008), of radical incrementalism and recursive empowerment. Here, again, design opens up just an enormous array of possibilities that are creative, engaging, fun, moving in terms of assessing what are the most strategic, what are the most technical options available in a much longer process in general. What is that calculus about something that is going to improve things without a radical rupture right away?

I also think design clarifies the problematic of sequencing. So one of the big problems in the sustainability discourse and in integrated development agenda is, "Where do you start? What goes first?" And it's paralyzing. Maybe design could help with prioritizing items in an agenda in the context of very poor cities with limited resources, deeply entrenched invested interests, and so on.

DAC: This begs the question, who can lead this process? Who would be part of the coalitions behind this kind of intervention?

EP: Well, it will depend a lot on the context. What I'm struck by in the South African context is that, if you think about it through the lens of the total public budget, probably a good 70, 75, maybe even 80 percent is predetermined with salaries and routine maintenance. And then there is just 2 or 3 percent of the overall budget for projects where you could really innovate. But that often goes to highly symbolic, flagship projects chosen by the mayor. But there's also another 15 percent of the budget for catalytic things, which is where the real transformative action is—for things like the BRT system in Cape Town, for example, or for saying that, within a decade, the city will transform its energy mix and energy system. Of course, that will be contingent on the actual coalitions' interests. At the moment, we're stuck with BRT and we're making all the mistakes: it's overcapitalized, we've gone for state-of-the-art buses with five-star environmental ratings, but it's a fiscal trap. We just can't afford to do it this way. So you need a coalition of interest groups that can understand this new economy and be strategic in mobilizing completely nontraditional stakeholders and actors, in a way that understands the constraints of the intergovernmental and multilevel government arrangements. Then you have to build a compelling narrative about what it means for an African city to be cutting-edge.

MINDY THOMPSON FULLILOVE
Professor of Clinical Psychiatry and Public Health at Columbia University

Background

Daniel Aldana Cohen (DAC): You're a psychiatrist working in a school of public health. How did you end up working on resiliency issues?

Mindy Thompson Fullilove (MTF): I got involved in AIDS research in 1986 at the request of the black and Hispanic community in San Francisco, who were aware that there was an excess risk for blacks and Hispanics. At that point, no research was being done to try to understand the situation. As our studies evolved, it became clear to us that the excess risk was due to urban processes that were destroying minority neighborhoods and spreading disease. The prominent one was planned shrinkage, which had been carried out in the middle of the 1970s in black and Hispanic neighborhoods in New York City and which had been an engine for the AIDS epidemic. What was to be done about this? How were these neighborhoods to be restored to health?

Like many people, I don't see any disaster as either purely natural or purely man-made. We can't separate the two. And it's people that have to respond to these problems. So planned shrinkage was a disaster made by people. But it played out in how we managed the environment. That said, I'm a huge critic of resiliency when it is used in an overly simplistic way. Much of resiliency discourse is kind of looking at people who have been through horrible times, who are barely standing, and saying, "My, aren't they resilient?" I find it just outrageously simplistic and detrimental.

Ecological Improvements and Displacement

DAC: You've written that social displacement is *the* problem the twenty-first century must solve. How does this relate to ecological crises and our responses to them?

MTF: Whole island nations are going to get wiped out. All of Bangladesh is under threat from sea level rise. There's no question there's going to be massive displacement, but for the most part, there's only lip service paid to what that means.

What's more, the ways in which we make massive investments or supposedly make things better have unintended consequences. In a city like New York, which is a hot spot for investment, any place you make modestly better, the first thing that happens is the rents go up. So all of the projects carried out with great hope for bettering communities for poor people have been blowing up in our faces. But more importantly, I think, the reason displacement is so bad is that it fractures social connections and it impoverishes people who were already impoverished, with weak social connections, because of earlier displacements. There's another part that's completely missing: How do we actually reknit a social fabric that we've been tearing apart for a long, long time, under the policies my team calls "serial forced displacement"?

DAC: One way people have at least tried to tackle displacement is to build places that are "just green enough," making improvements but not raising land values too much.

MTF: I've thought that, too, but I realized it's just silly. How do you say, "Oh, OK, the only way to solve this is that we won't make places top-notch"? Everybody deserves top-notch places. But it can't be that when you make a place top-notch, then the people who live there can't live there anymore, right? That defeats the purpose. Equity is the whole deal. It's what makes people healthy, what will enable us to survive.

Facing the Depth of the Crisis

DAC: So how do we get there?

MTF: People need to be able to talk to each other, and not just in neighborhoods. The scale issue is very important. The entire nation is facing climate change and is completely unable to have a conversation—a reasonable conversation. Three hundred million Americans are paralyzed in the face of grave changes that demand our attention. So the need for knitting communities together is intense. As a social psychiatrist, I find the situation terrifying. And I think that the people who are doing resiliency work, like the Rockefeller Foundation, could be very helpful if they would take this seriously. That would be real resilience. But I don't see that happening.

DAC: Do you mean in terms of a kind of shifting, jumping scale from the municipal to the national?

MTF: No, no, I don't mean that. You have to work on many levels of scale. You can work on it in cities and towns and villages and nationally all at the same time. I'm not making a comment about the level of scale. I'm making a comment about the level of seriousness. We aren't a functional nation; we're a nation that's socially paralyzed. We're going into a situation where there's going to be more storms. There's going to be more extreme weather, more of this deep economic depression we haven't come out of since 2008, and more social inequity. Our health care system, our education systems aren't functioning. These are deep crises that we can't talk about. . . . We've got to put this nation back together. If people really want to see resilience, to me, that's what they would deal with. This is a grave situation.

Design and Politics

DAC: You've played a key role in Rebuild by Design and also published a book about the nine elements of urban restoration, combining issues of design and social and political processes. How did you see design and politics coming together in a way that confronts serious challenges?

MTF: I thought Rebuild by Design had an incredible opportunity. There were hundreds of really smart people working on this problem—and they were literally volunteering much of the time they spent because they really cared. And it had the American people paying attention. The men and women who are leaders in many fields, engineering, architecture, and so on, came together and worked on a common analysis. Rebuild by Design could have said, "Here's what the issues are, and this is how we can move forward." But that wasn't done. In the end, the option of collaborating to make a coherent statement to the public was sacrificed for the competition about projects. But we already have too much competition. What we don't have is collaboration and consensus. Ultimately, what the government wanted was projects. So we end up with the concept that a dike around Lower Manhattan is going to solve the problems that are going on in New York City. And I just don't buy that.

I see a lot of problems. I don't think the Rebuild by Design process built social relationships. One of the new reports out of New Jersey showed that two years after Sandy, over thirty thousand people were still out of their homes. How do we get people money and get them back in their homes? What happens in those kinds of degrading social situations is it gets bloody. America's well armed. So a lot of people are going to start shooting each other. That's what I fear.

DAC: Do you see the design process as being intrinsically tied to this competitive project-oriented framework, or should there be more focus on cooperation and depth of intervention?

MTF: Design is inherently collaborative and cooperative—it is a long process. The first part of design in a situation is coming to understand the problem. During Rebuild by Design, there was a research stage where people sought to understand the problem. They collected huge amounts of data. That's design, right? Designing has to name and frame a problem. So having 250 people for three months naming and framing the problem, but then being directed to compete, rather than presenting a common perspective to the American people, was a huge waste of money. The government spent millions of dollars, with no return on that part of the investment, in my opinion. And all those architects, engineers, and designers knew incredible stuff! At least in the process that I'm familiar with as a psychiatrist, for example, when we have crises in medicine like hospital errors, we pull a team of top scientists together to create a consensus report. The whole National Academy of Sciences is about a consensus process. So I'm very familiar with that process. And I think that approach is a strength for our nation. And for questions like, Where's the best place to put a dike or a barrier, say, to keep water out?, we should have a consensus on what the science says. In getting the American people ready to respond to climate change, we needed Rebuild by Design to give us a consensus report on the nature of threat that we face.

Design and Time

DAC: In a disaster situation, political actors want speed, which can make design start to look like a luxury. I wonder how you think a political process can address this paradox.

MTF: I don't think we're in a political process at all. It's fake. It's ridiculous. Nothing's happening. So what speed are you talking about? Realistically, the nation's crumbling. So how much can you pay attention to somebody saying, "Oh, we're in a rush"? But it's a fake rush. We're rushed to get reelected, but nothing's actually happening. There's no rush when it comes to what people need. It's a difficult period. People aren't talking to each other. So whatever is called politics is just frozen. By contrast, design is not a luxury: the ability of designers to name and frame the problem is essential to getting us to move, to taking the next right step.

FERNANDO DE MELLO FRANCO
Secretary of Urban Development, City of São Paulo

Background

Daniel Aldana Cohen (DAC): You are the secretary of urban development in São Paulo, a politically complex portfolio. But your background is as an architect; my understanding is that you have no political experience. How did you find yourself in this position?

Fernando de Mello Franco (FMF): The mayor invited me to take this role precisely because I had no political background. And many of his other nominations to key secretariats also had academic backgrounds, just like the mayor himself (a professor of political science). Still, much of my previous work focused on the intersection of design research and public policy.

Designing the Master Plan

DAC: Your first major task has been to entirely review the master plan for São Paulo. What role has design played in shaping this plan?

FMF: First, let me frame this question in a historical perspective. During the 1970s, in Brazil, we lived through a military dictatorship; at that time, the debate in the School of Architecture and Urbanism at the University of São Paulo, where I studied, and also among architects and urbanists working across the country, was about whether our pencil could be an instrument of struggle, or if design would always be at the service of the dominating class, the bourgeoisie. The argument was that the only effective mechanisms of struggle were politics, social activism, and resistance against the dictatorship. There was a total detachment between design and politics. Design was regarded as a reactionary instrument, and this tension continues today. So one of our most difficult challenges now is to find a way to recombine these two fields: first, by understanding design also in terms of political processes; second, by revealing that politics can make use of design as a tool; and, third, acknowledging that design isn't necessarily an instrument of oppression.

DAC: And the master plan?

FMF: During the first half of the last century, the municipal government passed Francisco Prestes Maia's Plan of Avenues, which shaped the future of the city. The plan foresaw a series of expressways organized in a radial-concentric structure, in order to support the expansion of private motorized transport, strengthening the role of the city center and reinforcing, in fact, a monocentric city model. At the end of the 1960s, there was a plan that proposed the revision of that model, seeking to break with the radial-concentric model with a proposal of structuring the city through a grid, formed by a network of expressways. But, once again, this plan prioritized automobile transportation, and it also proposed that the flow of automobiles along those roadways would be more compatible with low density.

Our master plan reinforces the hypothesis of structuring the city as a grid. But with a crucial difference: this mobility grid that structures the city should no longer be oriented by individual transit but [should] instead [be oriented] by public transportation. Also, the goal now is precisely to have more density along this network. So imagine a grid where you have axes and interiors, that is, the space between the grid lines. In the 1960s–1970s, the concept was that the lines should have lower density, while the neighborhoods (the interior spaces of the grid) should be denser. We're proposing the opposite: because the grid lines are now organized by the network of bus corridors, and subway and train lines, they should also concentrate more people, jobs, and services, and ultimately be more dense than the spaces between these axes, guaranteeing that these interior spaces of the grid have their typical neighborhood identities and qualities preserved, especially considering that most of the city is already shaped and occupied. São Paulo can no longer sustain a process of urban sprawl, so it should now be improved and transformed from within. But, to be clear, we didn't have the ambition of planning and designing every square meter of the city. Alternatively, we have proposed a set of tools and regulations in the new master plan that can strategically transform the city, increasing density along the grid lines, or axes, and preserving the neighborhoods. So instead of providing a series of abstract regulations, as earlier plans did, we started with a spatial vision of the city and then developed proper tools and regulations embedded in the territory, so that vision could be realized.

Ecological Crisis in São Paulo

DAC: Of course, a key part of the plan is to increase density in strategic ways, and part of the reason is that, right now, there are sprawling informal sectors where people live in very precarious ecological situations. In São Paulo, there have been huge problems with flooding. And now there is also drought. Where does resilience fit into this planning approach?

FMF: My impression is that the concept of resilience, as it is used in the United States or Europe, cannot be directly applied to a developing or emerging country (however you want to term it) like Brazil. Its modernization process is incomplete. Our urban history is defined by a series of discontinuities, ruptures, tragedies, and crises associated with rapid urbanization. Each year there are floods and landslides affecting the favelas and shacks built over water streams and other risk areas. Crisis is not an exceptional condition in our country but a permanent one. The informal sectors, which are the most affected by energy and water shortages, and also flooding, have the greatest capacity for regeneration after these events. Our challenge is, therefore, not so much to prepare for unforeseen crises but rather to build a minimum, basic condition of social equality and infrastructure in the territory so that everyone can have a dignified life. So I think the term *resilience* has to be adjusted for our context.

DAC: In that case, what kinds of ecological concepts or discourses do you think can be combined with the social justice perspective in a useful way for a city like São Paulo?

FMF: The current water crisis is also becoming an energy crisis, because so much of our system is hydroelectric. We are projecting energy and water shortages in São Paulo and other cities. This is also generating an economic crisis and a social crisis. Water scarcity will be experienced in an unequal way, with the worst shortages in the territories with the greatest informality, where organized crime has even begun to seize water supplies. This vision might seem a bit catastrophic, generated in the heat of the moment, but I think this crisis will differ from the everyday crisis I was describing. This crisis should generate a new paradigm, a new model, not only of land use but also of infrastructural systems. All of this is related to the ecological question. But here the ecological question has to do less with the sensu stricto and more with its social dimensions, which are the main issues in our country and in São Paulo.

DAC: A new paradigm, redesigning infrastructure and land use—these are time-intensive projects. But as you point out, the situation is urgent. Is there time for design to provide solutions?

FMF: I believe that design will be a positive externality in this crisis, because I think we're reaching the conclusion that the imminent issue is not climate change but territorial uses and inequalities. Our urban design, our infrastructure design, our technical paradigms, our governance paradigms—these are the issues undergoing dilemmas. We should leverage this opportunity to persuade the political class that we need to reestablish the design imperative in this country. And why is that imperative weak?

Let's again look at history. In the 1980s, we experienced hyperinflation, reaching 80 percent a month. So the financial cost that design implied was unaffordable. Plus, the lack of design for public works served the interests of certain construction companies. We also had a discontinuity in shaping engineers, who massively abstained from the design field and went on to work in the financial market between the 1980s and 1990s. Design lost strength as the rhythm of cities' growth escalated, with the urgencies this entailed. The context now is different and so are the country's needs.

Today, in our balance of trade, we're great commodity exporters and increasingly service importers, including design services. There is thus a political decision to be made about how to achieve economic development. Which economic sectors should we privilege? What's the role of design at a time when inflation is under control, urbanization isn't accelerating at the rapid pace of the past century, and population growth has stabilized? I believe that there's space now for a return of planning and design. The problems that we're confronting will demand the revision of our governance paradigms, and design could provide some of the answers that we need. I think this is a promising field that could emerge from the present crisis.

DAC: Could you be a bit more concrete about the kinds of new paradigms in land use, urbanization, and modalities of economic development that you envision?

FMF: A concrete example is the issue of water supply, drainage, and sewage. We have always promoted a model that is highly concentrated, hub-and-spoke, and hierarchical. The interruption of a hub causes problems throughout the system. Right now, sewage is transported from the farthest points, over kilometers and kilometers, to be treated. In this process there is loss of water because such extensive networks are difficult to maintain, so you get leakages. We know that there are other possible setups, rhizomatic designs that enable shortcuts, bypasses, redundancy.

Also, there is little space in São Paulo for new water infrastructure, say, constructing water-retaining structures as we built in the past or building large, new sewage treatment plants. There isn't space for that scale of new constructions in a totally occupied territory like São Paulo's. So we need to rethink the current model and propose alternative ones, which necessarily entail a debate in which design plays a key role.

I believe that we should explore the possibility of another model, structuring these water services through a diffuse network of small-scale infrastructure artifacts, not heavily imposed in the local context but rather framing what can be called the landscape of infrastructure. I think that there are several groups discussing these issues and using these paradigms right now. So these are the issues we need to investigate and advance on, in order to overcome our strong modernist background.

Politics and Design

DAC: As you know, when it comes to design, one issue is the quality of design itself; the other is getting good design through the policy process. In your experience, what kinds of actors can be helpful allies in this process, and what are the barriers?

FMF: I understand design as a field of political articulation, a field of negotiation with society, a field for agreeing on how we are going to transform the city. So we need to think about design in terms of what the institutional and governance arrangements of a municipality should be. And within the design of the municipality of São Paulo, the department that is responsible for the political articulation of the government is not the Department of Urban Development but the Department of Government. Obviously these arrangements can be altered. But what I'm trying to say is that design should not be thought of as the assignment of any particular department. Instead, design should be thought of as a field for developing government policy. I believe that we must redesign the institutional matrix, that is, the systems of governance at the municipal, state, and federal levels. We need to connect those who formulate design to those who articulate the politics in some way so that design can make its best contributions. My point here is that, in our specific context, the first actor that has to be convinced of the importance of design is the public sector.

DAC: Speaking more concretely about the actors involved, in São Paulo we know that there are sectors of real estate and construction that are very powerful. There are housing movements, middle-class civil society groups, and so on, often contesting that dominance. Are there any groups in particular you have found it helpful to work with?

FMF: In order to get our master plan passed, we needed to speak to all sectors of society. The master plan is interesting because it reveals the conflicts of the city. As a result, it is a social pact signed by the city. I believe that there are no particular groups that we especially spoke with. We are now in a process of revising the zoning law, and this is not anymore about organized groups but about each individual in the city. The debate is almost block by block, house by house. There is no privileged dialogue. The city is a field of struggle where all stakeholders act. Some with more or less force, but all actors are relevant. Urban politics is contaminated by all of the interests.

DAC: OK, but beyond the importance of talking to everybody, did anything surprise you in terms of how you overcame resistance to get the plan passed? What kinds of lessons could you pass on to others?

FMF: I think that in any democratic regime, it's impossible to conceive of technocratic and authoritarian processes of design. Even in a democracy under consolidation, like Brazil's, the participation of society and its awareness about the territory are growing. And yet this is a new process for Brazil. First, because we left a military dictatorship just over thirty years ago; second, because this process will require considerations not only from the political class, as was common practice, but also from designers, architects, engineers, and other professionals. What we mean by design today is different from what my generation, for instance, learned about design a few decades ago.

For example, take architecture competitions. What are they after? They are looking for the best design. And since these processes are competitive, the design is always secret and the author is also secret. You only find out when the competition is done. If we understand that for urban design a democratic process is needed, the architecture competition cannot be used to select only the best design, the best architectonic solution, but should also choose the best method of participation and consultation that, once chosen, will establish a contact with the population that is affected by the design. The prevailing model of developing and promoting urban design, in my view, is in contradiction with the need to strengthen participatory processes for redesigning our cities.

Democratic Design

DAC: Could you say a bit more about what democratic design means to you?

FMF: Democratic design is desirable and it's an imperative. For example, there is a great issue to be faced regarding how public projects can transform public space. In my view, it's not about the construction of a tangible space but more about envisioning how space could be used in the public domain. That is the main question. If society has no sense of belonging in the public space that is built, there will be unhealthy conflicts. So the centrality of redesigning public space does not fall necessarily on the choice of materials or technologies of construction but falls more on establishing pacts on how different actors want to use this space. Another design focus is needed, based on the search of the necessary infrastructure to support the variety of uses of public space in time.

There is also an issue of scale, as exemplified by the process of developing the new master plan. A participatory process can be very different in a community of thirty thousand residents in the American Midwest, in the interior of the Brazilian northeast, or in a municipality of 12 million inhabitants. In this case, as with São Paulo, you cannot organize a direct, participatory process. It's always representative at some level, with a small proportion of the population actually showing up to participate. For the master plan, we had four, five thousand contributions. For a municipality with 12 million inhabitants, it's a tiny percentage of the population. So participatory processes are restricted; they have limits. As the scale increases, we end up with a conflict between the processes of direct democracy and those of representative democracy. That's an issue not just of design but of politics more broadly. There's enormous dissatisfaction with our representative system because our legislative body no longer responds to the wishes of the population. There's a great distance between elected city council members and the population in general. Even in São Paulo, to move toward direct democracy is very difficult.

DAC: Do you feel that the challenge, then, is to deepen democratization or to become reconciled with the limits of that representative democracy?

FMF: When we formulated our master plan, we saw that in all of the events for engaging the public, there was much less participation in person than online. A public meeting had two hundred, three hundred people, while two thousand, three thousand watched online. So we need to rethink the instruments of public engagement to broaden the channels of democratization. Public meetings are no longer the only adequate solution for participatory processes. In order to face this challenge, we created, for instance, a digital platform with all of the materials and news under discussion, the studies we were using, maps and tables in open format. We also embedded in this platform a series of participatory applications, where every citizen with access to a computer could actively engage in the elaboration of the master plan. It was a fundamental tool for democratizing and making transparent our planning process.

Investment and Displacement

DAC: Finally, I want to ask about displacement and ecology. There's an argument worldwide now that ecological improvements tend to lead to social displacement. What kinds of tools do you think are available for improving the quality of life of people without displacing the poorest and most vulnerable?

FMF: It's effectively a rule that any investment, when successful, results in an increase of value. I invest in my education to increase my value on the labor market, for example. The city is the same. This paradox of investment and displacement is very difficult to face, a contradiction inherent to the capitalist system. Because of that, our great concern must be toward those who are in more vulnerable situations. Such people are, in fact, often seduced to realize real estate profits when a public investment raises the value of their homes (in São Paulo, most public housing is owner occupied, sold to low-income residents at a massive discount). One idea we are working on is the idea of social housing owned by the state, so that residents have no incentive to move by selling their homes. I believe this would be similar to the US system of public housing.

MAARTEN HAJER
Chief Curator of the 2016 International Architecture Biennale Rotterdam

Background

Daniel Aldana Cohen (DAC): Could you say something about how you came to focus on the intersection of urbanism, design, and resiliency?

Maarten Hajer (MH): I'm both a political scientist and an urban planner by training and have always worked on that intersection of cities and public policy. I have always been intrigued by how design is also a special form of political practice. There is a political moment in creating imaginaries of new futures. Particularly if such new imaginaries are cocreated. Then design becomes part of the democratic process. The interesting thing is that designers use different tools and techniques in that process. I've tried to figure out why it is that designers can deliver on very complex political, contextual situations, provide solutions that people like, whereas people who were trained as public policy mediators fail.

Design and Complexity

DAC: Why do you think that is?

MH: Designers are oriented towards the middle; they try to bring stakeholders together. I think one of the classic qualities of designers is that they tend to do precisely the opposite of what an economist does. The economist would always try to solve a problem by reducing the complexity and turning everything into a form of monetary value. A designer tends to solve problems by making them more complex.

  With designers, you also have a more diverse understanding of what knowledge is. They are used to working in interdisciplinary situations. Research by design is to me a powerful notion of how you can achieve democratic outcomes, allowing a role for stakeholders, and consequently mobilizing all sorts of knowledge when that is required. Of course, there is always a special role for politicians. They are the ones who decide whether to allocate the money or not. But research for design allows for a much more fluid and much more dynamic way of organizing democratic deliberations. Let's not forget it does not have the problem of democratic territorial boundaries. Finally, I think research by design is helpful for complex issues because people are allowed to experience the cultural values that they find are important and [it] let[s] them speak to what should happen to a particular area. All this makes research by design a good proposition for contemporary planning issues and, in particular, issues like climate adaptation.

Discourse and Coalitions

DAC: In your book *Smart about Cities: Visualizing the Challenge for Twenty-First Century Urbanism*, you have a memorable phrase: "The discourse is the glue of coalitions" (Hajer and Dassen 2014: 16). And you cite the idea that planning is about telling persuasive stories about the future. It sounds like what you're saying is that one of the key aspects of this design process is communicative storytelling, which then enables coalitions that might otherwise not find each other or not find their points in common.

MF: I think that's a fair representation. Mind you, I always use "discourse" in a pair with "dramaturgy": it is important "what" is said, but it is just as important "where" something is said. The role of dramaturgy in policy making comes out in the way you actually stage meetings. Again, I think that design is such a powerful practice because it's not purely textual. Public participation is often all about text, often even legal language. It excludes and shapes conversations. Design, on the other hand, may communicate through images or drawings.

And these are communicative tools that allow more of the public in. People don't feel disenfranchised or alone. Language can be difficult or excluding. The political theorist Iris Marion Young wrote beautifully about this. So indeed, planning and design may be about telling persuasive stories about the future, but in languages that allow for a broad coalition of actors to shape up around them. This is an art that we desperately need to support.We need a planning approach that illuminates alternative possible worlds.

The Dimensions of Resiliency

DAC: So what about resiliency? There's a frequent criticism that resiliency is a big and vague concept, utopian and splashy, but not like concrete or steel. Do you think it's an idea that can still provide a narrative to bring people together?

MH: It is definitely a very powerful notion because it suggests elasticity. It's not concrete. It's being able to bounce back, to not be knocked down. So in that sense, it has more to do with judo than with boxing, if you see my point. So that makes it an elegant notion. More specifically, I would emphasize two dimensions. You can think about the city being resilient, being able to really restore itself quickly or not be knocked out literally after disaster strikes. That's one notion. That's the physical one. The second understanding of resiliency is of course the process. The idea is engaging people in finding solutions. If you speak to four hundred people like an old-style planner, they will wait for you to provide a solution. A better participatory process can make society more resilient because people will then also take responsibility. What is more, it can also help to create and maintain the social network that will help people prepare and respond to unhappy situations.

I also think it's important that a term resonate. As an academic, you can try to find the ideal term, but *resiliency* resonates very well with decision makers for the moment. And that's a quality that's important, too.

Design and Politics

DAC: In your research, have you found particular kinds of actors to be especially receptive to the research-by-design and resiliency agendas?

MH: We live in a time where the traditional roles of "academic," "layperson," "designer," and "politician" increasingly get blurred. We are all subjects nowadays. In that sense it is crucial to acknowledge the role of reflective practitioners within organizations, people who are not higher up in the bureaucracies. They might not sit in front of a computer, but they have good empirical knowledge of the field. These people and their knowledge about how to get things done are often overlooked. It is often "tacit" knowledge, experience based, not written down but in their heads. Here I find the work of Donald Schön, and his book *The Reflective Practitioner*, to be very helpful. His understanding of how you learn is, I think, essential for thinking about resiliency and research by design. A second thing that strikes me as an important topic is that in cases where we have been able to get results with resiliency, academic institutes and knowledge initiatives play a crucial role. Not for classical "evaluations" but to help thinking along. I think it was very interesting that the Rockefeller Foundation, in New York, chose to partner with the Institute for Public Knowledge at New York University to lead the research phase of Rebuild by Design.

DAC: With respect to the reflective practitioner, are we talking about coastline ecological inspectors, people in the fire services, or community leaders who might not be in charge of their organization?

MH: Primarily the former. People with their wellies on. The street-level bureaucrats. But the reflective practitioner is nowadays more an attitude than it is a hierarchical level. There are people who are constantly trying to improve their practice, are open for critique and suggestions, and have a wish to learn and improve.

References

Hajer, Maarten, and Ton Dassen. 2014. *Smart about Cities: Visualizing the Challenge for Twenty-First Century Urbanism*. Rotterdam: Nai/010 Publishers.

Klinenberg, Eric. (2002) 2015. *Heat Wave: A Social Autopsy of Disaster in Chicago*. 2nd ed. Chicago: University of Chicago Press.

Pieterse, Edgar. 2008. *City Futures: Confronting the Crisis of Urban Development*. London: Zed Books.

Schön, Donald. 1983. *The Reflective Practitioner: How Professionals Think in Action*. New York: Basic Books.

....

Henk Ovink is special envoy for international water affairs for the Kingdom of the Netherlands and is principal of Rebuild by Design, the resilience innovation competition he developed and led for the US Presidential Hurricane Sandy Rebuilding Task Force, where he was senior adviser to the chair. He has been director-general for planning and water affairs and director for national spatial planning for the Dutch Ministry of Infrastructure and the Environment. He teaches at the Harvard University Graduate School of Design and is a member of the International Advisory Board for the City of Rotterdam.

Edgar Pieterse is founding director of the African Centre for Cities (ACC) at the University of Cape Town. He is consulting editor for *Cityscapes*—an international biannual magazine on urbanism in the global South. His most recent coedited books are *African Cities Reader III: Land, Property and Value* (2015), *Africa's Urban Revolution* (2014), and *Rogue Urbanism: Emergent African Cities* (2013).

Mindy Thompson Fullilove is a research psychiatrist at New York State Psychiatric Institute and a professor of clinical psychiatry and public health at Columbia University. She has conducted research on AIDS and other epidemics of poor communities, with a special interest in the relationship between the collapse of communities and decline in health. Her books include *Urban Alchemy: Restoring Joy in America's Sorted-Out Cities* (2013), *Root Shock: How Tearing Up City Neighborhoods Hurts America, and What We Can Do about It* (2004), and *The House of Joshua: Meditations on Family and Place* (1999).

Fernando de Mello Franco is São Paulo's secretary of urban development. He is an architect and holds a PhD from the University of São Paulo. He taught architecture and urbanism at several schools, including Harvard as a visiting professor. He was managing partner of MMBB Arquitetos and project curator of the Institute of Urbanism and Studies for the Metropolis (URBEM).

Maarten Hajer is chief curator of the 2016 International Architecture Biennale Rotterdam. He is also Distinguished Professor of Urban Futures at Utrecht University, since October 2015. Before that he was professor of public policy at the University of Amsterdam and director-general of PBL, the Netherlands Environmental Assessment Agency.

The Perfect Storm:
Heat Waves and Power Outages
in Buenos Aires

Valeria Procupez

In December 2013, and then again in mid-January 2014, thermometers in Buenos Aires hit their highest marks in over half a century. In relentless heat waves that affected almost all of Argentina, the city endured peaks of around 39°C (102.2°F) and a "real feel" of 47°C (116.6°F) due to persistent humidity.[1]

The duration of the heat waves set a historic record. The first one started on December 16, 2013, and lasted eighteen days, the longest since Buenos Aires began recording temperatures in 1906 (Villalonga 2014). Another heat wave hit in January 2014 and turned the month into the hottest January since 1961. Ever since Buenos Aires instituted color alerts, this was the longest period of consecutive days of red alert in the city (SMN 2014).[2] Authorities called for people to remain at home or in the shade, drink plenty of liquids, and wear hats and sunscreen.

And in tandem with these events . . . the lights went off. This outage was to yield yet another record in the history of the city, in this case regarding the length of the blackouts. Over two hundred thousand households, in which there were eight hundred thousand inhabitants, were left without electricity (*Infobae* 2013), in some cases for ten consecutive days and in others with recurrent power outages for as long as forty days. Blackouts were registered in over sixteen neighborhoods

1. According to the Servicio Meteorológico Nacional (SMN), the National Weather Service, under the Secretary of Science, Production, and Technology, a "heat wave" in Buenos Aires occurs when temperatures persist above a minimum of 22°C (71.6°F) and above a maximum of 32°C (89.5°F) for a period of more than three days (SMN 2014).

2. Color alerts regarding temperatures are issued daily by the SMN during conditions of extreme heat. The color indicates increments in the daily mortality risk, yellow being the lowest (a 10 percent increase) and red the highest (indicating a 60 percent increase).

Public Culture 28:2   DOI 10.1215/08992363-3427475

throughout the city, as well as in municipalities of the greater Buenos Aires metropolitan area (*InfoNews* 2013).

Initial frustrations and formal complaints to the authorities quickly fueled protests around the city. Technical crews failed to respond or, worse, proved unable to reestablish or sustain power supplies, and external generators distributed by energy companies were not enough to provide service for all the affected clients. Technicians reported severe problems in distribution, not just the overheating of wiring but also extensive damage to transformers and substations. No one offered convincing explanations of what was happening. Accusations flew back and forth among the national and local administrations (of opposing political affiliations), both of which claimed that the private sector was responsible for failing to invest in system upgrades to meet increased demand in the city (*InfoNews* 2013).

Extreme weather conditions and a sudden increase in power demand often lead to temporary blackouts (Harris 2011: 60–62). Buenos Aires has had its share of utility outages throughout the years, too, but the prolonged system outages in recent years have highlighted the underlying situation of an electrical grid already working at its limit capacity. The intense heat waves revealed a broader spectrum of shortcomings regarding energy in Buenos Aires, including a steady increase in demand that has not been matched by investment in supply, aging infrastructure, and a manifest inability to confront challenges such as those brought about by climate change.

. . . .

Argentina has one of the largest electricity systems in South America, with an electrification rate of almost 90 percent, an installed capacity in the public power grid of around thirty-three hundred megawatts, and a high per capita consumption (Enerdata 2013). When the system was privatized in the 1990s, during a period of neoliberal reforms, the previously state-owned electricity model was unbundled. Functions such as generation, transmission, and distribution were separated, which broke down vertical integration and combined ownership of production and distribution (Datamonitor 2011). While the other functions were open to a competitive market, distribution to clients was assigned to private companies as regulated monopolies. As a consequence, today clients cannot choose their provider, but prices are regulated (Recalde 2011; Haselip and Potter 2010).

Electricity provision for the city of Buenos Aires was divided between two distribution companies, Edenor and Edesur, which thus serve a captive market yet offer controlled prices. After the economic crisis of 2002 provoked the demise of the national government and the debt default, the incoming authorities issued a utility tariff freeze to prevent oscillation in energy prices from affecting household economies (De Santis 2013) and established a government subsidy to cover companies' operating costs. Since then, the economy has recovered and electricity demand in the city has soared, but subsidies have remained in place—even with increasing modifications—and clients in Buenos Aires pay the lowest rates in the country even though they consume a high percentage of the energy produced nationally (CEDEM 2014).[3] Some critics argue that the tariff freeze has discouraged the companies' investment in upgrades (De Santis 2013), since their earnings fell despite the sharp increase in demand. Others lament that within the current market structure, the government is unable to fully control commitments to invest in infrastructure (Recalde 2011). As an example, at the peak of the heat waves, the national government seized the administration of an underused fund it had created the previous year, with the aim of allowing Edenor and Edesur to perform repairs, maintenance, and upgrades to the grid.[4]

By the same token, the fragmentation and deregulation of the system have also complicated long-term planning. The high dependence of Argentine energy supply on thermal production—basically on natural gas—makes it vulnerable to the severe decline in reserve margins due to local consumption but also due to exports, which were only cut down around 2006, when the government decided to regulate them to protect local demand.[5] Some kind of centrally planned energy policy is needed that takes into account the various aspects of the system as a whole and makes provisions accordingly, such as diversifying production by developing renewable energy sources (Recalde 2011).

. . . .

3. The Argentine economy grew at a steady rate of 7–9 percent annually between 2004 and 2009, but it has since decreased due to the effects of the international financial crisis (Enerdata 2013). As the report by the Center for Economic Development (Centro de Estudios para el Desarrollo Metropolitano [CEDEM 2014]) notes, Buenos Aires's population constitutes 7 percent of the total population of the country, but electricity consumption reaches 12 percent. The same study indicates, however, that even though Buenos Aires has a per capita consumption rate of 4.1 megawatt hours compared to the national average of 2.5 megawatt hours, the city has a much larger population during the day than at night—since people come to work but do not reside in the city.

4. To raise money for the Fund for Works to Consolidate and Expand Electrical Distribution (Fondo de Obras de Consolidación y Expansión de Distribución Eléctrica, or FOCEDE), in 2012 the companies had been allowed to charge consumers a fixed amount with the specific purpose of performing repairs to the grid. When the government took over, it planned to increase the funds with contributions from other sources and force companies to perform over four hundred repairs or upgrades, raise the number of on-call work crews to solve emergencies, and maintain a twenty-four-hour call center to respond to customer demands (La Nación 2014).

5. Although the energy mix in Argentina comes from several sources, 60 percent of the energy produced is thermal (using nonrenewable fossil fuels—88 percent of which is natural gas), producing large emissions of carbon dioxide (CO_2).

353

A similar lack of coordination between programs carried out by different agents contributes to the failure of curbing consumption or making energy use in Buenos Aires more efficient. This adds to a pervasive *cortoplacismo*, or "collective short-term mentality" (Grimson 2004: 189), a trait that appears to guide not only policy making but also Argentines' attitudes and behaviors. Possibly the effect of recurrent experiences of uncertainty, this temporal frame of actions foregrounds immediacy and overlooks long-term planning (Procupez 2012: 166), leading to the overlapping of measures with conflicting outcomes and the stretching in time of temporary solutions. Below are some examples of how those different effects and behaviors combine into insurmountable disjunctions in the system.

Demand for energy in the city has grown steadily since roughly 2004, mostly due to economic growth in commercial activities and residential consumption (CEDEM 2014). However, the low price of energy for consumers has not encouraged energy saving, and different campaigns promoted by both the city and the national governments have not entirely succeeded in promoting a more rational use of electricity. Thus the indirect subsidies that have protected household economies for a long time might also be held accountable for the overuse of electricity (De Santis 2013). As expected, demand rises in periods of extreme weather (usually winter and summer months), as happened during the heat waves when it rose to the city's maximum power demand (around twenty-four thousand megawatts), much higher than for the same months the previous and following years (CNEA 2015).

Argentines have taken advantage of sustained economic growth to purchase appliances and other consumer goods. The government incentivized consumption, too, with programs that facilitated installment payments for certain products.[6] Since 2011, the sharp restrictions on purchasing US dollars (D'Avella 2014), combined with a generalized distrust in saving in the local currency, further encouraged spending. Air conditioners, which are emerging as a hallmark of First World modernity, are becoming massively popular, with sales increasing by a remarkable 36 percent in 2013. The increasing incidence and frequency of heat waves in Buenos Aires has made air-conditioning all the more popular (SMN 2014).

Recent economic prosperity has also propelled a construction boom in Buenos Aires, and weak regulation has led to indiscriminate construction of residential towers in some neighborhoods, building densification (D'Avella 2014), and a sig-

6. This could have been an opportunity to add an incentive to purchase high-efficiency appliances and thus contribute to the efficient use of energy, but it was also part of the uncoordinated efforts (Gil 2014).

nificant increase in electricity demand.[7] In some places, as many as half of the new buildings are "electric," meaning they lack connection to gas pipelines and depend on electricity as the only source of energy (*Clarín* 2014a).[8] Substations, however, have not been upgraded to sustain the higher demand, and many urban neighborhoods where construction was concentrated—such as Flores and Almagro—were among those most affected during the blackouts (*Página 12* 2014). Among more affluent residents, one popular response to these outages has been to purchase portable generators—the city has seen record numbers sold since 2013—yet this temporary solution contributes to an increase in CO_2 emissions, exacerbating the long-term problem of heat (*La nación* 2013). In all these examples, the unanticipated effects of uncoordinated measures and actions converge into the perfect storm of the blackouts.

....

The local government reports that 56 percent of all emissions in Buenos Aires are from energy consumption, and in recent years, as part of its policy on climate change (Resolution 3.871, 2011), the city has designed programs to promote energy efficiency. It offers credits for local industry and service companies that improve efficiency and environmental protection. It has attempted to curb electricity consumption in public buildings, with the objective of achieving a 20 percent reduction. It has also established measures to reduce emissions in transportation and industry.

The national government, for its part, launched a program for the rational and efficient use of energy in 2007, which included an educational section to promote clean generation activities and labeling of appliances. In addition, it has declared its intention to increase the nation's share of renewable energy by 2016 and to invest in research and development of alternative energy sources (Enerdata 2013).

These initiatives, however, appear as discrete plans rather than integral parts of a coherent and coordinated national policy and are undermined by the unanticipated consequences of related developments in other policy domains. Despite promises to reduce Argentina's carbon footprint, CO_2 emissions from energy com-

7. Nicholas D'Avella (2014) nicely shows that the boom in construction was related to a notion of building as investment, in the sense of providing (relatively) stable assets—bricks—instead of the volatile Argentine currency.

8. Electric buildings are considered a "world tendency" because they are cheaper to build, require fewer certifications, and offer more possibilities for architectural design and because gas is a nonrenewable fuel that, in addition, is not particularly safe. However, the city does not seem to keep records of the permits it has granted for construction of this kind of building or to have made provisions to request the upgrading of infrastructure (*Clarín* 2014b).

bustion have been rising rapidly since 2002, reaching a level 80 percent higher than in 1990 (Enerdata 2013).

During heat waves, the problems with Argentina's infrastructure planning and climate change adaptation strategy become abundantly visible, and citizens respond with passionate protests. But when the weather cools so does popular outrage, and other urban issues—poverty, housing, inflation, corruption, even traffic—displace concerns about the climate. The city moves on as if global warming is a distant problem, until things heat up again.

References

CEDEM (Centro de Estudios para el Desarrollo Económico Metropolitano). 2014. "El consumo de energía en la Ciudad de Buenos Aires en 2013" ("Energy Consumption in the City of Buenos Aires in 2013"). Informe de resultados no. 633. Buenos Aires: Ministerio de Hacienda GCBA.

Clarín. 2014a. "Cada vez se construyen más edificios eléctricos" ("Increase in Construction of Electrical Buildings"). January 17.

———. 2014b. "Daños en la red eléctrica" ("Damage in Electrical Grids"). January 13.

CNEA (Comisión Nacional de Energía Atómica). 2015. *Síntesis del mercado eléctrico mayorista* (*Summary of the Wholesale Electricity Market*). March. Buenos Aires: CNEA.

Datamonitor. 2011. "Electricity Industry Profile: Argentina." London: Marketline.

D'Avella, Nicholas. 2014. "Ecologies of Investment: Crisis Histories and Brick Futures in Argentina." *Cultural Anthropology* 29, no. 1: 173–99.

De Santis, Juan Pablo. 2013. "Causas y responsables de los cortes del electricidad en Buenos Aires" ("Causes and Responsibilities for Electricity Outages in Buenos Aires"). *La Nación*, December 13.

Enerdata. 2013. "Argentina Energy Report." February. London: Enerdata.

Gil, Salvador. 2014. "Plan ahora eficiencia 12" ("High Efficiency 12-Installment Plan"). *Página 12*, October 1.

Grimson, Alejandro. 2004. "La experiencia Argentina y sus fantasmas" ("The Argentine Experience and Its Ghosts"). In *La cultura en las crisis latinoamericanas* (*Culture in the Latin American Crises*), edited by Alejandro Grimson, 177–93. Buenos Aires: El Consejo Latinoamericano de Ciencias Sociales (CLACSO).

Harris, Anne. 2011. "Avoiding Future Electricity Shortfalls." *Engineering and Technology* 6, no. 10, 60–63.

Haselip, James, and Clive Potter. 2010. "Post-Neoliberal Electricity Market 'Re-Reforms' in Argentina: Diverging from Market Prescriptions?" *Energy Policy* 38, no. 2: 1168–76.

Infobae. 2013. "Continúan los cortes de luz y la ola de calor amenaza con extenderse." ("Power Outages Continue and the Heat Wave Threatens to Extend"). December 29.

Infonews Tiempo Argentino. 2013. "El calor no cesa, los cortes de energía tampoco" ("Heat Does Not Cease, Neither Do Power Outages"). December 28.

La Nación. 2013. "Los precios y las claves para comprar un grupo electrógeno" ("Prices and Clues to Purchase Portable Power Generators"). December 18.

———. 2014. "Prometen obras en el sector eléctrico" ("Promises of Improvements in Electric System"). January 11.

Página 12. 2014a. "La demanda eléctrica sigue encendida" ("Electrical Power Demand Is Still On"). February 19.

———. 2014b. "Otro mes de caída en las ventas minoristas" ("Another Month of Decreasing Retail Sales"). February 18.

Procupez, Valeria. 2012. "Inhabiting the Temporary: Patience and Uncertainty among Urban Squatters in Buenos Aires." In *The Anthropology of Ignorance: An Ethnographic Approach*, edited by Casey High, Ann H. Kelly, and Jonathan Mair, 163–88. New York: Palgrave Macmillan.

Recalde, Marina. 2011. "Energy Policy and Energy Market Performance: The Argentinean Case." *Energy Policy* 39, no. 6: 3860–68.

SMN (Servicio Meteorológico Nacional, Argentina). 2014. "Informe especial debido a la ocurrencia de una ola de calor excepcional en Argentina durante Diciembre de 2013" ("Special Report Due to the Occurrence of an Exceptional Heat Wave in Argentina during December 2013"); "Informe especial debido a la ocurrencia de temperaturas extremadamente altas. Enero 27 2014" ("Special Report Due to the Occurrence of Extremely High Temperatures, January 27, 2014"). www.smn.gov.ar/serviciosclimaticos/clima/archivo/Olasde Calor_BuenosAires.pdf.

Villalonga, Juan Carlos. 2014. "Camino al desastre" ("On the Way to Disaster"). *Los verdes* (blog), January 14. www.losverdes.org.ar/blog/?p=1238.

....

Valeria Procupez is a visiting scholar in the Department of Anthropology at Johns Hopkins University. Her publications include articles and book chapters on issues of social housing, urban infrastructure, and public policy in Argentina.

The Case for Retreat

Liz Koslov

Most people say, "I'm not leaving." You know, it's what
Americans do: they wave a flag and say, "We are strong, we'll
persevere, we'll build it back, we'll be better, we'll be stronger."
[But] we knew different. We knew different.
—Member of the Oakwood Beach Buyout Committee,
Staten Island, New York (July 2013)

"I issue a challenge to anyone here to come up with a bet-
ter word than *retreat*." These words, uttered in a glass-walled conference room
in Lower Manhattan in early 2015, rouse predictable laughter from the audience of urban planners, policy makers, real estate developers, and academics,
assembled here for a roundtable discussion of strategies to adapt the New York
City region to climate change. "Retreat is like defeat," a man's voice intones to
murmurs of assent. "People do not want to give up their homes," the first speaker
acknowledges. There are nods all around. The conversation moves on. *Retreat*, I

My thanks to Klaus Jacob and to one anonymous reviewer for insightful feedback that helped
make this a stronger piece. For comments on earlier drafts, I would like to thank Shane Brennan,
Dorothy Huey, Eric Klinenberg, Ariel Schwartz, and Daniel Aldana Cohen (whom I must also thank
for the title). Thanks are due as well to Ayasha Guerin, who incorporated Harold Fisk's maps for
the Army Corps of Engineers into her installation *Sushi, Maki / A Sudden Change in Course* (2012,
www.ayashaguerinworks.com/installation/) and first showed them to me, and to Nicholas Pinter and
Paul Osman for background information on the relocation of Valmeyer, Illinois. Above all, I am
grateful to the many residents of Staten Island who have shared their experiences with me over the
past several years. I would also like to acknowledge and thank the Department of Media, Culture,
and Communication and the Institute for Public Knowledge at New York University for supporting
this research.

hear again and again in meetings like this, is a bad word for an unpopular, if not unthinkable, concept. To suggest that people move away from the water is, I am repeatedly told, "politically toxic," "infeasible," and even "impossible."

This is common sense, something I too would once have hesitated to question. Retreat, it seemed to me, was likely to play out as an all-too-familiar story of government-planned relocation proceeding against the will of people forced to move. But nearly two years to the day prior to that roundtable in Manhattan, I attended a community meeting in another New York City borough, Staten Island, which upended my assumptions. Just over four months had passed since Hurricane Sandy struck the city, killing forty-four people—all but one of them on Staten Island's south shore. The storm ravaged the homes of thousands more, those at this meeting among them. To my surprise, though, the mood at the meeting belied the recent devastation. People were anxious, yes, but many were smiling. There was a palpable sense of relief and even optimism. Several times, people referred to themselves as "blessed" and others agreed. They were blessed, they said, because New York State governor Andrew M. Cuomo had announced that he would support a home buyout program on Staten Island. Should enough homeowners in a neighborhood agree, the state would purchase and demolish their damaged houses and restore the wetlands that once flourished along much of the city's coastline. While many south shore homeowners had lived in these neighborhoods for decades, if not generations, this meeting established that at least some of them were prepared to give up their waterfront property so that it could become public land and provide protection from future storms. In other words, these homeowners were ready to retreat.

So too, it turns out, were hundreds of other homeowners on Staten Island, where residents organized their own "buyout groups" after Sandy to lobby for parts of at least eight different neighborhoods to be unbuilt. But Staten Islanders seeking a move to higher ground were fighting an uphill battle. Aside from Cuomo, most political leaders refused to acknowledge retreat as a possibility, let alone a necessity, and dismissed those who wanted buyouts as anomalous, out of step with the city at large. "The only place where more than just a small handful want to relocate is a couple of communities on Staten Island," said Senator Charles Schumer. "Otherwise just about everybody—you take Nassau, Suffolk, Queens—they all want to rebuild and come back, and I think that's great. That shows the spirit of New York" (quoted in Kaplan 2013). Then mayor Michael R. Bloomberg spoke similarly at the launch of the city's climate change adaptation plan the summer after Sandy. In his speech, Bloomberg (2013) was adamant: "As New Yorkers, we cannot and will not abandon our waterfront. It's one of our greatest assets. We must protect it, not retreat from it." He surveyed many "layers of defense"—nearly $20 billion worth—proposed for the city, but gave no mention to the more than twenty-five hundred New Yorkers who had already formally preregistered their interest in a state buyout (New York State Homes and Community Renewal 2013: 20). For those who wanted to move to higher ground, retreat was not an abandonment of the waterfront, as Bloomberg put it, but rather an investment in it, one that would strengthen its natural resources while assuring the recovery and long-term safety of its present inhabitants.

Although retreat, often called "managed retreat," remains on the fringes of conversations about climate change adaptation, people throughout the world are already moving away from the water out of fear or necessity. There are many more who want to move but lack the resources to do so, from New York City's Staten Island to Papua New Guinea's Carteret Islands (Edwards 2013), from Panama (Displacement Solutions 2014) to Alaska (Shearer 2012). In each of these places, groups of residents are working to organize their own retreat from environments they perceive as uninhabitable. Despite vastly different circumstances, these residents are engaged in a similar struggle for recognition and support from, paradoxically, the very governments and institutions responsible for planning, implementing, and managing retreat once it becomes necessary. Government officials with the power to plan retreat tend to dismiss it as an option to be averted at any cost, however. Retreat, for them, is not a valuable adaptation strategy but a useful threat to encourage alternate courses of action, such as timely reductions in greenhouse gas emissions or investments in the "hard" defenses of levees and seawalls.

In this article, I contrast dominant official representations of retreat as marginal, unpopular, and infeasible with existing cases of collective movement away from rising waters that demonstrate just the opposite. First, I define *retreat* and address the core concerns that make many officials hesitate to talk about it. I then situate retreat in relation to an emerging body of research on relocation and climate change, before delving into cases of collective retreat in Valmeyer, Illinois, after the Great Midwest Flood of 1993, and in Oakwood Beach, Staten Island, after Hurricane Sandy in 2012. I have selected these cases because they are counterintuitive, serving to challenge common misconceptions about retreat. Some of these misconceptions are geographical: namely, that climate-related migration is a phenomenon external to the United States and that if retreat does occur, it will be confined to peripheral sites on coastal edges. Some of these misconceptions are political and social: that retreat will be a top-down process, one inevitably resisted by local communities. And some of these misconceptions are cultural: that retreat equals failure and defeat, while conquest and growth equal progress.

For the long-standing communities of Valmeyer and Oakwood Beach, by contrast, retreat proved an empowering process and a remarkable achievement, even as it entailed loss.

Nearly twenty years apart, these cases reveal how the growing awareness of climate change alters the meaning of this kind of collective movement. When Valmeyer moved to higher ground it was neither called retreat nor understood as a response to climate change. Rather than taken as a sign of defeat, Valmeyer's relocation was represented as progress and as a patriotic act. Two decades later, when Sandy devastated Staten Island, to move away from the water was instead represented as capitulation. Political speeches and media coverage portrayed retreat as an admission of weakness rather than as a show of strength in the face of irreversible climate change. Retreat is a powerful and controversial concept whose cultural and political significance will grow as the planet warms and the seas rise, and it is already a valuable and necessary addition to the language of climate change adaptation. Without taking retreat seriously as a concept, strategy, and existing practice, meaningful conversation and action around climate change adaptation will continue to prove illusory. Understanding community-organized relocation efforts as forms of retreat unifies this emerging practice with other social movements and political projects that seek more sustainable ways of settling on earth.

Defining Retreat

The term *managed retreat* once referred primarily to ecological rather than social change. When a shoreline retreats due to erosion or sea level rise, one option is to manage that retreat instead of attempting to prevent it. In this context, managing retreat means removing hard coastal defenses to create space for the coastline to move, for water to come in, and for intertidal habitats such as wetlands and salt marshes to flourish. These habitats in turn can provide "soft" defense by acting as sponges and buffering storm surge. Retreat is an established coastal management strategy in rural and agricultural areas, and it is now also being debated as a strategy to adapt to climate change in more densely populated places. Hence, *retreat* increasingly refers to the relocation of people to higher ground and associated efforts to plan and manage that movement. In practice, however, this often means restricting movement as much as facilitating it.

Government officials who resist retreat share core political, social, and economic concerns. Retreat is distinct from other kinds of climate-related migration in that it entails not just relocating a group of people but also unbuilding land

and returning it to nature in perpetuity. Relocation on its own is a politically and socially fraught process, though this has not stopped governments from forcing people to move for countless development and regeneration projects in the name of economic and social progress. With retreat, it is thus the latter act of unbuilding that stirs special fears, even as evidence suggests that those fears are misguided. Local officials in the United States, for instance, fear lost income from property taxes on top of the added costs of maintaining acquired land as open space. But residential development is itself an expense that easily outweighs its presumed economic benefits, because the cost of providing services for more people is greater than the additional taxes they pay. Restoring open space, meanwhile, increases adjacent property values and provides numerous other economic, social, and health benefits, particularly in otherwise dense urban areas (Active Living Research 2010), not to mention the extensive savings that result from mitigating flood damage.

For governments, buying people out once is a far more effective and less expensive means of flood protection than building and maintaining structural defenses, such as levees and seawalls, that will become obsolete as floods worsen and sea levels rise.[1] Hard defenses, moreover, have been shown to increase rather than decrease the costs of flooding, since the sense of safety they provide works to attract further development (the so-called levee effect), ultimately placing more people and property at risk. These defenses also have negative impacts on the environment and on neighboring areas to which they displace water (Tobin 1995). Despite these costs, many officials treat unbuilding land and removing it from the market as the greater risk, though the profits to be gained from remaining in dangerous places are more uncertain and short-lived than the rewards of retreating from them are (Jacob 2015; Polefka 2013).

Even if officials and the general public were to appreciate the numerous benefits of retreat, concerns would persist that it is too costly to support the movement of vast numbers of people living in places vulnerable to the effects of climate change. To succeed, retreat certainly requires substantial government financing and organizational support in conjunction with grassroots efforts, both at the site of retreat itself and in the communities to which people relocate. At the same time, concerns about costs may be overstated. Estimates of vulnerable popula-

---

1. A US Army Corps of Engineers study after the Great Midwest Flood of 1993, for example, found that more than $6 billion in levee improvements would have been needed to reduce the damage that occurred, compared with a FEMA estimate that $209 million for voluntary buyouts would have done much the same and done it "with no adverse impact to the environment and without inducing future development" (quoted in Conrad, McNitt, and Stout 1998: 40).

tions generally incorporate not just those who are most immediately in danger but also those who potentially face longer-term risk. For instance, data on the global population in low-lying coastal zones include everyone living up to ten meters above sea level. But potentially only people within two or three meters of sea level may want or need to retreat from the water in the near future. Estimates that half of the US population lives on the coast count entire coastal counties, whereas only approximately 3 percent of the population actually lives in a high-risk coastal flood zone (Crowell et al. 2010). Retreat also acts to lower the number of vulnerable people beyond those who themselves relocate, by creating a protective buffer zone of open space that reduces risk further inland.

The costs of retreat, though undeniable, are relative and should not be seen as prohibitive. In the United States, there are precedents for voters supporting tax increases to pay for buyouts of local flood-prone property (Conrad, McNitt, and Stout 1998). Meanwhile, every year the government gives billions of dollars in subsidies to the fossil fuel industry, which arguably should be on the hook for at least some of the costs of climate-induced relocation, as the village of Kivalina, Alaska, argued in a recent lawsuit (Siders 2012). Another notion is to fund buyouts by selling development rights in upland areas or transferring them from low-lying land to higher ground (Drake 2013). There are, in short, many ways to make retreat financially viable.[2] A focus on the potential problems of retreat should not outweigh consideration of its possibilities and promise.

Resistance to retreat also stems, however, from deeper concerns that are more conceptual than practical, bound up with the meaning of the word itself. The prevailing definition of *retreat* is a military one: "movement by soldiers away from an enemy because the enemy is winning or has won a battle" (*Merriam-Webster* 2015)—retreat, indeed, as defeat. Etymologically, the earliest meaning of the word *retreat*, dating from around 1300, is "a step backward" (*Online Etymology Dictionary* 2015). Additional definitions cast *retreat* more positively, as a refuge or a spiritual retreat providing a safe place and span of time for reflection. Breaking the word down, *re-* means "back to the original place; again, anew, once more" and *-treat* "an attempt to heal or cure," making retreat a process of going back, of returning, in order to heal. Contained within the word *retreat*, then, are not solely negative connotations of defeat and loss but also a positive potential for the process of giving in and giving up to prove reparative rather than harmful—particularly as societies begin considering more sustainable forms of settling and organizing.

2. For an overview of legal, policy, and regulatory tools for managing retreat, see Siders 2013.

This affective ambivalence lends *retreat* its rhetorical power and permeates debates over its meaning as a climate change adaptation strategy. In the context of climate change, *retreat* has come to form part of a broader military metaphor: other strategies to respond to flooding and sea level rise include building seawalls to "defend" ourselves or going on the "attack" by building land farther out into the water (Building Futures 2010). Here water is positioned as the immediate enemy; it is less clear whether ultimately the war is being waged against the forces of nature or the forces of anthropogenic (human-caused) climate change. This distinction matters: Does retreat mean giving in to the power of Mother Nature, or does it mean acquiescing to the human forces destroying nature? Is it possible to adapt to a changing climate while still fighting climate change?

The latter question has dogged debates over the relationship between adaptation and mitigation, which aims to curtail climate change by cutting greenhouse gas emissions. At this point, few doubt the need both to adapt to the already ensuing impacts of climate change *and* to minimize future impacts. But these endeavors do not necessarily go hand in hand; as a well-known climate science contrarian once enthusiastically explained to me, "Adaptation is agnostic!"—meaning, regardless of whether people accept that humans are causing climate change, they will want to adapt to its effects.[3]

Relocation as Adaptation

What constitutes adaptation remains subject to heated debate. Human movement in particular can be taken as both a negative result of climate change and a positive response to it. J. A. G. Cooper and Jeremy Pile (2014) point out that much of what is commonly called "adaptation" in fact works to modify the environment so as to preserve human activities. For instance, they note that in coastal cities "adaptation to climate change is typically viewed simply as a need for better defences to protect human settlements, infrastructure, and activities from future flooding" (ibid.: 92). This approach, they argue, "is better termed 'resistance' than 'adaptation,'" which they instead hold to mean modifying human activities to adapt to a changing environment (ibid.: 90). By this definition, retreat, which couples human relocation with land-use changes, is one of the most adaptive responses to climate change.

Until recently, though, scholars and activists alike framed human move-

---

3. For a thorough discussion and critique of "agnostic adaptation" in relation to the latest Intergovernmental Panel on Climate Change (IPCC) report, see Kuh 2015.

ment primarily as a failure to adapt, or even as a kind of maladaptation. Ben Orlove (2005: 599) calls the lack of attention to migration in discussions of climate change adaptation "a striking form of silence" considering the central role migration played for past societies confronted by climate variability (including the United States during the 1930s dust bowl). Migration "lies entirely outside the acceptable range of proposals" for adaptation, Orlove writes, in part because it would "contradict the political frameworks under which the contemporary debate over global warming takes place" (ibid.). Within these frameworks, premised on state sovereignty and national borders, climate migration is treated as a threat to regional stability and global order—as one of the risks posed by climate change rather than as a process with the power to reduce risk (Podesta and Ogden 2007).

Work on migration and climate change has since demonstrated that there is little empirical support for the oft-dire predictions of climate-induced mass movement. Migration, first of all, is not driven by any one force in isolation but depends on a range of social, political, and economic factors as well as environmental ones (Hunter, Luna, and Norton 2015; Tacoli 2009). Second, climate change is more likely to intensify existing patterns of migration than to radically alter them, such that the vast majority of movement will continue to be internal and over relatively short distances rather than international. Third, not all of those people who live in places vulnerable to the effects of climate change will want to move or be able to do so; "migration," as Cecilia Tacoli (2009: 516) points out, "requires financial resources and social support, both of which may decline with climate change, which may thus result in fewer rather than more people being able to move." These dynamics, together with the challenge of forecasting the regional- and local-level effects of climate change, make it exceedingly difficult to predict the scale and distribution of population movements that will result, let alone to determine their outcomes based on numbers alone.

The circumstances under which relocation proves adaptive for those who do move remains an open question. Recent studies highlight the benefits of voluntary, temporary migration for individuals and households faced with environmental pressure (Hunter, Luna, and Norton 2015; Tacoli 2009).[4] Little is known, however, about the effects of permanent planned relocation, "a relatively uncharted topic in the context of climate change" (Ferris 2014: 5). In other contexts, though, the devastating consequences of forced relocation are clear, whether this relocation results from disasters (Erikson 1976), urban renewal (Fullilove 2004), or large-

4. For a critique of the promotion of circular migration as a response to climate change, see Felli 2013.

scale development projects such as dams (Weerasinghe et al. 2014). But as climate change renders certain places uninhabitable, relocation plans that enable people to move in advance of disaster offer a positive alternative to sudden displacement (Bronen 2011). The uncertainty that inheres in determinations of whether, or when, a place has become unsafe creates at least some room for agency on the part of those making relocation decisions (Weerasinghe et al. 2014). Yet it is not necessarily or exclusively the people who may have to move who are making these decisions. Retreat depends on support from governments and institutions that have their own interests and stakes in the outcome of climate-related relocation.

The Politics of Climate-Related Relocation

When people decide to migrate they do so for a range of reasons that extend beyond environmental change. Governments tasked with managing relocation are likewise motivated by a number of factors. While governments and related institutions may develop and implement relocation plans primarily in response to climate change, these plans are also likely to serve other, existing agendas. In the Maldives, for instance, a government-mandated relocation program after a 2004 tsunami served the purpose of "clearing entire areas for tourism," a use that the government viewed as "more profitable" than the subsistence fishing practiced by present inhabitants (Maldonado 2014: 74). The Maldives government also recently revived a controversial decades-old plan to resettle the population onto a smaller number of islands (Burkett 2015; Kothari 2014). "Environmental exigencies," Maxine Burkett (2015: 82) explains, "now fuel a plan that was once a strategy based on economic and political pressures."[5] Planning relocation is not a disinterested act, nor is it one oriented solely toward future environmental conditions. Rather, desire for relocation, both on the part of those seeking to move and of those seeking to manage that movement, arises and gains meaning within a particular political, historical, and cultural context.

This context also determines who is seen as a "climate migrant" and, by implication, as someone whose relocation *needs* to be managed. Carol Farbotko (2012:

---

5. Relatedly, in New Orleans after Hurricane Katrina, proposals from planners and government officials to return parts of some neighborhoods to open space "were viewed by many as extensions of the old urban renewal policies that had decimated communities around the United States" (Fields 2009: 335). "Public skepticism over current debates about reducing the urban footprint [or] reintroducing wetlands into the city in the form of new urban parks," write Rachel Breunlin and Helen A. Regis (2006: 744), "is informed by a mindfulness of long histories of urban renewal and interstate highway and park construction, which caused their own form of devastation in mostly black residential neighborhoods."

833) points out that managing climate-related migration is presented as "largely a project of managing the poor" rather than managing "those likely to be displaced from their waterfront mansions."[6] Certainly, climate change will disproportionately affect the poor, who will also need more resources in order to move. But management may serve less as a way to equitably distribute those resources than to restrict migration not deemed profitable, or to enforce it in places inhabited by poorer people, places deemed more valuable when put to another use. As Giovanni Bettini (2014: 187) argues, the growing acceptance of migration as a viable way to adapt to climate change remains premised on the firm belief "that migration flows . . . need to be (if not curbed) 'combed' through management." This management works to differentiate "those able to render their mobility a fruitful investment and those fleeing because of desperation (or unable to move)" (ibid.: 188). Climate migration becomes a development project, meaning that its management is not just about keeping people safe but also about "*transforming* the 'vulnerable'" to ensure that environmental sustainability dovetails with enhanced economic productivity (ibid.: 189).

When framed in terms of development, climate-related migration is considered necessary and adaptive only for particular people and places. Retreat from the small islands of New York City, for instance, appears impossible, while retreat from the small island nations of the Pacific and Indian Oceans seems inevitable. Extensive media coverage depicts these latter islands as on the verge of disappearance and life on them as a constant crisis. Ethnographic studies, however, demonstrate that the evacuation of these nations is not a foregone conclusion but an actively contested one (Farbotko and Lazrus 2012; Mortreux and Barnett 2009; Rudiak-Gould 2013). Farbotko (2010) critiques the dominant representations of disappearing islands as "wishful sinking," noting that these nations have long been described as economically unsustainable in colonial and development discourses (whereas the subsistence practices of many inhabitants make their lifestyles significantly more *environmentally* sustainable than those of most New York City residents). Environmental discourse, she argues, continues to treat the "islands as expendable," even as more valuable if they vanish, because "only after they disappear will the islands become an absolute truth of the urgency of climate change, and thus act as a prompt toward saving the rest of the planet" (ibid.: 47–48). Thus, Farbotko explains, "conceptions of the islands as fundamentally impoverished and

6. The figure of the climate migrant is racialized as well as classed, argues Andrew Baldwin (2013). Climate migrants are conceived alternately as threat and victim, each of which "mark[s] the migrant as different from some purportedly normal, unmarked body" and serves to "authorise some form of moral intervention—whether increased policing or humanitarian assistance" (ibid.: 1475).

dependent became the basis of their meaning as spaces of climate change," giving rise to the view that "rising sea levels merely hasten a preordained exit toward spaces of modernity, such as Australia" and other mainland economies (ibid.: 52). Small island nations and their inhabitants are repeatedly represented as natural victims of climate change, bound eventually to retreat, regardless of the reality on the ground.[7] Meanwhile, retreat in the United States remains relatively invisible, even as people are moving away from the water en masse.

Retreat from the River: Valmeyer and the Great Midwest Flood

By contrast with the low-lying atoll islands of the South Pacific, the cornfields, prairies, and rocky bluffs of the American Midwest are probably the last landscape that comes to mind upon imagining retreat. Yet despite the usual depiction of retreat as a coastal phenomenon, people in the United States have predominantly moved away from its rivers. It was the bursting Mississippi and Missouri Rivers during the Great Midwest Flood of 1993 that spurred the expansion of federal funding to buy out flood-prone property and return floodplains to open space (Chagnon 1996; Wilkins 1996). The Great Midwest Flood was the costliest disaster ever to befall the United States until Hurricane Katrina (Watson 1996). Spawned by snowmelt and record-breaking rains that dramatically raised river levels, it flooded over thirty thousand square miles of land across nine states (Ayres 1993), breaching more than one thousand levees (FEMA 2003: xiii). This massive failure of structural flood control measures launched a "revolution in social policy" in favor of nonstructural ways of reducing risk, such as home buyouts (Conrad, McNitt, and Stout 1998: 44). There were ten thousand buyouts after the 1993 floods (ibid.: 34), and by 1998 an estimated twenty thousand home buyouts and relocations were under way or completed across at least thirty-six states (ibid.: 123). Over the past decade, the Federal Emergency Management Agency (FEMA) has continued to provide the bulk of financial support for more than seven thousand additional buyouts, with inland states receiving the majority of funding (Cater and Benincasa 2014).

The risks of climate change, like its causes, are not solely external but also spring from within. River flooding currently affects in excess of 21 million people per year worldwide, a number expected to more than double by 2030, primarily due to climate change (Luo et al. 2015). This is because warmer air holds more moisture, leading to heavier rains; extreme precipitation events have already

7. The latest science, in fact, suggests atoll islands may be growing in response to sea level rise (Warne 2015), while New York is going under at more than twice the global rate (Gerken 2015).

increased over midlatitude regions, such as the American Midwest, where they are very likely to become more frequent and intense in the years to come (IPCC 2014: 11). Even those parts of the United States projected to suffer from worsening droughts may still see their flood risk increase (AECOM 2013: ES-6). When the rains do fall, they will do so in more concentrated bursts, leaving dried-out land unable to absorb the water.[8]

Despite these risks, and the reality of already devastating floods, riverine retreat attracts little attention compared with coastal retreat. Perhaps the congruence of coastlines and national borders incites greater anxiety about the loss of territory that will accompany retreat from the rising seas. Certainly, the density and rapid development of oceanfront property stokes added worry over the costs of giving it up and the shortage of comparable space. The special challenges facing coastal cities with complex and aging infrastructure also warrant considerable attention. There is, as well, a sense that the path of rivers has always shifted, giving their erratic movement a more natural feel than that of the oceans coming in, even with this movement increasingly subject to the effects of anthropogenic climate change.

Moving along with rivers thus signals historical continuity more than it does novel and irreversible change. "One who knows the Mississippi," wrote Mark Twain ([1883] 2015), "will promptly aver . . . that ten thousand River Commissions, with the mines of the world at their back, cannot tame that lawless stream, cannot curb it or confine it, cannot say to it, Go here, or Go there, and make it obey; cannot save a shore which it has sentenced; cannot bar its path with an obstruction which it will not tear down, dance over, and laugh at." Nevertheless, there have been repeated attempts to channelize and control the flow of rivers such as the Mississippi in order to open proximate land to stable, permanent uses. The feeling of security that results leads more to move into harm's way, even as it proves illusory time and again.

One of the many places that the Great Midwest Flood submerged in 1993 was the southern Illinois town of Valmeyer, population nine hundred, about thirty miles downstream from St. Louis along the Mississippi River. The town's name reveals the importance of land and family to its residents; short for "Valley of the Meyers," *Valmeyer* denotes both the town's location in the American Bottom

8. These conditions additionally increase the risk of mudslides, another danger that is prompting retreat from certain areas. Buyouts are supported, for instance, by most property owners in Oso, Washington, the site of the deadliest landslide in US history in 2014 (Kamb and Brunner 2015). County officials actually considered buyouts for Oso a decade prior to the slide, but the option was not approved, nor was it discussed with residents (Le 2014). Mudslides are further exacerbated by wildfires, which are also becoming more frequent due to climate change (USGS 2015).

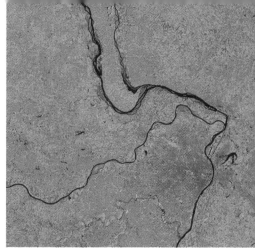

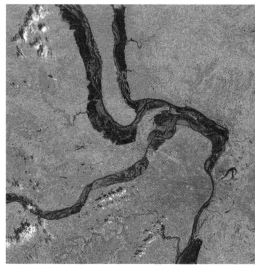

Figure 1   One of Harold Fisk's maps of the Mississippi River's historical meandering, created in 1944 for the US Army Corps of Engineers. Retrieved June 5, 2015, from lmvmapping.erdc.usace.army.mil.

Figure 2   National Aeronautics and Space Administration (NASA) images showing the Mississippi River before and during the Great Midwest Flood of 1993. Created by Jesse Allen, Earth Observatory, using data provided courtesy of the Landsat Project Science Office. Retrieved May 14, 2015, from earthobservatory .nasa.gov/IOTD/view.php?id=5422.

floodplain and one of its founding families of German immigrants, from whom a number of present-day inhabitants descend (Wilkerson 1993). Historical flooding of the Mississippi provided the town's farmers with fertile soil and its older residents with childhood memories of amphibious boats, front-yard fishing, and washing away the mud that the river left in its wake, as recounted in *Valmeyer, IL: The Documentary* (dir. Danny Moore; 2015). By the 1940s, however, the floods had grown deep enough for Valmeyer to seek protection from the US Army Corps of Engineers (fig. 1). The corps constructed a large levee system, effectively rendering the three-mile-distant river "out of sight, out of mind" for nearly fifty years (Knobloch 2005: 41). Until 1993, that is, when the Mississippi burst its banks and overtopped Valmeyer's levee, coursing through the town and filling houses with up to sixteen feet of floodwater that took months to fully subside, only to flood once again (fig. 2).

"There's not a book out there that says, 'This is how you move a flooded town,'" then mayor of Valmeyer Dennis M. Knobloch says in *Valmeyer, IL*. But move the town was exactly what they did; rather than rebuild in place, after the flood Valmeyer's residents voted to relocate to the top of a nearby bluff. A series of community meetings had made the preference for a collective relocation plan clear. Individual buyouts would disperse the community, while rebuilding to FEMA floodplain elevation standards was undesirable for some and unaffordable for others. "We felt that the only way we could keep the town together, and continue to have *a* Valmeyer," Knobloch explained in the documentary, "would be trying to relocate the town."

Approximately two-thirds of the town's nine hundred residents eventually moved to the new site. All told, the relocation took twenty-two government agencies (Watson 1996) and $35 million in federal and state funding (Brown 1996). Many residents, however, attribute the success of the relocation to their mayor—as one resident states in *Valmeyer, IL*, "He was the one that pretty well pushed FEMA and all the other organizations that you had to go through to get stuff done"—while Knobloch himself views it as the result of residents' collaborative efforts: "The people sat down at the table and planned all of this," he recounts in the documentary, explaining that they formed seven citizens' committees to facilitate designing and moving to the new town. An article in *Smithsonian* magazine described the complex and collaborative work involved: "Farmers found themselves plowing through state and federal building codes. Bank tellers and businessmen mastered blueprints. Secretaries and school teachers decided details from sewers to streetlamps" (Watson 1996). The *New York Times* put it like this: "Almost as therapy, ordinary people are remaking a town from scratch" (Wilkerson 1993). The picture that emerges from these accounts is of an ideal democratic process that brings together people from all walks of life to debate and ultimately deliver their vision of a better collective future, with the support of a government acting on the wishes of those it represents.

Accounts of Valmeyer's relocation depict the town's move as the means to recover an American dream, one thought lost in the muddy waters. "'There we were,'" said a resident recalling life before the flood, "'living the quote unquote American dream. . . . Both working, paying the mortgage, two kids in school. And like that, we're homeless" (quoted in Watson 1996). Two years later, this resident was one of the "old Valmeyer" inhabitants to move into homes in the "new Valmeyer." Life began afresh, and in many ways alike: "The first school prom. The first church bell. The first community garage sale. The first grass" (Brown 1996). Bucolic, all-American images abound; there is no hint that helping this community regain and even improve on what they had before could be controversial in any way. Nor is there any sense, yet, that global climate change presents a more fundamental and existential challenge to this way of life than the river alone does. It is still possible to move away from the threat and move on, to return to normal.

Media coverage emphasized the historical continuity of Valmeyer's move, making it appear as natural as the Mississippi's cresting waves. The *Smithsonian* article lauded Valmeyer residents as "new pioneers" who, after the flood, rediscovered an earlier "pioneer spirit" (Watson 1996). The *New York Times* framed them similarly: "Like the original Swiss settlers on the rich Mississippi River bottom land at the turn of the century, residents of Valmeyer are homesteaders in a strange new land" (Brown 1996). With development no longer constrained by floodplain building regulations, the new Valmeyer grew "from blueprint to boomtown" with old Valmeyer left "clogged by weeds, flat as an ocean floor . . . again what the river made it—a floodplain" (Watson 1996). Those who opted to remain behind seem in this telling like the ones consigned to the past. Those who moved to higher ground, meanwhile, maintained their traditions but embodied a brighter future. With retreat reconfigured as Manifest Destiny, a tale of supposed triumph through territorial expansion, it remained able to support rather than challenge the dominant ideology of unstoppable growth and progress.

In the case of Valmeyer, Illinois, as well as in neighboring Missouri where two smaller towns likewise relocated after the Great Midwest Flood, retreat was considered a success and even valorized. However, countless other places that have sought government support for buyouts and relocation fared less well and received scant attention. This is especially true of coastal cities, and particularly of poorer areas. A report on buyouts issued in 1998 notes the eagerness of New Orleans residents for flood mitigation measures such as buyouts seven years prior to Hurricane Katrina. The report points out, however, that in an urbanized area with a lack of undeveloped space, "the voluntary buyout option may have limited utility" despite having "clearly aroused considerable local interest" (Conrad, McNitt, and Stout 1998: 172).

"There are more offers from flood victims to sell than funds available," the report states, explaining that there are "numerous poorer communities and neighborhoods where residents with repetitive loss and substantially damaged properties have signed up for buyouts, but the communities have no funds" to pay the share required by the federal government (ibid.: 163–64). In these places, people may be more likely to be displaced but less likely to be fairly compensated, leaving them unable to rebuild their lives somewhere safer. Meanwhile, there is little awareness of retreat as a viable option not because there is no public desire for retreat but because government support has been lacking and government policies are inadequate to accomplish it.[9] Hence retreat winds up as a road not taken more often than it does a historical precedent.

Retreat in a Climate-Changed City: Staten Island after Sandy

Twenty years after retreat from the rural, riverine town of old Valmeyer was seen as progress, retreat from New York City took on a very different meaning. "The future of the city lies along its coastline," Mayor Bloomberg (2013) announced at the 2013 launch of his administration's climate change adaptation plan. The year before, Hurricane Sandy had flooded over fifty square miles of the city's five boroughs (New York City Special Initiative for Rebuilding and Resiliency 2013: 13). But Bloomberg assured his audience that climate change was not going to halt the pace of growth and development. "Demand for housing in Lower Manhattan," where Sandy submerged streets, sparked blackouts, and shut down subways, "has never been stronger," the mayor said as he laid out a vision in which the city would not retreat but would build even *farther* out into the water, filling new land along Manhattan's Lower East Side to provide space for a "Seaport City" with "thousands of new residents and hundreds of businesses" (Bloomberg 2013). This was progress, in the mayor's view. Bloomberg reminded listeners that before his time in office, "the city allowed the waterfront to become polluted, degraded, and

9. The Stafford Act, for instance, restricts the amount of FEMA disaster relief that can be spent on mitigation activities, including buyouts. As Robin Bronen (2011: 367) notes, government funding "is designed to help rebuild individual homes in their current location, not rebuild communities in a new one."

abandoned." By contrast, his mayoralty was dedicated to "reversing that history and reclaiming the waterfront," a project that was "not going to stop now" (ibid.). Indeed, new buildings—along with rents and property values—had soared along New York City's waterfront under Bloomberg, as industrial areas were rezoned for residential redevelopment (Rosenberg 2014). From the perspective of those profiting from these changes, to reclaim the waterfront for nature rather than for development was to abandon the city's tried-and-true path of economic—if not social or environmental—progress.

Progress looks very different on the south shore of Staten Island, the city's so-called forgotten borough, where I have spent the past two and a half years conducting interviews and ethnographic research on Sandy's aftermath. Instead of postindustrial-gone-luxury high-rise, Staten Island's south shore neighborhoods retain the feel of the seasonal beach communities they once were. There are still narrow streets of small wooden bungalows surrounded by stalks of towering phragmites. Though there are also plenty of newer, larger houses, attached duplexes, and condominium complexes, buildings that began encroaching on the wetlands in force after the Verrazano-Narrows Bridge linked Staten Island to Brooklyn in 1964. The ensuing decades of private development, coupled with soaring population growth and inadequate public infrastructure, proved the source not of progress but of problems—most notably flooding, which grew worse and worse in the years leading up to Hurricane Sandy. From the vantage point of many residents who experienced these changes firsthand, unbuilding the waterfront undoes a costly and destructive mistake. Retreat would chart a wiser course for the future, strengthening the waterfront rather than abandoning it—and abandoning them.

Abandoned was how residents had long felt in one Staten Island neighborhood, Oakwood Beach, where recurrent flooding came to a head years before Sandy. In 1992 a powerful nor'easter—the Storm of No Name, some call it—struck the city. Nearly five feet of water inundated Oakwood Beach, leading residents to organize a flood victims committee to lobby government for better coastal protection. The government eventually agreed to do a series of studies, but funding ran out and little changed. Building continued on wetlands adjacent to the neighborhood despite community opposition. Flooding grew worse. When Sandy struck on the night of October 29, 2012, the highest water levels citywide were recorded in Oakwood Beach, which was hit with a ferocious fourteen-foot storm surge. After the storm, residents once again organized a committee—the Oakwood Beach Buyout Committee. The time had come, they decided, to get out.

The Oakwood Beach Buyout Committee, with unanimous support from nearly two hundred neighboring households, created a buyout plan and began pushing it to local officials. Working through the city turned out to be "a dead end," in the words of one committee member, and so they focused their efforts on the state. And they succeeded: less than three months after Sandy's landfall, Governor Cuomo announced a state buyout program for affected homeowners. "Climate change is real," Cuomo said (2013). "There are some parcels that Mother Nature owns. She may visit once every few years, but she owns the parcel and when she comes to visit, *she visits*." The state designated the streets selected by the Oakwood Beach Buyout Committee the first "enhanced area" eligible for the program. Homeowners opting to participate would receive prestorm fair market value for their damaged houses plus incentives for being in a target area and for relocating within New York City. "It's just amazing," one Oakwood Beach resident said to me later that year. "We are so lucky." The governor's support of Oakwood Beach encouraged homeowners in at least seven other Staten Island neighborhoods to organize their own buyout groups, in the hopes of showing that they too shared the will to retreat and thus should also be included in the program and offered buyouts (figs. 3 and 4).

Figure 3 Photograph taken by the author, October 5, 2013

Figure 4 Photograph taken by the author, April 26, 2014

Shortly after the launch of the state buyout program, however, the city announced its own program for homeowners wishing to relocate. This program preempted the state's program for all city residents, including Staten Islanders living outside the already designated Oakwood Beach buyout area. Unlike the state buyout program, the city's program was not retreat. While a state buyout would return purchased land to nature and prohibit any future construction, the city would retain the right to turn acquired land over to developers, so long as they rebuilt in a more flood-resistant way. Though participants in both programs would receive roughly the same amount of money to relocate, redeveloping rather than retreating from the land altered the meaning of moving in consequential ways that made the city's program far less appealing for many.

Staten Island is a borough with a culture of sacrifice, notable for its high number of firefighters, police officers, 9/11 first responders, sanitation workers, and other public servants. Residents who wanted to retreat emphasized that they were not seeking safety solely for themselves but believed that their actions would also help protect their broader community. "If this is an area that takes in water, that becomes a sponge, that goes back to nature," one resident explained to me, "everybody wins. It's a hell of a sacrifice for the greater good." Another homeowner noted that the benefits of buyouts would extend beyond Staten Island to taxpayers at large, because "if you buy the houses out, you never have to pay flood insurance [claims], you're not gonna have to pay a [disaster] payment again, so the United States is actually saving money." The advantages of retreat would thus accrue to all, whereas the redevelopment plans favored by the city would likely advantage only an elite few. Moreover, redevelopment threatened to harm those whom retreat would protect, both by potentially worsening flooding for people who remained living near acquired areas and by placing prospective new residents at risk. "I would prefer the land going back to nature than to see some other family ten, twenty, thirty years from now going through this kind of thing," one man told me. "It's gonna happen again." While retreat would be a personal sacrifice for the public good, redevelopment would sacrifice others for private gain—a stark and unpalatable contrast.

Months of meetings, petitions, and demonstrations eventually resulted in just two additional neighborhoods winning buyouts from the state. Yet even these successful efforts were framed as defeat. For instance, when the *New York Times* N.Y./Region section ran a front-page feature on the Oakwood Beach buyout, it depicted the neighborhood as a place where people had simply given up. "This is the way a neighborhood ends," read the first sentence, printed alongside a large photograph showing a darkened street of shuttered houses awash in an eerie red

377

glow. The article casts the story of retreat in a similarly grim light: "In the storm's aftermath, many people here vowed that they would return," it narrates, but then "the state announced a [buyout] program" and "Gov. Andrew M. Cuomo said the area should be returned to nature." "One by one, people have been accepting the offers, emptying out their houses, turning out the lights for the last time" (Gregory 2013). Rendering completely invisible the sustained and dedicated community action that achieved the buyout, this article instead depicts passive residents individually relenting in the face of a government directive.

Retreat is neither a passive act nor a defeatist one, though it is often represented as such. In part, this may be wishful thinking—or another form of "wishful sinking"—that as places disappear due to climate change the people who live in them will quietly dissipate too. One Oakwood Beach resident put it to me like this: "Men didn't get smarter and egos didn't diminish. So it's hard [for officials] to say, 'We made a mistake.' . . . It's much easier for them to say, 'Let's just let them go away.'" She and other Staten Islanders may be physically going away, but the movement for retreat that they advanced is not. "The game changed" with Sandy, this resident believes, and now the experience of Oakwood Beach can "help other communities" that decide they too want to retreat. She hopes their experience will also help government officials to "really, really, really recognize that community effort and involvement plays a role in this."

Acknowledging demands for retreat and the grassroots activism that plays a crucial role in its success, however, threatens the political status quo and its financial bottom line. It challenges dominant interests and business-as-usual approaches that have, themselves, contributed to the need for retreat by exacerbating the larger problem of anthropogenic climate change and by being persistently unwilling to admit and mitigate it. But on Staten Island after Sandy, residents could see that it is worth fighting for retreat and worth fighting for those whose actions place people in harm's way to finally take responsibility for it.

Connecting Movements in the Context of Climate Change

Flood buyouts like those I describe above are not generally recognized as climate-related migration. They are located in places not seen as the "front lines" of climate change. They occur after disasters, not necessarily in anticipation of them. They also are actually happening, albeit in a limited way, whereas many community-led efforts to relocate due to climate change have received far less support. Accounts of these efforts tell less of movement than of the near insurmountable obstacles to it. In Alaska, for instance, a number of indigenous villages have for decades voted repeatedly to relocate yet have been unable to garner the resources to do so, despite multiple government studies attesting to the imminent danger they face (Bronen 2011; Marino 2015; Shearer 2012). In Papua New Guinea, meanwhile, residents of the Carteret Islands finally took relocation planning into their own hands after years of government inaction (Edwards 2013). An indigenous community in Panama did likewise but found it difficult to leverage enough external support and funding to actually make the move (Displacement Solutions 2014).

Retreat might reasonably be expected to follow from physical geography, to be based on factors such as elevation and proximity to the coast. Yet these cases show that it is based as much, if not more, on political and social geography. Retreat is restricted for reasons of political and financial risk even in places with extreme environmental risk. A report issued five years after the Great Midwest Flood found that the twenty thousand buyouts under way nationwide "stem largely from community-led (and federal- and state-assisted) efforts" but that many fewer people receive resources to move than want to do so (Conrad, McNitt, and Stout 1998: 124). This condemns some to live through multiple disasters. Five hundred households in Manville, New Jersey, for example, applied for buyouts after Hurricane Floyd in 1999. Of these, the town selected 274, a number that FEMA subsequently reduced to 42 (Hanley 2000). After Hurricane Irene struck Manville in 2011, the year before Sandy, only nineteen of four hundred applicants received a buyout (Tyrrell 2012). Manville is now the site of nearly one hundred post-Sandy buyouts. Even where retreat is widely viewed as necessary, there remain political and financial barriers to its achievement.

The effects of climate change are rendering retreat increasingly imperative, but relocation remains largely unrecognized "as an adaptation strategy rather than a 'last resort,'" Burkett (2015: 78–79) notes. On an international level, she explains, this makes it difficult to use funding specifically for adaptation in order to finance retreat. Furthermore, this adaptation funding tends to be disbursed to national governments, not local communities, though research shows effective adaptation is most often a bottom-up rather than top-down process. Top-down adaptation funding may enable governments to pursue projects that are counter to the interests of those they represent. It may also allow them to avoid engaging in difficult, but vital, conversations about retreat. All told, retreat is messy. It takes democratic debate and collective decision making. Once a decision is reached, it requires acknowledgment, cooperation, and substantial support from multiple levels of government. "Voluntary buyouts are more complicated than building levees," reports the National Wildlife Federation (Conrad, McNitt, and Stout 1998: 35). Yet they are also more effective, sustainable, and scalable.

Because retreat arises from local efforts, it tends to be treated as an isolated, ad hoc phenomenon. Diverse communities, however, are beginning to connect with one another as they confront climate-related relocation. The month before Hurricane Sandy, community leaders from Newtok, Alaska, visited with Carteret Islanders to discuss their respective fights for community-based relocation (Crump 2012). After Sandy, I heard the story of Valmeyer from an Illinois floodplain manager on a bought-out street in Oakwood Beach. He had traveled to Staten Island with a team of researchers hoping to learn lessons applicable back home. We met that day with a member of the Oakwood Beach Buyout Committee, who spoke of the indigenous peoples contending with the need to retreat from the Louisiana coast. Though retreat has a landscape of meanings as vast and varied as the diverse geographies in which it takes place, those grappling with it, despite their differing sites and circumstances, have begun to recognize one another as bound in a common struggle.

The Case for Retreat

What do we gain by calling this a struggle for *retreat*? Leaving home in the context of climate change is not a neutral act. Relabeling retreat to make it *sound* more neutral is, I argue, counterproductive. Euphemisms may abound, but each carries baggage of its own. Adding "planned" or "managed" to *retreat* makes it sound like a rebranded version of policies such as managed decline and planned shrinkage that withdrew public resources from places deemed "at risk," to deleterious and discriminatory effect. "Planned relocation" and "resettlement" insert retreat squarely into a history of forced population movements that have likewise been devastating for the people and communities involved (McAdam 2015). This history undeniably sets the scene for retreat—many of those living in the most vulnerable places do so as the direct or indirect result of forced relocation, sedentarization, or displacement—but this is a history from which retreat should depart. Examples of successful community-organized relocation provide retreat a different history and suggest ways it can have a more just, sustainable future.

Discussions of retreat are stymied in part because they do not distinguish government-supported, but community-organized, collective movement from government-dictated mass relocation or disaster- and climate-induced displacement. Forced relocation and displacement are already resulting from—and in the name of—climate change, not least from government-sponsored adaptation and mitigation schemes (de Sherbinin et al. 2011). Use of the term *retreat* maintains space for another kind of movement in the context of climate change, one that aligns less with top-down interventions that displace people and abandon places in the name of progress than with a whole range of grassroots efforts to democratize and transform space and place—from right-to-the-city movements (Harvey 2012), to those for the right to relocate from places contaminated by industrial pollutants (Auyero and Swistun 2009; Lerner 2006), to stay put in the face of rising rents and gentrification (Newman and Wyly 2006), or to return home after disaster (Bullard and Wright 2009).

To bring together collective movements in the context of climate change under the term *retreat* suggests that the time has come to retreat not only from particular places but also from particular ways of life that are likewise proving unsustainable. The complexity and ambivalence of retreat serves as a reminder that there are no easy solutions and that it is not possible to rebuild forever or to wall ourselves off from the problems we face. *Retreat* is a powerful and evocative word, one that signals a change in direction—something we share the need for as a society even though we do not all live in places that are immediately vulnerable.

References

Active Living Research. 2010. "The Economic Benefits of Open Space, Recreation Facilities, and Walkable Community Design." May. San Diego, CA: Active Living Research. atfiles.org/files/pdf/Economic-Benefits-Active.pdf.

AECOM. 2013. "The Impact of Climate Change and Population Growth on the National Flood Insurance Program through 2100." June. Arlington, VA: AECOM. www.aecom.com/deployedfiles/Internet/News/Sustainability/FEMA%20Climate%20Change%20Report/Climate_Change_Report_AECOM_2013-06-11.pdf.

Auyero, Javier, and Débora Alejandra Swistun. 2009. *Flammable: Environmental Suffering in an Argentine Shantytown*. New York: Oxford University Press.

Ayres, B. Drummond, Jr. 1993. "The Midwest Flooding: What's Left from the Great Flood of '93." *New York Times*, August 10. www.nytimes.com/1993/08/10/us/the-midwest-flooding-what-s-left-from-the-great-flood-of-93.html.

Baldwin, Andrew. 2013. "Racialisation and the Figure of the Climate-Change Migrant." *Environment and Planning A* 45, no. 6: 1474–90.

Bettini, Giovanni. 2014. "Climate Migration as an Adaption Strategy: Desecuritizing Climate-Induced Migration or Making the Unruly Governable?" *Critical Studies on Security* 2, no. 2: 180–95.

Bloomberg, Michael R. 2013. "Mayor Bloomberg Presents the City's Long-Term

Plan to Further Prepare for the Impacts of a Changing Climate." City of New York, Office of the Mayor, June 11. www1.nyc.gov/office-of-the-mayor/news/200 -13/mayor-bloomberg-presents-city-s-long-term-plan-further-prepare-the-impacts -a-changing.

Breunlin, Rachel, and Helen A. Regis. 2006. "Putting the Ninth Ward on the Map: Race, Place, and Transformation in Desire, New Orleans." *American Anthropologist* 108, no. 4: 744–64.

Bronen, Robin. 2011. "Climate-Induced Community Relocations: Creating an Adaptive Governance Framework Based in Human Rights Doctrine." *N.Y.U. Review of Law and Social Change* 35, no. 2: 357–407.

Brown, Patricia Leigh. 1996. "Higher and Drier, Illinois Town Is Reborn." *New York Times*, May 6. www.nytimes.com/1996/05/06/us/higher-and-drier-illinois -town-is-reborn.html.

Building Futures. 2010. "Facing Up to Rising Sea Levels: Retreat? Defend? Attack?" www.buildingfutures.org.uk/projects/building-futures/facing-up.

Bullard, Robert D., and Beverly Wright, eds. 2009. *Race, Place, and Environmental Justice after Hurricane Katrina: Struggles to Reclaim, Rebuild, and Revitalize New Orleans and the Gulf Coast*. Boulder, CO: Westview.

Burkett, Maxine. 2015. "Lessons from Contemporary Resettlement in the South Pacific." *Journal of International Affairs* 68, no. 2: 75–91.

Cater, Franklyn, and Robert Benincasa. 2014. "Map: FEMA Is Buying Out Flood-Prone Homes, but Not Where You Might Expect." NPR, October 20. www.npr.org/sections/thetwo-way/2014/10/20/357611987/map-femas-buying -out-flood-prone-homes-but-not-where-you-might-expect.

Chagnon, Stanley A., ed. 1996. *The Great Flood of 1993: Causes, Impacts, and Responses*. Boulder, CO: Westview.

Conrad, David R., Ben McNitt, and Martha Stout. 1998. "Higher Ground: A Report on Voluntary Property Buyouts in the Nation's Floodplains; A Common Ground Solution Serving People at Risk, Taxpayers, and the Environment." July. Washington, DC: National Wildlife Federation. www.nwf.org/pdf /Water/199807_HigherGround_Report.pdf.

Cooper, J. A. G., and Jeremy Pile. 2014. "The Adaptation-Resistance Spectrum: A Classification of Contemporary Adaptation Approaches to Climate-Related Coastal Change." *Ocean and Coastal Management* 94: 90–98.

Crowell, Mark, et al. 2010. "An Estimate of the U.S. Population Living in 100-Year Coastal Flood Hazard Areas." *Journal of Coastal Research* 26, no. 2: 201–11.

Crump, John. 2012. "Community Leaders Meet to Discuss Relocation in the Face of Climate Change." *Many Strong Voices* (blog), September 12. manystrong voices.org/blogs.aspx?id=5288.

Cuomo, Andrew M. 2013. "Transcript of Governor Andrew M. Cuomo's 2013 State of the State Address." Governor of New York State, January 9. www.governor .ny.gov/news/transcript-governor-andrew-m-cuomos-2013-state-state-address.

de Sherbinin, Alex, et al. 2011. "Preparing for Resettlement Associated with Climate Change." *Science* 334, no. 6055: 456–57.

Displacement Solutions. 2014. "The Peninsula Principles in Action: Climate Change and Displacement in the Autonomous Region of Gunayala, Panama." July. Geneva: Displacement Solutions. displacementsolutions.org/wp-content /uploads/Panama-The-Peninsula-Principles-in-Action.pdf.

Drake, Susannah. 2013. "Transfer Development Rights to Upland Areas." In *Next New York: A Sketchbook for the Future of the City*, by Forum for Urban Design, 32–33. New York: Forum for Urban Design. nextnewyork.org/#/transfer -development-rights-to-upland-areas-susannah-drake.

Edwards, Julia B. 2013. "The Logistics of Climate-Induced Resettlement: Lessons from the Carteret Islands, Papua New Guinea." *Refugee Survey Quarterly* 32, no. 3: 52–78.

Erikson, Kai T. 1976. *Everything in Its Path: Destruction of Community in the Buffalo Creek Flood*. New York: Simon and Schuster.

Farbotko, Carol. 2010. "Wishful Sinking: Disappearing Islands, Climate Refugees, and Cosmopolitan Experimentation." *Asia Pacific Viewpoint* 51, no. 1: 47–60.

———. 2012. Review of *Climate Change and Displacement: Multidisciplinary Perspectives*, edited by Jane McAdam. *Progress in Human Geography* 36, no. 6: 833–36.

Farbotko, Carol, and Heather Lazrus. 2012. "The First Climate Refugees? Contesting Global Narratives of Climate Change in Tuvalu." *Global Environmental Change* 22, no. 2: 382–90.

Felli, Romain. 2013. "Managing Climate Insecurity by Ensuring Continuous Capital Accumulation: 'Climate Refugees' and 'Climate Migrants.'" *New Political Economy* 18, no. 3: 337–63.

FEMA (Federal Emergency Management Agency). 2003. "The 1993 Great Midwest Flood: Voices Ten Years Later." Washington, DC: FEMA. www.fema .gov/media-library/assets/documents/3799.

Ferris, Elizabeth. 2014. "Planned Relocations, Disasters, and Climate Change:

Consolidating Good Practices and Preparing for the Future." Background paper, Sanremo Consultation, Sanremo, Italy, March 12–14. Washington, DC: Brookings Institution. www.brookings.edu/~/media/research/files/papers /2014/03/14-planned-relocations-climate-change/planned-relocations-background -paper-march-2014.pdf.

Fields, Billy. 2009. "From Green Dots to Greenways: Planning in the Age of Climate Change in Post-Katrina New Orleans." *Journal of Urban Design* 14, no. 3: 325–44.

Fullilove, Mindy. 2004. *Root Shock: How Tearing Up City Neighborhoods Hurts America, and What We Can Do about It.* New York: One World / Ballantine Books.

Gerken, James. 2015. "Sea Levels along the Northeast Rose Almost Four Inches in Just Two Years: Study." *Huffington Post*, February 25. www.huffingtonpost .com/2015/02/25/sea-level-rise-northeast_n_6751570.html.

Gregory, Kia. 2013. "Deciding Whether It's Lights Out." *New York Times*, October 25. www.nytimes.com/2013/10/27/nyregion/deciding-whether-its-lights -out.html.

Hanley, Robert. 2000. "Not Waiting for the Next Floyd: A Year Later, Flooded New Jerseyans Take U.S. Buyout." *New York Times*, September 15. www .nytimes.com/2000/09/15/nyregion/not-waiting-for-the-next-floyd-a-year-later -flooded-new-jerseyans-take-us-buyout.html.

Harvey, David. 2012. *Rebel Cities: From the Right to the City to the Urban Revolution.* New York: Verso.

Hunter, Lori M., Jessie K. Luna, and Rachel M. Norton. 2015. "Environmental Dimensions of Migration." *Annual Review of Sociology* 41: 377–97.

IPCC (Intergovernmental Panel on Climate Change). 2014. "Climate Change 2014: Synthesis Report; Contribution of Working Groups I, II, and III to the Fifth Assessment Report of the Intergovernmental Panel on Climate Change." Edited by the Core Writing Team, Rajendra K. Pachauri, and Leo A. Meyer. Geneva: IPCC. www.ipcc.ch/pdf/assessment-report/ar5/syr/SYR_AR5 _FINAL_full.pdf.

Jacob, Klaus H. 2015. "Sea Level Rise, Storm Risk, Denial, and the Future of Coastal Cities." *Bulletin of the Atomic Scientists* 71, no. 5: 40–50.

Kamb, Lewis, and Jim Brunner. 2015. "Year after Oso Disaster, Land-Use Rules Slow to Change." *Seattle Times*, March 21. www.seattletimes.com/seattle -news/even-after-oso-disaster-land-use-rules-slow-to-change.

Kaplan, Thomas. 2013. "Homeowners in Flood Zones Opt to Rebuild, Not Move."

New York Times, April 26. www.nytimes.com/2013/04/27/nyregion/new-yorks
-storm-recovery-plan-gets-federal-approval.html.

Knobloch, Dennis M. 2005. "Moving a Community in the Aftermath of the Great
1993 Midwest Flood." *Journal of Contemporary Water Research and Education* 130, no. 1: 41–45.

Kothari, Uma. 2014. "Political Discourses of Climate Change and Migration:
Resettlement Policies in the Maldives." *Geographical Journal* 180, no. 2:
130–40.

Kuh, Katrina Fischer. 2015. "Agnostic Adaptation." In "A Response to the
IPCC Fifth Assessment," by Sarah Adams-Schoen et al. *Environmental Law
Reporter* 45, no. 1: 10027–48.

Le, Phuong. 2014. "Washington Mudslide Death Toll Rises to Thirty as Officials
Piece Together Lives of Those Lost." *Huffington Post*, April 3. www.huffington
post.com/2014/04/03/washington-mudslide-death-toll_n_5084294.html.

Lerner, Steve. 2006. *Diamond: A Struggle for Environmental Justice in Louisiana's Chemical Corridor.* Cambridge, MA: MIT Press.

Luo, Tianyi, et al. 2015. "World's Fifteen Countries with the Most People
Exposed to River Floods." World Resources Institute (blog), March 5. www
.wri.org/blog/2015/03/world%E2%80%99s-15-countries-most-people-exposed
-river-floods.

Maldonado, Julie Koppel. 2014. "A Multiple Knowledge Approach for Adaptation
to Environmental Change: Lessons Learned from Coastal Louisiana's Tribal
Communities." *Journal of Political Ecology* 21: 61–82.

Marino, Elizabeth. 2015. *Fierce Climate Sacred Ground: An Ethnography of Climate Change in Shishmaref, Alaska.* Fairbanks: University of Alaska Press.

McAdam, Jane. 2015. "Relocation and Resettlement from Colonisation to Climate
Change: The Perennial Solution to 'Danger Zones.'" *London Review of International Law* 3, no. 1: 93–130.

Merriam-Webster. 2015. "Retreat." www.merriam-webster.com/dictionary/retreat
(accessed June 14, 2015).

Mortreux, Colette, and Jon Barnett. 2009. "Climate Change, Migration, and
Adaptation in Funafuti, Tuvalu." *Global Environmental Change* 19, no. 1:
105–12.

New York City Special Initiative for Rebuilding and Resiliency. 2013. "A Stronger, More Resilient New York." June 11. New York: Office of the Mayor. www
.nyc.gov/html/sirr/html/report/report.shtml.

New York State Homes and Community Renewal. 2013. "State of New York

Action Plan for Community Development Block Grant Program Disaster Recovery." April 25. New York: New York State Homes and Community Renewal. www.nyshcr.org/Publications/CDBGActionPlan.pdf.

Newman, Kathe, and Elvin Wyly. 2006. "The Right to Stay Put, Revisited: Gentrification and Resistance to Displacement in New York City." *Urban Studies* 43, no. 1: 23–57.

Online Etymology Dictionary. 2015. "Retreat." www.etymonline.com/index.php?term=retreat (accessed June 14, 2015).

Orlove, Ben. 2005. "Human Adaptation to Climate Change: A Review of Three Historical Cases and Some General Perspectives." *Environmental Science and Policy* 8, no. 6: 589–600.

Podesta, John, and Peter Ogden. 2007. "The Security Implications of Climate Change." *Washington Quarterly* 31, no. 1: 115–38.

Polefka, Shiva. 2013. "Moving out of Harm's Way." Washington, DC: Center for American Progress. cdn.americanprogress.org/wp-content/uploads/2013/12/FloodBuyouts-2.pdf.

Rosenberg, Eli. 2014. "How NYC's Decade of Rezoning Changed the City of Industry." *Curbed*, January 16. ny.curbed.com/archives/2014/01/16/how_nycs_decade_of_rezoning_changed_the_city_of_industry.php.

Rudiak-Gould, Peter. 2013. *Climate Change and Tradition in a Small Island State: The Rising Tide.* New York: Routledge.

Shearer, Christine. 2012. "The Political Ecology of Climate Adaptation Assistance: Alaska Natives, Displacement, and Relocation." *Journal of Political Ecology* 19: 174–83.

Siders, Anne. 2012. "Ninth Circuit Affirms Dismissal in Kivalina v Exxon-Mobil." *Climate Law Blog*, September 26. blogs.law.columbia.edu/climatechange/2012/09/26/9th-circuit-affirms-dismissal-in-kivalina-v-exxonmobil.

———. 2013. "Managed Coastal Retreat: A Legal Handbook on Shifting Development away from Vulnerable Areas." New York: Columbia Law School Center for Climate Change Law. web.law.columbia.edu/sites/default/files/microsites/climate-change/files/Publications/Fellows/ManagedCoastalRetreat_FINAL_Oct%2030.pdf.

Tacoli, Cecilia. 2009. "Crisis or Adaptation? Migration and Climate Change in a Context of High Mobility." *Environment and Urbanization* 21, no. 2: 513–25.

Tobin, Graham A. 1995. "The Levee Love Affair: A Stormy Relationship?" *Water Resources Bulletin* 31, no. 3: 359–67.

Twain, Mark. (1883) 2015. *Life on the Mississippi.* Reprint of the edition pub-

lished by James R. Osgood and Company of Boston, Project Gutenberg. www
.gutenberg.org/files/245/245-h/245-h.htm (accessed June 5, 2015).

Tyrrell, Joe. 2012. "Conflicting Priorities Slow Efforts to Save NJ Towns from
Floods." *NJ Spotlight*, June 28. www.njspotlight.com/stories/12/0627/2027.

USGS (United States Geological Survey). 2015. "Post-Wildfire Landslide Hazards." landslides.usgs.gov/research/wildfire (accessed June 15, 2015).

Warne, Kennedy. 2015. "Will Pacific Island Nations Disappear as Seas Rise?
Maybe Not: Reef Islands Can Grow and Change Shape as Sediments Shift,
Studies Show." *National Geographic*, February 13. news.nationalgeographic
.com/2015/02/150213-tuvalu-sopoaga-kench-kiribati-maldives-cyclone
-marshall-islands.

Watson, Bruce. 1996. "A Town Makes History by Rising to New Heights." *Smithsonian*, June. www.smartcommunities.ncat.org/articles/smithsonian.

Weerasinghe, Sanjula, et al. 2014. "Planned Relocations, Disasters, and Climate
Change: Consolidating Good Practices and Preparing for the Future." Report,
Sanremo Consultation, Sanremo, Italy, March 12–14. Geneva: United Nations
High Commissioner for Refugees. www.unhcr.org/54082cc69.pdf.

Wilkerson, Isabel. 1993. "350 Feet above Flood Ruins, a River Town Plots
Rebirth." *New York Times*, October 31. www.nytimes.com/1993/10/31/us/350
-feet-above-flood-ruins-a-river-town-plots-rebirth.html.

Wilkins, Lee. 1996. "Living with the Flood: Human and Governmental Responses
to Real and Symbolic Risk." In Chagnon, *The Great Flood of 1993*, 218–44.

....

Liz Koslov is a PhD candidate in media, culture, and communication at New York
University. Her dissertation, an ethnographic study of collective retreat on Staten Island
after Hurricane Sandy, examines what mediates the ability to adapt to climate change.

Adaptive Publics:
Building Climate Constituencies
in Bogotá

Austin Zeiderman

In May 2013, the mayor of Bogotá, Gustavo Petro, announced his intention to revise the city's master plan.[1] The Plan de Ordenamiento Territorial, or POT for short, had undergone minor revisions since it was established in 2000, but nothing on the scale Petro had in mind. The city council initially refused to discuss the proposal, leading Petro to pass it by decree. This infuriated his longtime adversaries, who promptly filed suit. A judge sympathetic to the opposition suspended the plan, and over a year later it was still hung up in court. While various dimensions of the proposal provoked discontent, one proved especially incendiary: Petro's desire to reorganize the master plan around climate change. In the words of a critic, though his supporters would agree, the mayor's goal was to make adaptation "the core principle guiding the planning of the city" (Behrentz 2013).

I am grateful to the Robert Wood Johnson Foundation for supporting this collaboration and to LSE Cities for facilitating it. My thanks go especially to Eric Klinenberg for inviting me to participate and for his editorial guidance. Nikhil Anand, Gökçe Günel, Andrew Lakoff, Robert Samet, Jerome Whitington, and two anonymous reviewers generously commented on the article or the ideas within it. An earlier version was presented at the Institute for Public Knowledge, New York University, where I received invaluable feedback. In Bogotá, my gratitude goes to Laura Astrid Ramírez for her research assistance and to Juan David Ojeda and Andrés Romero for allowing me to accompany them in their work. Without Germán Durán's logistical help, Bogotá's *quebradas* would have been inaccessible. Some of the names of those quoted in the text were changed to protect their anonymity, and all translations from the Spanish are my own.
1. The Plan de Ordenamiento Territorial (POT) is the set of rules and regulations that determines much of what can and cannot be done within the municipal boundaries. At least in theory, the POT designates areas in which the city can expand, identifies zones to be protected, dictates the relationship between the city and the surrounding region, controls the use of land by different sectors, and establishes guidelines for public transportation, parks, utilities, schools, and hospitals.

Public Culture 28:2   DOI 10.1215/08992363-3427499

Petro began his political career with the left-wing M-19 and spent two years in prison before participating in the militant group's demobilization. Once elected to the House of Representatives and eventually the Senate, he became a key opponent of the conservative political establishment. Petro made a name for himself as a fiery critic of corruption, persistently condemning the intimate relationship between elected politicians, drug traffickers, paramilitary forces, and other private interests. As mayor of Bogotá from 2012 to 2015, he expanded his political horizons: in his first year in office, he became an outspoken advocate of the imperative to adapt to the changing climate. This represented a sharp change, since until recently Bogotá was considered to be lacking an adaptation strategy.[2] In contrast, Petro's (2012) position was remarkably unambiguous for a political leader: "Global warming is irreversible. The damage is done, and we can't undo it. It may be possible to slow it down. But if we don't do something now, we're all dead."

The mayor's attention to climate change has angered many, especially those who saw Bogotá's future through the lens of capital investment, and his revised master plan was a lightning rod for criticism. Though he did not achieve all of his goals, he clearly raised climate change to the top of the political agenda. Despite a cloud of uncertainty hanging over city hall—Petro's opponents tirelessly sought to remove him from office—his administration took action. The municipal agency that once specialized in disaster prevention and response was given the broad mandate of climate change adaptation. Along with a new title, the District Institute for Risk Management and Climate Change (Instituto Distrital de Gestión de Riesgos y Cambio Climático, or IDIGER) was promoted within the city's governance structure and given a budget commensurate with its elevated importance. This allowed the agency to begin implementing a range of adaptation initiatives: from early warning systems and participatory budgeting workshops to bioengineering experiments and watershed management plans. Based on recent fieldwork within IDIGER, and building upon long-term research in Colombia, this article examines the new technopolitical responsibilities, capabilities, and collectivities accompanying these initiatives. It shows how the imperative to adapt to climate change actively reconfigures both urban infrastructures and politics in Bogotá.[3]

2. For a review of climate change adaptation and mitigation policies before Petro took office, see Lampis 2013a.

3. Over a twenty-month period from August 2008 to April 2010, I conducted both ethnographic and archival research in Bogotá on the politics of security and the government of risk. My specific focus was the field of disaster risk management, in particular a municipal government program working to relocate households from what in the early 2000s had been designated *zonas de alto riesgo*, or "zones of high risk." I returned for follow-up visits of between one and two months in January

In what follows, "adaptive publics" serves as a way to conceptualize the political constituency assembling around the problem of climate change in the city. The article situates Bogotá's recent experiments in urban climate governance within the politics of security in late twentieth-century Colombia, whereby victimhood and vulnerability are both targets of governmental intervention and frames of political recognition. The article shows how these innovative adaptation strategies challenge notions of the "public" associated with the liberal democratic politics of North American and European cities. It argues that the politics of climate change in Bogotá aims to link a redistributive economic agenda to the technical project of adaptation in the service of a broad program of social inclusion. The article's analysis of interventions aimed at building social infrastructure throughout the city's hydrological systems highlights a form of "metrological citizenship," whereby the inclusion of the urban poor within the political community of the city is predicated on (and enacted through) practices of measurement. While urban politics in Latin America have long revolved around popular demands to be counted, this article shows climate change adaptation to be the most recent idiom in which claims to recognition-through-enumeration are being articulated. However, looking ahead to the future, the political uncertainty plaguing Bogotá's adaptation agenda parallels the ecological uncertainty to which it responds.

From Endangered City to Resilient City

Throughout the 2000s, crime and violence in Bogotá dramatically decreased and security steadily improved. Yet there was something paradoxical about this change. Although the general atmosphere is now more relaxed, Bogotá remains, to some degree, in the grip of Colombia's violent past. It continues to be understood as an endangered city—that is, as a threat-ridden place.[4] Though immediate dangers have declined, a more general sense of endangerment remains. Colombia's history of conflict, violence, and instability continues to orient both popular sentiments and political rationalities toward the ultimate pursuit of security. Governmental authority, national unity, and social order are framed primarily in these

---

2012, December 2013, and August 2014. My objective during these visits was to understand how techniques of disaster risk management had since merged with the imperative of climate change adaptation.

4. Further elaboration on the concept of "endangerment" and on the relationship between histories of security in Colombia and contemporary urban politics and government in Bogotá may be found in my book *Endangered City: The Politics of Security and Risk in Bogotá* (Zeiderman, forthcoming).

terms. The persistence of everyday concerns about insecurity has many implications. One is that democracy and security have been fused such that a number of rights and entitlements have been reconfigured by the imperative to protect life from threat (Rojas 2009; Zeiderman 2013; cf. Goldstein 2012). Another is that elected officials across the political spectrum must position themselves within the national security landscape, such that the moderate and radical Left seek to promote their own versions of security in order to prevent the Right from monopolizing this key political terrain (Villaveces Izquierdo 2002; Rivas Gamboa 2007; Llorente and Rivas Gamboa 2004).

The constitutive relationship between politics and security has its parallel in the domain of urban politics and government, in the relationship between the state and the urban citizen, and in the formation of the city as a political community. Over the past two decades, a political consensus—a governing pact—has formed around the imperative to protect vulnerable populations from threats of both environmental and human origin.[5] Risk management is accepted across the political spectrum as a governmental framework that can encompass a range of objectives. Interventions throughout the urban periphery have focused on reducing vulnerability, mitigating risk, and protecting life in order to deal with problems as diverse as informality, criminality, and marginality (Zeiderman 2015). In risk management, a series of mayoral administrations with varying political commitments and different visions for the future of Bogotá have found an ostensibly neutral, "postpolitical" way to address the social and environmental problems of the urban periphery and to build a political constituency among the urban poor. This has enabled left-of-center administrations to articulate a progressive approach to security that insulates them from the conservative establishment's efforts to criminalize, persecute, or annihilate anything resembling radical ideology. The politics of security in late twentieth-century Colombia has set the parameters by which urban life can be governed and lived.

Responses to climate change in contemporary Bogotá emerge out of this history. For it has shaped how progressives like Petro pursue a viable political idiom in which to govern. Like disaster risk management before it, climate change adaptation is a platform from which to address a range of political objectives. Reverberations of longer histories of insecurity are also evidenced by the current emphasis

5. There is academic and political debate in Colombia over the right definition and measurement of "vulnerability." For a review of these debates in the context of climate change adaptation, see Lampis 2013b.

on adaptation over mitigation.[6] Organized around categories of "victimhood" and "vulnerability" and the identification of threat and danger, security and adaptation share a common logic. The concept of "resilience," now firmly established in the lexicon of government in Bogotá, also makes intuitive sense in this context; if "endangerment" indexes the condition of existence whereby threats of human and nonhuman origin are always looming, then "resilience" names the capacity to withstand them or to bounce back after they materialize. There are other reasons why adaptation and resilience are favored over mitigation at the present moment in Bogotá.[7] But this orientation is shaped fundamentally by the horizon of security and risk that structures politics and governs everyday life in Colombia. The endangered city slides easily into the resilient city.

That said, Petro and members of his administration often defied the adaptation/mitigation dichotomy by articulating the dual benefits of any single initiative. In scientific and policy discourses, there is a general shift toward recognizing the positive feedback loops that link mitigation and adaptation, and in Bogotá new urban policies were justified on similar grounds (Bulkeley 2013). Densification of the city center is one example: the goal of cutting emissions from motorized transport by moving people closer to their jobs was linked to the objective of reducing the number of people living in areas vulnerable to environmental hazards on the urban periphery.[8] In climate change, Petro found a political discourse that could unify a broad range of policies and plans for urban development.

In 2013 I returned to Bogotá to find out more about this surge in climate change politics. A number of people I spoke with discussed Petro's concern for the risks associated with extreme weather events and his support for the relocation of families living in "zones of high risk." Around the same time, he issued a decree ordering twelve thousand additional households to be resettled over three years. This was a dramatic increase both in the scale of the relocation program and

6. It is important to note that, before Petro took office, climate change policy on the national and municipal levels was focused almost exclusively on mitigation (Lampis 2013a).

7. Scientific consensus on the irreversibility of climate change is one reason governments cite for emphasizing adaptation over mitigation. Another is the moral argument that mitigation should be the responsibility of the largest contributors to greenhouse gas emissions. Economic justifications also support the decision to spend limited resources on initiatives that will save lives or prevent disasters at home rather than those that will help the planet as a whole. The political expediency of adaptation over mitigation is always an important factor. For a broader review of these issues, see Wamsler 2014.

8. Various mitigation goals have also been announced recently, such as the progressive reduction of carbon emissions by 2020, 2038, and 2050 and the intention to increase the amount of the city's energy supply from alternative sources to 25 percent over the next thirty-five years (*El Tiempo* 2013a).

in the housing subsidy the municipal government would provide to each family (now Col\$45 million, or about US\$16,000). Petro explained to the media that this decision was long overdue. Thanks to inaction on the part of previous administrations, he said, "thousands of families have settled in immitigable high-risk zones. Living in a *zona de alto riesgo* means an increased probability of death due to environmental risks. . . . [Col\$]45 million is the amount required to speed up the process of relocation and completely undo a decade of delay in the city of Bogotá" (*El Tiempo* 2013b). Petro was clearly committed to expanding the resettlement program in the self-built settlements of the urban periphery—to using techniques of risk management to respond to the precarious living conditions of those on the margins of Colombian society. But I wanted to hear directly from those managing this program how they understood city hall's new enthusiasm for their work.

The program director confirmed what I had read in the newspapers: "The budget for relocation has quintupled under Petro! Initially, we were in charge of relocating about three thousand households annually, but this number has now increased to fifteen thousand." I then asked him why he thought Petro found this program so important. He told me: "As you know, the guiding principle behind our work is to save lives. This hasn't changed. Everything else follows that principle. Petro knows that every four months or so we're hit hard by heavy rains and landslides. He's got that clear. He says time and time again that he doesn't want to lose a single life in the *zonas de alto riesgo*." Until this point we were on familiar ground, and I told the director of the resettlement program that each of his predecessors had said the same thing. "But," he retorted, "Petro understands what no previous mayor of Bogotá has: that climate change is absolutely real and serious and that what we're doing here with the resettlement program could become the foundation for a citywide strategy of adaptation."

The municipal government's position could be understood as an expansion of established approaches to governing risk in Bogotá, whereby what began as a relatively limited experiment was becoming a generalized strategy of urban government. But the escalation of interventions in high-risk areas also signals a shift in how these interventions were framed. What was once a way to protect poor and vulnerable populations from regularly occurring disasters had morphed into a citywide response to the potentially dire consequences of climate change. The problem was no longer the relatively constant periodicity of the rainy season in Colombia and its rather predictable effects in the city's steep hillside settlements. Petro recognized that global warming would increase the severity and frequency of extreme weather events, thereby intensifying pressure on urban infrastructure and housing. The compounded uncertainty inherent to climate change meant that existing techniques for governing risk in Bogotá were necessary but insufficient.[9] This required not only expanding the resettlement program throughout the self-built settlements of the urban periphery but also using this program as a guide for how to plan, build, and govern the city as a whole.

Between Victimhood and Vulnerability

I went back to Bogotá in August 2014 to see how the politics of climate change was playing out on the ground. My visit coincided with the Rio+20 Summit, which followed the United Nations Conference on Sustainable Development that had taken place in 2012 in Brazil. For three days, Bogotá would play host to high-level dialogues between scientists, policy makers, and nongovernmental organizations from around the world. The delegates were expected to share their knowledge and experience with climate change adaptation and mitigation. But the international visitors, who traveled from as far as Egypt and China, were allocated a small amount of time relative to their local hosts. Capitalizing on Bogotá's global reputation as a "success story" for its innovations in urban governance, the event's organizers positioned themselves as leaders in the field of climate change adaptation. As such, the summit was an opportunity for Petro's administration to showcase its agenda, perhaps even to mobilize international support for the revised master plan, which remained suspended.

I awoke early to get to the conference venue before the proceedings began. During the taxi ride, I noticed something not terribly unusual in Bogotá: a line of over fifty people waiting single file outside a nondescript office building. Five blocks later I passed a similar scene, except this time the line stretched down the block and around the corner. I asked the taxi driver what was going on. It turned out that each building housed a *centro dignificar* (a literal translation is impossible; *dignificar* means simply "to dignify"). These were centers set up after the 2011 passage of the Law of Victims and Land Restitution to house representatives of the national and local government agencies responsible for protecting the rights of and providing reparations to victims of violence. Since the 1960s, Colombia's armed conflict has caused an inordinate amount of death, destruction, and displacement. Those lined up were hoping to register or advance their claims to land restitution. Waiting to be recognized as beneficiaries of a state that adjudicates

9. There is not space here to comment on the distinction between *risk* and *uncertainty* or on the claim that there has been a global shift from the former to the latter in the domain of urban and environmental governance. These are topics I have analyzed extensively elsewhere.

rights on the basis of victimhood, they were subjects of what Didier Fassin and Richard Rechtman (2009) have called the "empire of trauma."

I arrived at the summit in time to catch the mayor's welcome address. His message was plain: climate change, as he put it, is "killing the poor" (Caracol Radio 2014). Petro's speech was also an opportunity to take shots at the national government's housing policy. President Juan Manuel Santos had recently declared his intention to build one hundred thousand new homes, mostly on the periphery of Colombian cities, and give them away to members of the urban poor who were also victims of armed conflict (a benefit accessed at the centers I had just passed). The national government's housing policy conflicted directly with Petro's plan for densification. The mayor's goal was to build new housing in the city center for people currently living on the edges of the city, especially vulnerable populations at "high risk" for landslide and flooding. What Petro did not emphasize in his opening remarks was the common ground he and the president shared. Despite their disagreement over where, when, and how new housing should be built, both proposals forged a connection between plans for the city and the lives (and deaths) of the urban poor.

This unremarked congruence reveals the degree to which the politics of security sets the conditions of possibility for everything from climate change adaptation to housing policy. But there were two important differences between the competing visions. Santos's plan understood the poor as *actual* victims, while Petro's alternative saw them as *potential* victims (in other words, as vulnerable), and while the former focused on the past threat of *armed conflict*, the latter targeted the future threat of *climate change*. These distinctions notwithstanding, both politicians—despite their professed opposition—emphasized threats to life and positioned the victim and the vulnerable as the unassailable moral subjects of Colombian politics and as the deserving recipient of the state's official beneficence. The categories of victimhood and vulnerability shape the field of governmental intervention for climate change adaptation in Bogotá.

Adaptive Publics

The rest of the Rio+20 Summit was a platform for the Petro administration to showcase its climate change agenda. Details of that agenda are discussed below. The overarching message communicated to the audience was the goal of assembling a political constituency through the imperative of adaptation. Everyone I heard speak onstage, everyone I talked to face-to-face, seemed to agree: the city government's guiding mission, and in particular that of IDIGER, the newly created risk management and climate change agency, was to build a public around the goal of adapting to a decidedly unpredictable and potentially violent urban ecological future.

That said, the term *lo público* did not figure prominently in these discussions. This fact should not be overlooked. Better yet, it should be cause to consider some of the problems involved in focusing the lens of "publics" on climate politics in Bogotá. A critical approach to such concepts is surely necessary when dealing with what postcolonial scholars have shown to be societies perpetually divided between those who belong to the imagined collectives of liberal democracy and those who do not (Chatterjee 2011; Chakrabarty 2000). In Latin American cities, categories like the "citizenry," the "public," and the "commons" have often competed with other notions of the body politic and have long been internally stratified along lines of race, ethnicity, gender, education, language, sexuality, class, and religion (Sabato 2001; de la Cadena 2000). A similar point can be made about the linear privatization narratives central to critiques of neoliberalism and their supposed reversal in a "post-neoliberal" era (Yates and Bakker 2013; Bakker 2013). Again, the category of "public" often occludes more than it reveals.

Caution is even more warranted when we recognize that for those on the margins of civil society, liberal democratic institutions and ideals are often circumscribed by and subordinated to other rationalities of rule (Chatterjee 2004). Many uses of "publics" as an analytical frame begin with a rather taken-for-granted notion of democracy. One example would be science studies scholars, who sometimes commit this error even as they rethink democracy in order to make room for nonhuman things.[10] For they often fail to engage with histories and geographies of "disjunctive democracy," as Teresa Caldeira and James Holston (1999: 692) call it, "where the development of citizenship is never cumulative, linear, or evenly distributed for all citizens, but is always a mix of progressive and regressive elements, uneven, unbalanced, and heterogeneous." Automatically resorting to notions like "publics" limits our ability to think through the politics of climate change in decidedly illiberal or nondemocratic circumstances. This is no doubt the case in places like Colombia, where political liberalism has always been contested

10. Bruce Braun and Sarah Whatmore (2010: xiv) note that science studies scholars could benefit from greater precision in their political analyses: "Citizenship, democracy, representation, and politics are constantly invoked in [the science and technology studies (STS)] literature, [yet] it is not always clear to what these terms refer, which traditions in political theory inform them, or where these traditions might need revision." Noortje Marres's (2012) work is an example of recent attempts to deepen the exchange between STS and political theory by inquiring further into the role of materiality in politics and democracy.

and incomplete. Perhaps the same concern applies even to the "advanced" liberal democracies of Europe and North America.

If not in the idiom of "publics," how was the imperative to create a political constituency around climate change adaptation imagined and discussed in Bogotá? More prevalent were collective categories such as *la gente* (the people), *la comunidad* (the community), *la población* (the population), and *lo popular* (the popular). These categories were often foregrounded in political discourse, pointing to the populist orientation of climate change adaptation in Bogotá. If the "public" was invoked, it was when Petro and other members of his party talked about *la alianza público-popular* (the public-popular alliance). Here the state is synonymous with the "public," and the political constituency it seeks to mobilize is the "popular." It's tempting to understand climate politics in Bogotá as populist—that is, as a politics based on the will of "the people" as the "rightful source of sovereign authority" (Samet 2013: 526).

Nevertheless, there are good reasons to adopt "publics" as an analytical lens while recognizing the potential problems involved in doing so. Central to Petro's adaptation agenda was the goal of addressing a fragmented and somewhat privatized urban infrastructure. For example, the city's water supply, sewage, and drainage systems were run by a public agency, but that agency contracted out much of the construction and management of infrastructure to private firms, which maintained it unevenly across the city. Starting with drainage (or garbage, actually, but that's another story), Petro wanted the city's vital systems brought back fully under public management, or rather into an arrangement whereby the city government partnered with neighborhood associations (here again, the "public-popular alliance" was invoked). Thinking through "publics" highlights the degree to which adaptation in Bogotá aimed to reorient spaces of urban collective life around the common good.

This, in turn, directs our attention to questions of rights and citizenship. On many occasions in Bogotá (and on Twitter), I encountered the slogan *¡El cambio climático es un hecho, adaptación es un derecho!*—"Climate change is a fact, adaptation is a right!" What a few years earlier might have been framed as the "right to the city" was now expressed as the right to a city adapted to future (climate) uncertainty. "Citizenship" (in this securitized form) was the idiom within which the rights and responsibilities of adaptation were discussed.

Another reason to conceptualize the politics of climate change in Bogotá through the lens of "publics" has to do with the boundaries of political discourse in Colombia. As Robert Samet (2013: 526) observes: "The term *populism* has decidedly negative overtones. To call someone a 'populist' is to accuse him or her of pandering to 'the masses,' whipping up anti-institutional fervor, and using social unrest for personal political gain." *Populist* is a damning word in Colombian political discourse regardless of whatever analytical neutrality it may have for social scientists and is automatically how Petro's opponents characterized his initiatives. It immediately draws connections to clientelism, patronage, and corruption, delegitimizing its participants as delusional masses irrationally following a charismatic leader (cf. ibid.). The analytical category of "publics," however, is less freighted.

Finally, "publics" facilitates comparison, not in the sense of searching for equivalence but rather of thinking across difference. Approaching issues of adaptation in Bogotá through this lens offers points of connection with cities elsewhere, both North and South. In the following sections, "adaptive publics" refers to the hybrid collectives assembling around the problem of climate change adaptation in the city and the technical and political projects they are pursuing or that are being pursued in their name. I discuss some of Bogotá's new adaptation initiatives, highlighting the key conceptual and practical issues they present. Each, I argue, contributes to the creation of a new political constituency, an "adaptive public." But the public assembled around the problem of climate change, in contrast to the public of liberal democratic theory, is predicated on threats to life, stratified by categories of vulnerability and victimhood, and summoned by promises of protection.

Hydrosocial Infrastructure

Since Petro was elected mayor, one of city hall's key objectives was to foster "social infrastructure" in the self-built settlements of the urban periphery. Special priority was given to areas adjacent to hydrological features, such as wetlands, canals, rivers, drains, and ravines. The stated goal was to reduce concentrated vulnerability among the urban poor by strengthening their collective capacity to manage the risks associated with climate change. *Participación popular*, or "popular participation," was its guiding principle.

In late 2013, I attended a launch event for the Red Social de Gestión de Riesgo, or the Social Network of Risk Management. The event was held at Bogotá's main convention center and hosted by IDIGER. Present were voluntary associations of all sorts, some of which were Juntas de Acción Comunal (Community Action Councils, the lowest level in the city's governance structure), while others were neighborhood organizations focused on the environment, culture, or security. Over a thousand people took part, most of them inhabitants of the self-built settlements of Bogotá's urban periphery. The day began with a general assembly, in which IDIGER's director, Javier Pava, outlined the program. A series of workshops followed on themes ranging from participatory risk management and community-based vulnerability assessment to grassroots environmental education and bottom-up solid waste reduction. Group leaders spoke about organizing in their neighborhoods, about working in both partnership with and resistance to IDIGER, and about what others could learn from their experiences. These were the self-appointed spokespeople for the adaptive public. Though they did not speak with one voice—in fact, disagreements arose over how best to manage risk and reduce vulnerability—they consistently took a critical but collaborative stance relative to the municipal government's adaptation agenda.

The overarching themes of the event were popular participation and *autogestión* (self-governance). These values sat in tension with the fact that most of the participants (even some children accompanying their parents) were wearing jackets, hats, and bandanas emblazoned with IDIGER's name and logo. However, this did not stop many neighborhood leaders from denouncing the city government's relocation program for households in "zones of high risk" or from proposing their own alternatives. Again, the members of the adaptive public participating in this event positioned themselves as both belonging to and critical of the official adaptation program. Even when disparaging IDIGER, they were applauded vigorously by invited participants and government officials alike. As the day progressed and strategies were shared, contact information exchanged, and potential collaborations discussed, calling this a "social network" of risk management began to make sense. Compared to the heavily technocratic approach to governing risk I had seen a few years before, the objective of creating a political constituency around climate change—an adaptive public—stood out.

The Rio+20 Summit took place nearly a year after this launch. One of my reasons for attending the later event was to see whether anything initiated at the earlier one had materialized. To find out what had become of the "social network" of risk management, I sat down with Priscila, one of the creators of IDIGER's Community Initiatives Program. She explained to me that the program began in 2012 as "a way to work directly with the *comunidades de base* [grass roots], to encourage participation from the bottom up. The objective is *convocarlos a todos* [to bring together, or summon, everyone] to do something about risk." She told me, "Adaptation is impossible without the communities. They can organize themselves and make their own decisions, but they also require close accompaniment to organize in an adequate—that is, an adaptive—manner."

The Community Initiatives team, Priscila said, supports this approach. It works to find synergies between the activities of existing social organizations adjacent to waterways and the broader goal of climate change adaptation. Her team starts by offering training in capacity building before getting into exercises designed to identify threats, risks, and vulnerabilities. An IDIGER representative eventually discloses a budget set aside for the group (somewhere around Col$200 million, or about US$70,000) to conduct remediation works. The organization has to contribute Col$20,000 or about US$7,000, but in-kind donations are encouraged (use of a meeting room, for example). Throughout the process, IDIGER staff members help the group to formulate a plan, allocate the budget, and contract workers—that is, to become an adaptive public.

"What sort of concrete initiatives have been done thus far?" I asked. Priscila responded: "Since climate change is upon us, we have to make sure the streams and canals are in the best possible condition. So we clear out and reforest areas surrounding bodies of water, working with communities so they don't go back and put more solid waste or rubble into the system." She then went on to define infrastructure as a hydrosocial system: "The canal is not just a physical thing—it's also made up of people, and with a bit of support we find that the community organizes around it to monitor the water level, to clear out debris, to work together on these sorts of problems but also on others that have less to do with the canal, with infrastructure, or with adaptation." The maxim "people as infrastructure" (Simone 2004) was implicit.

Priscila was describing a process by which the ideas introduced at the 2013 event—social networks, hydrosocial infrastructures—were put into practice. Implicit was the fact that IDIGER's training sessions communicated to community groups the need to organize around the collective condition of vulnerability and the overarching imperative of climate change adaptation. By doing so, these groups could enter into partnerships with municipal government, making them subcontractors rather than simply beneficiaries. Responsibility was devolved to individuals, households, and communities. Yet it was also through this process that people on the margins of society could belong to a political constituency. In return, they benefited from a novel form of distribution-via-adaptation, whereby public funds designated for climate change responses are put directly in the hands of those at the bottom of the political system and the social order (cf. Ferguson 2015).

Metrological Citizenship

To better understand this process, I accompanied the Community Initiatives team on a number of *recorridos* (tours or rounds). One cold, rainy Saturday morning, we traveled to a low-income neighborhood called Nueva Delhi on Bogotá's far southeastern edge. We were greeted by the head of the local junta, who welcomed everyone with a round of coffee from the corner bakery. The purpose of today's exercise, he announced, was to unite those committed to organizing an intervention in the adjacent *quebrada* (ravine).[11] He introduced Tomás from IDIGER. After providing some background on his agency's coordinating role within the city's climate change adaptation efforts, Tomás got down to business. He went around the room, appointing each person a category of object to measure or count (square meters of stream edges to be reinforced, cubic meters of garbage to be removed, number of trees to be felled). Once duties were assigned, the group took off on foot. We ascended until the sidewalks turned to dirt tracks and the houses gave way to dense thickets of alpine scrub.

We spent the rest of the day—close to eight hours total—traversing the *quebrada* from top to bottom (see fig. 1). Dropping nearly a thousand feet in elevation, the group paused every few minutes to measure an area of erosion, count leaking water supply pipes, or register an illegal dumpsite. The team worked tirelessly to construct a systematic inventory, which they carefully recorded in their Social Network of Risk Management notebooks. The data gathered would eventually be incorporated within the official adaptation strategy for the area and guide the distribution of resources for specific projects.

These acts of measurement can be understood as acts of citizenship, since the collection of data is also the assembly of a certain kind of public. Tomás assigned responsibility to each person to count something, and it was through these counts that they could themselves be counted as members of a political constituency—in this case, one organized around the imperative of climate change adaptation. Expanding upon Andrew Barry's (2011) "metrological regimes," this is an expression of something we might call "metrological citizenship," whereby political recognition and entitlement are predicated on (and enacted through) performances of enumeration, quantification, calculation, and measurement (cf. Appadurai 2012; Townsend 2015). Barry (ibid.: 274) insists that metrology is not antithetical to politics: "Measurement and calculation do not only have antipolitical effects." After all, being counted as a member of the public is one of the basic procedures of liberal democracy. But there is nothing necessarily liberal about the politics of metrology (cf. Schnitzler 2008). The constitutive relationship between recognition and measurement in metrological regimes (whether liberal or

---

11. *Quebradas* are essentially ravines, but due to Bogotá's rainfall patterns they are rarely (if ever) dry. Since the local usage of the term implies a body of water as much as a landform, I will mostly retain the Spanish name.

illiberal, democratic or populist) sets the boundaries of the body politic and shapes struggles over inclusion and exclusion.

Figure 1 A *quebrada* cutting through a hillside on Bogotá's southern periphery. Photograph by the author, 2013

The *Quebrada* and Its Public

During these *recorridos*, new political ecologies came to life. The groups gathered together were united by the *quebrada*. Their participants were not from the same junta or even the same neighborhood, but from opposite sides of the ravine, from different juntas, from a range of community organizations. Stopping frequently, the group grew as it descended, doubling in size by the end of the day. The *quebrada* was assembling a political constituency that differed from any that existed before the exercise began.[12]

Yet hard political work was still to come. Before an intervention could begin, the group had to designate one organization legally responsible. Difficult ques-

12. Recent work in STS is helpful for understanding such processes. In the introduction to a particularly generative set of articles, Marres and Javier Lezaun (2011: 491) outline an approach to the study of politics that "queries how objects, devices, settings and materials, not just subjects, acquire explicit political capacities, capacities that are themselves the object of public struggle and contestation, and serve to enact distinctive ideals of citizenship and participation."

tions arose about how best to organize, socially and politically, in order to execute the project: Who speaks on behalf of the group? Who is in and who is out? Does the *quebrada* itself have any say? If not, who should adjudicate the rights and resources now attached to it? The gender imbalances endemic to neighborhood-level politics in Bogotá were front and center. The junta leaders were predominantly men, whereas the women present mainly represented voluntary, issue-based organizations. When Gladys, the spokeswoman for an environmental group, challenged Don Orlando, the president of the junta, in his bid for the leadership role, she was told: "Why don't you just participate as an individual, as a citizen, as a member of the community adjacent to the *quebrada*? There's no need for your whole organization to get involved." Gladys would not be sidelined. Her questioning persisted until the group agreed that Don Orlando's junta would be named on the paperwork, but all decisions would be made collectively and horizontally.

At the center of these negotiations was the *quebrada*. Due to its unconventional political geography—it conformed neither to an existing jurisdiction nor to an established institutional form—the *quebrada* disrupted customary relations of authority and reconfigured familiar territorial arrangements. Without ascribing autonomous, intentional agency to the nonhuman world, we can nevertheless say that the *quebrada* politicized people and place in new ways. Its ability to assemble a public was enhanced, of course, by the fact that money was involved. But there was an affective dimension to the action the *quebrada* inspired.

In some cities, like Medellín, *quebradas* are spaces of conflict and danger. Separating one neighborhood from another, they have often served as battlefields for warring paramilitary groups or drug cartels. Clashes flare up, shootouts go down, and bodies are dumped there. People have learned to fear and avoid them. Bogotá's *quebradas* have never had quite the same stigma, but people still approach them with caution. They are believed to shelter drug addicts, thieves, the homeless, and others on the urban margins.

But as security in urban Colombia has improved, people in the hillside settlements abutting *quebradas* have begun to see these "no-go zones" in a different light. Feeling safe to traverse them again—albeit always accompanied and only during daylight hours—residents of the urban periphery have started imagining new relationships with the waterways bisecting their neighborhoods. They are also attuned to shifts in governmental priorities and the openings and opportunities that accompany them. And many have firsthand experience with *quebradas*' potential to overflow and cause damage if not properly maintained. As a result, Bogotá's *quebradas* are matters of concern around which a public has begun to assemble.

Although adaptation was actively reconfiguring the politics of the urban periphery, this was not a smooth, fast, or seamless process. After all, when concrete entitlements are at stake, metrological politics often involves contentious debates over who and what should be counted. The adaptive public was heterogeneous and fragmented. There were tensions between competing metrics—disputes over how, when, and where measurements should be done. On one survey, some participants fixated on recently built shacks perched on the edge of the ravine. They marked down the location of the shacks, noted that they were discharging sewage directly into the stream, and began to inquire about their occupants, who were identified as recent arrivals of modest means and unknown pedigrees. Implied was the need to relocate, or perhaps evict, them. A faction within the group objected on the grounds that they should be consulted, not displaced. Ultimately, these households were counted, but as part of the problem rather than as part of the political constituency empowered to solve it. The politics of metrology can assemble a participatory, democratic public; it can also slide in the direction of illiberal, vigilante justice.

Early Warnings

Metrological citizenship was deepened during IDIGER workshops in which residents were trained to participate in the city's early warning systems. These workshops began with a conceptual discussion of the verb *prevenir*, which combines elements of "anticipation," "foresight," "warning," and "prevention." They quickly got technical, covering rainfall meters, stream-flow gauges, river-level sensors, and weather monitoring stations. The immediate objective was to educate neighborhood groups on the city's meteorological instruments and how their measurements are communicated via text message. Using examples, the trainers focused on how to interpret these alerts, when to take them seriously, and how to warn others. The ultimate goal was to strengthen collective resilience by making those living alongside waterways integral to the function of the city's early warning system. At stake were issues of vulnerability and responsibility, both central to the formation of an adaptive public.

Álvaro, an IDIGER technician, instructed the group: "You have to learn how to read these alerts and know when they require serious action on your part. . . . We're not going to tell you that." He gave an example: "You know that it's been raining heavily for the past few weeks and that the *quebradas* are filling up with garbage and rubble, so you can assume that there's a risk of flooding. It could be a quick, heavy rain (five millimeters over ten minutes) or a slow, light one (ten millimeters over three hours), but since you know the *quebrada*, you know both are potentially problematic." After this lesson in vulnerability, Álvaro moved to responsibility: "This is when you have to alert others in the community and start taking preventive measures. We're not always going to be able to come and save you. Every citizen of Bogotá has to do his or her part."

Like the practices of enumeration discussed above, these measurements belong to the domain of political metrology. Fluency in the technical idiom of early warning systems is necessary for establishing one's level of vulnerability and knowing how to act accordingly. These are membership criteria for belonging to the public assembled around climate change adaptation. When rights and responsibilities are predicated on such information, entitlements depend on proficiency in meteorological measurement and monitoring.

Equipped with such data and the ability to interpret it, residents were presumed by IDIGER to share the responsibility of preparing for or responding to emergencies. Incorporating people into the function of the early warning system recognized the importance of intuitive, noncalculative knowledge for the anticipation of threat and the management of infrastructure. But this also enabled them to make demands on or wage critiques of the government, for the data could be used to hold authorities accountable for actual or potential climatic events. Metrological citizenship implies the ability to mobilize measurements in order to call for the construction or repair of infrastructure in preparation for the next storm. It involves pushing to be recognized as vulnerable in order to access the opportunities made available by adaptation.

Much of what we know about enumeration and urban politics comes from commentary on the benefits and dangers of "smart cities" in the global North (Kitchin 2014; Greenfield 2013). Intelligent technologies, infrastructures, and buildings are seen to require a population willing to relinquish ownership of sensitive personal information and to acquiesce to values embedded with the design of the devices themselves. Individual privacy and freedom are opposed to government surveillance and corporate control. When city dwellers enter the equation, it is as "hackers" or "citizen scientists" independently collecting data to demand public or private accountability (Townsend 2015). These analyses sit in tension with the politics of metrology in Latin America, where urbanization and democratization have long depended on popular demands to be counted by the state. For inhabitants of the informal, self-built settlements of the urban periphery, political incorporation has been predicated on enumeration and measurement. By demanding inclusion in official surveys, maps, and plans, and eventually street addresses, bus routes, and land titles, they have fought to join the political community of the city.

In Bogotá, climate change adaptation is the most recent idiom in which claims to recognition-through-enumeration are being articulated. In the 1970s and 1980s, inclusion was sought in terms of development, modernization, legalization, and formalization. In the 1990s and 2000s, imperatives such as security, sustainability, and disaster risk management took center stage. With the rise of climate politics, struggles for urban citizenship now mobilize metrics associated with adaptation, vulnerability, and resilience.

Budgeting Adaptation

With trainings completed, inventories conducted, and agreements signed, the allocation of resources could begin. This is where the data collected during the surveys described above would guide the distribution of funds for specific interventions. To this end, IDIGER organized participatory budgeting workshops in community meeting houses throughout neighborhoods adjacent to *quebradas*. One took place in a single-room storefront with a roll-up metal door. Since the interior space was too limited for the forty-odd attendees, plastic chairs spilled out onto the sidewalk.

Equipped with laptop and projector, two IDIGER representatives, Álvaro and Camila, introduced the exercise. A spreadsheet prepared specially for the workshop was beamed onto a blank white wall. The spreadsheet contained a column of key roles, such as "general coordinator" and "accountant," and one of sample interventions: pruning bushes, fixing stream margins, extracting fallen trees, fixing plumbing leakages, and so on. Further down the list were cultural and educational activities, such as inauguration and closing celebrations, outreach events, and mural painting workdays. Álvaro explained, "The question is: Which risks do you want to invest in mitigating, and which are most likely to cause problems in the future?" He then encouraged the group by predicting that they would be more careful and effective with their intervention than a hired contractor. "This is why city hall wants to work directly with you," he stressed. "If we start from your ideas, adaptation is more likely to succeed. The best way to reduce vulnerability is by building knowledge and then converting it into practice."

Guided by Álvaro, the group traversed the spreadsheet cell by cell. Consulting the inventories recorded during their surveys, they called out measurements of the amount of work needed in each category. Estimated costs for each line item were tallied automatically. As totals accumulated at the bottom of the spreadsheet, the exercise took on a more serious tone. Álvaro then unveiled the overall budget: "We have allocated [Col$]214,790,014 . . . (about [US]$80,000) for this *quebrada*."

The adaptive public assembled now had to decide on the specific interventions on which these funds would be spent.

But the group also had to agree who among them was going to be hired to perform the work. Tensions flared between those who spoke in the name of redistribution and those concerned about issues of accountability. Some argued that everyone present should get a fair share. A few expressed concern about the junta leadership distributing funds in exchange for political loyalty. Others wanted assurances that the work would truly get done. Álvaro finally intervened: "There will be full transparency and zero corruption." Using a term that means "to regulate," "inspect," "control," and "supervise" all at once, he said: "You can be sure that we are going to *fiscalizar.*"

In the truck on the way back to IDIGER headquarters, Álvaro and Camila elaborated this point with candor. They told me that these initiatives, which were still in their infancy, would undoubtedly be barraged by allegations of populism, clientelism, and corruption. Camila foresaw members of the opposition demanding investigations by the Contraloría, Colombia's Government Accountability Office. But, Álvaro stressed, "there are just as many if not more thieves in private companies with government contracts than among the community." "Better to put a small amount of resources in the hands of people whose lives are affected by the problem," he said, "than to put a large sum in the pockets of contractors who have no stake in it whatsoever." Regulating the process was necessary not only to ensure results but also to buffer adaptation initiatives from the opposition's attempts to undo them.

Among those present, an irony was lost on no one: it was Petro himself, as senator, who scrutinized and eventually uncovered extensive corruption in the city government. His predecessor, Samuel Moreno, was ultimately jailed for his illegal relationships and backroom deals with private contractors. By increasing public awareness of corruption, Petro was partly responsible for creating the climate of suspicion that now surrounded his administration. This added another dimension to the politics of vulnerability in Bogotá. Petro's adaptation initiatives were organized around the imperative to protect vulnerable lives but were themselves vulnerable to being overturned by his political opponents.

An Uncertain Future

In recent years, Bogotá has clearly been the site of an innovative climate change adaptation agenda. But that agenda faces serious challenges as it moves forward. The vision for the future of Bogotá expressed by Petro's administration foregrounded adaptation within nearly all sectors of urban governance, planning, and development: from densification of the city center and alternative transportation networks to social housing schemes and water management systems. It did so not only to prepare the city for a future of ecological uncertainty but also to transform the institutional structures that could lead to a more resilient Bogotá. As Daniel, a top-level IDIGER coordinator, explained, "resilience" for Petro was "a new paradigm of governance that strengthens public instructions, reduces the influence of the private sector, and challenges the tyranny of the market." This upends academic critiques that treat resilience and neoliberalism as homologous (Walker and Cooper 2011). Here the logic is reversed: resilience is used to confront neoliberalism and the paradigm of market order on which it rests.[13] Whether Petro succeeded is another matter. What's significant is that he linked resilience to a broad program of social inclusion that sought to bring essential urban services under public management and to redistribute resources to the urban poor (cf. Ferguson 2010). This is not to say that adaptation was simply a means to a different end—a social agenda in an ecological disguise—but that we must pay attention to what it comes to mean and do at specific conjunctures. Indeed, adaptation can be harnessed to a program of socioenvironmental change that refuses such dichotomies altogether.

What this emerging politics of climate change will ultimately mean for Bogotá depends on whether the broader political program underpinning it will have longevity. The adaptation initiatives discussed above may be ephemeral if they are further compromised by legal battles in the courts and political skirmishes with the city council. Will they all disappear into thin air now that Petro's term has come to an end and Enrique Peñalosa, one of his most persistent critics, has taken his place? The political future of these adaptation initiatives is as uncertain as the ecological future they confront (cf. Zeiderman et al. 2015).

The fact that the politics of disaster risk management of the 1990s and 2000s enjoyed relative stability under a handful of different mayors, even some with quite different approaches to governing the city, suggests that something similar could be expected here. This seems all the more likely if we consider the historical conjuncture in which the politics of adaptation has taken root in Bogotá. Whether in the hands of Petro or his successor, climate change will remain a strategic way of governing the urban poor and building a political constituency that responds

13. A similar point has been made by Stephen J. Collier and Andrew Lakoff (2015) in their genealogy of "vital systems security." They, too, suggest an alternative view of the emergence of "resilience" and its political implications relative to neoliberalism.

both to international pressures and priorities and to the politics of security on a national level.

Even if these adaptation initiatives are soon disavowed or discarded, they nevertheless offer an important lesson about contemporary climate politics. In recent years, philosophers and social theorists have declared the arrival of two new periods: the "postpolitical" and the "Anthropocene." Some have argued that they are interconnected and that climate change is one of the key domains in which the postpolitical condition is produced and sustained (Swyngedouw 2010). It is easy to find evidence to support this argument. However, we must not foreclose the possibility that another climate politics is possible—one that identifies strategies for radically reconfiguring the unequal social and economic relations underpinning the ecological crisis confronting the present.[14]

The politics of adaptation in Bogotá has such potential. There are currents of thought within it that seek to respond to the dire consequences of climate change with ambitious and transformative strategies of social transformation—for example, reducing entrenched marginality and widespread economic inequality, strengthening social infrastructure and collective resilience among vulnerable communities, opening spaces of political debate and participation for previously excluded sectors of society, making vital infrastructures work in the interest of people rather than profit, and promoting democratic values of transparency, justice, and accountability. While powerful forces seek to derail these initiatives, what is perhaps more difficult to suppress is the potential for the adaptation agenda in Bogotá to stimulate experiments in climate politics elsewhere.

References

Appadurai, Arjun. 2012. "Why Enumeration Counts." *Environment and Urbanization* 24, no. 2: 639–41.

Bakker, Karen. 2013. "Neoliberal versus Postneoliberal Water: Geographies of Privatization and Resistance." *Annals of the Association of American Geographers* 103, no. 2: 253–60.

Barry, Andrew. 2011. "The Anti-Political Economy." *Economy and Society* 31, no. 2: 37–41.

Behrentz, Eduardo. 2013. "Concejo debe hundir el POT" ("The Council Should Sink the POT"). *El Tiempo*, May 28.

14. Matthew Gandy (2014: 16) has observed that the "politics of inevitability" associated with the rise of neoliberalism today looks less predetermined: "A more polarized landscape is emerging in which some cities have successfully won control back from underperforming private-sector providers and even developed new models of public participation in technological politics."

Braun, Bruce, and Sarah Whatmore. 2010. *Political Matter: Technoscience, Democracy, and Public Life.* Minneapolis: University of Minnesota Press.

Bulkeley, Harriet. 2013. *Cities and Climate Change.* New York: Routledge.

Cadena, Marisol de la. 2000. *Indigenous Mestizos: The Politics of Race and Culture in Cuzco, Peru, 1919–1991.* Durham, NC: Duke University Press.

Caldeira, Teresa P. R., and James Holston. 1999. "Democracy and Violence in Brazil." *Comparative Studies in Society and History* 41, no. 4: 691–729.

Caracol Radio. 2014. "Se instaló e inauguró cumbre Río+20 en Bogotá" ("Rio+20 Summit in Bogotá Set Up and Inaugurated"). caracol.com.co/radio/2014/08/10 /bogota/1407675840_361124.html.

Chakrabarty, Dipesh. 2000. *Provincializing Europe: Postcolonial Thought and Historical Difference.* Princeton, NJ: Princeton University Press.

Chatterjee, Partha. 2004. *The Politics of the Governed: Reflections on Popular Politics in Most of the World.* New York: Columbia University Press.

———. 2011. *Lineages of Political Society: Studies in Postcolonial Democracy.* New York: Columbia University Press.

Collier, Stephen J., and Andrew Lakoff. 2015. "Vital Systems Security: Reflexive Biopolitics and the Government of Emergency." *Theory, Culture and Society* 32, no. 2: 19–51.

El Tiempo. 2013a. "Bogotá fija metas para reducir 20% de emisiones de carbono, al 2020" ("Bogotá Sets Goals to Reduce Carbon Emissions by 20% by the Year 2020"). March 25. www.eltiempo.com/bogota/cambio-climatico-bogota-fija-metas -para-reducir-emisiones-de-carbono/15459235.

———. 2013b. "Petro ordenó reubicar 12 mil familias que viven en zonas de riesgo" ("Petro Ordered the Relocation of 12,000 Families Living in Zones of High Risk"). June 17. www.eltiempo.com/colombia/bogota/ARTICULO -WEB-NEW_NOTA_INTERIOR-12876819.html.

Fassin, Didier, and Richard Rechtman. 2009. *The Empire of Trauma: An Inquiry into the Condition of Victimhood.* Princeton, NJ: Princeton University Press.

Ferguson, James. 2010. "The Uses of Neoliberalism." *Antipode* 41, no. S1: S166–S184.

———. 2015. *Give a Man a Fish: Reflections on the New Politics of Distribution.* Durham, NC: Duke University Press.

Gandy, Matthew. 2014. *The Fabric of Space: Water, Modernity, and the Urban Imagination.* Cambridge, MA: MIT Press.

Goldstein, Daniel M. 2012. *Outlawed: Between Security and Rights in a Bolivian City.* Durham, NC: Duke University Press.

Greenfield, Adam. 2013. *Against the Smart City.* New York: Do Projects.

Kitchin, Rob. 2014. "The Real-Time City? Big Data and Smart Urbanism." *Geo-Journal* 79, no. 1: 1–14.

Lampis, Andrea. 2013a. "Cities and Climate Change Challenges: Institutions, Policy Style, and Adaptation Capacity in Bogotá." *International Journal of Urban and Regional Research* 37, no. 6: 1879–901.

———. 2013b. "Vulnerabilidad y adaptación al cambio climático: Debates acerca del concepto de vulnerabilidad y su medición" ("Vulnerability and Adaptation to Climate Change: Debates Surrounding the Concept of Vulnerability and Its Measurement"). *Revista colombiana de geografía* 22, no. 2: 17–33.

Llorente, María Victoria, and Ángela Rivas Gamboa. 2004. "La caída del crimen en Bogotá: Una década de políticas de seguridad ciudadana" ("The Drop in Crime in Bogotá: A Decade of Policies of Citizen Security"). In *Seguridad ciudadana: Experiencia y desafíos* (*Citizen Security: Experiences and Challenges*), edited by Lucía Dammert, 311–41. Valparaíso: Municipalidad de Valparaíso.

Marres, Noortje. 2012. *Material Participation: Technology, the Environment, and Everyday Publics.* New York: Palgrave Macmillan.

Marres, Noortje, and Javier Lezaun. 2011. "Materials and Devices of the Public: An Introduction." *Economy and Society* 40, no. 4: 489–509.

Petro, Gustavo. 2012. Address at the "Cities and Climate Change" summit, Bogotá, November 19.

Rivas Gamboa, Ángela. 2007. *Gorgeous Monster: The Arts of Governing and Managing Violence in Contemporary Bogotá.* Saarbrücken: VDM Verlag Dr. Müller.

Rojas, Cristina. 2009. "Securing the State and Developing Social Insecurities: The Securitisation of Citizenship in Contemporary Colombia." *Third World Quarterly* 30, no. 1: 227–45.

Sabato, Hilda. 2001. "On Political Citizenship in Nineteenth-Century Latin America." *American Historical Review* 106, no. 4: 1290–1315.

Samet, Robert. 2013. "The Photographer's Body: Populism, Polarization, and the Uses of Victimhood in Venezuela." *American Ethnologist* 40, no. 3: 525–39.

Schnitzler, Antina von. 2008. "Citizenship Prepaid: Water, Calculability, and Techno-Politics in South Africa." *Journal of Southern African Studies* 34, no. 4: 899–917.

Simone, AbdouMaliq. 2004. "People as Infrastructure: Intersecting Fragments in Johannesburg." *Public Culture* 16, no. 3: 407–29.

Swyngedouw, Erik. 2010. "Apocalypse Forever? Post-Political Populism and the Spectre of Climate Change." *Theory, Culture and Society* 27, nos. 2–3: 213–32.

Townsend, Anthony. 2015. "Cities of Data: Examining the New Urban Science." *Public Culture* 27, no. 2: 201–12.

Villaveces Izquierdo, Santiago. 2002. "Seguridad" ("Security"). In *Palabras para desarmar: Una mirada crítica al vocabulario del reconocimiento cultural* (*Words to Disarm: A Critical Look at the Vocabulary of Cultural Recognition*), edited by Margarita Rosa Serje de la Ossa, María Cristina Suaza Vargas, and Roberto Pineda Camacho, 373–77. Bogotá: Ministerio de Cultura, Instituto Colombiano de Antropología e Historia.

Walker, Jeremy, and Melinda Cooper. 2011. "Genealogies of Resilience: From Systems Ecology to the Political Economy of Crisis Adaptation." *Security Dialogue* 42, no. 2: 143–60.

Wamsler, Christine. 2014. *Cities, Disaster Risk, and Adaptation*. New York: Routledge.

Yates, Julian S., and Karen Bakker. 2013. "Debating the 'Post-Neoliberal Turn' in Latin America." *Progress in Human Geography* 38, no. 1: 62–90.

Zeiderman, Austin. 2013. "Living Dangerously: Biopolitics and Urban Citizenship in Bogotá, Colombia." *American Ethnologist* 40, no. 1: 71–87.

———. 2015. "Spaces of Uncertainty: Governing Urban Environmental Hazards." In *Modes of Uncertainty: Anthropological Cases*, edited by Limor Samimian-Darash and Paul Rabinow, 182–200. Chicago: University of Chicago Press.

———. Forthcoming. *Endangered City: The Politics of Security and Risk in Bogotá*. Durham, NC: Duke University Press.

Zeiderman, Austin, Sobia Ahmad Kaker, Jonathan Silver, and Astrid Wood. 2015. "Uncertainty and Urban Life." *Public Culture* 27, no. 2: 281–304.

....

Austin Zeiderman is an assistant professor of urban geography at the London School of Economics and Political Science (LSE) and a research associate at LSE Cities. He holds a PhD in anthropology from Stanford University and specializes in the cultural and political dimensions of cities in Latin America. His forthcoming book, *Endangered City*, focuses an ethnographic and historical lens on the politics of security and risk in Bogotá, Colombia.

Modernist Infrastructure and the Vital Systems Security of Water: Singapore's Pluripotent Climate Futures

Jerome Whitington

The anticipation of climate change as matter for urban planning has precipitated a substantial return to large-scale infrastructure development. Major development banks now routinely frame classical development interventions such as roads, dams, or power grids with a climate change rationale, while developing country governments are busy setting up bureaus to access Green Climate Fund monies, which, in the United Nations climate negotiations, have been promised on a par with current development aid spending (on the order of $100 billion per year by 2020). Urban design has followed suit by taking climate change as a framing logic for frequently large-scale urban infrastructure and construction programs, such as Bangkok's $12 billion flood control spending package or Jakarta's plans for a vast redesign of its coastal seascape (Whitington 2013; Goh 2014). Built in low-lying floodplains, such postcolonial cities have become paradigmatic of a unique historical conjuncture that brings together global capitalism, localized ecological processes such as land subsidence or urban hydrological transformation, and the longer-term trajectories of a climate changing in unpredictable ways. Singapore likewise has been hailed as a model of urban climate change planning due to its long-standing commitment to detailed urban planning and precise (if sometimes authoritarian) implementation (Chua B. H. 2011). Asian processes of urbanization are constituted by what Aihwa Ong (2011: 10) calls heterogeneous "milieus of intervention" including in Singapore's case a powerful demand for reordering nature and a revitalized modernist vision of infrastructural urbanism. But to what extent can an infrastructure predicated on

Public Culture 28:2   DOI 10.1215/08992363-3427511

the wholesale reordering of nature adequately grapple with the uncertain possibilities of a planet warming at a historically unprecedented rate?

In this article, I consider the main features of Singapore's urban water infrastructure adaptation to climate change forecasts in order to stress the unique kind of problem climate change represents to cities and their management. Planning discourses in the early 2000s assumed major climate change impacts were to be expected at some point in the relatively distant future. However, a shift in perspective accompanied major climatic events such as the European heat wave of 2003 or Hurricane Katrina in 2005 and was further confirmed by events as diverse as the grain market crisis in 2007–8; historically unprecedented drought and forest fires in Syria, Texas, Russia, Australia, and California; precipitous Arctic ice loss; catastrophic flooding in Thailand in 2011; and "superstorm" cyclones Sandy and Haiyan. Typhoon Haiyan was historically perhaps the largest directly observed storm to make landfall (Daniell et al. 2013). Increasingly, the de facto scale for contending with environmental disasters is the urban, and city governments have raced to grapple with the shifting timescales in which climate change runs up against long-term localized ecological changes to multiply existing urban vulnerabilities.

By viewing urbanization processes as emergent within a unique historical conjuncture, this research draws on the concept of vital systems security (Collier and Lakoff 2008, 2014) to foreground the modes of governmental reason, including urban planning, which incorporate specific repertoires of knowledge to anticipate and manage unprecedented futures. Urbanization in Singapore or New York is viewed not simply as an outcome of abstract world-historical processes such as capitalism or climate change. On the contrary, as Bruce Braun (2014: 58) argues, urban resilience infrastructure maintains and expands the apparatus of power through which life is imbricated with state and capital. Cities and their attendant planning practices form a site in which planetary-scale ecology and biopolitical processes of urbanization are dynamically and mutually interrelated.

The sections that follow describe the basic role of Singapore's vital systems security commitments for planning and implementing its climate adaptation agenda for water infrastructure. Situating environmental and climate planning within the country's history of postcolonial urbanism and securitization, I show that the three core adaptation infrastructures for water—water supply, coastal protection, and flood drainage—each can only be understood in terms of the island nation's approach to population security taken broadly. For example, since Singapore imports a large proportion of its drinking water from Malaysia, water supply diversification has the clearest military resonances of the three. But coastal protection and flood drainage also demonstrate key features of Singapore's long-standing politics of security and emergency. Vital infrastructures and their attendant political logic of security draw into relief the way emerging threats like climate change are constituted by uncertainty (Mayer 2012; Whitington 2013, 2016). Invoking a biomedical metaphor, I introduce the idea of pluripotential climate futures as a critique of Singapore's deterministic engineering for future climate risks and its centralized control approach to adaptation planning. Singapore's planners assume that forecasted climate changes will be limited to small, quantitative increases in set variables (temperature, rainfall, sea level rise) and, by placing too much confidence in deterministic predictions of what climate change will turn out to be, fail to consider the likelihood of potentially nonlinear or chaotic impacts on vital systems security (see NCCS 2012; MEWR 2014). The error is particularly blatant when the government, economically dependent on fossil fuel industries, has plans for a 60 percent increase in national carbon emissions to at least sixty-five metric tons from 2005 to 2020 (NCCS 2012; my calculation).[1] I am not arguing that climate change will turn out to be catastrophic or that we should be convinced prima facie of worst-case scenarios. Rather, pluripotentiality describes a situation in which prediction and control per se of the burdens of climate change cannot be taken for granted.

Vital Systems Infrastructures

Stephen J. Collier and Andrew Lakoff (2014) identify vital systems security as a "general diagram" of governmental power that emerged in the context of Cold War planning in the twentieth century. To extend and deepen discussions of risk and complex sociotechnical systems (Beck 1992; Barry 2001), they develop the concept of preparedness (Collier and Lakoff 2008; Collier 2008, following Foucault 2007) as a political rationality in which a conventional understanding of risk as social insurance can no longer provide a guide for the governmentalization of society. Among other things, there is a shift in emphasis from the population as the object or target of power toward what they call vital systems such as food, fuel and water supply, critical industries, transportation and communication, health care, and so forth. As a rationality of governmental preparedness, vital systems security emerged in the context of what they call a period of biopolitical urban-

---

1. Emissions in 2005 were 41 metric tons; the 2020 business as usual projection is 77.2 metric tons (NCCS 2012: 35, 43). Industry and nonhousehold building emissions account for 74.1 percent of the projected increase; transportation, which includes domestic maritime and commercial travel, accounts for another 14.5 percent. The government of Singapore consistently represents this as an emissions reduction.

ization (Collier and Lakoff 2014: 21–22; Foucault 2007: 63–65) in which cities' support of biological life increasingly came to be understood as thoroughly dependent on complex webs of industrial production vulnerable to systemic disruption. While drawing on Ulrich Beck's (1992) understanding of risk society, they depart from Beck's arguments about antitechnological or precautionary subpolitics in order to emphasize a biopolitics "designed to assess the vulnerability of vital systems and to ensure their continued functioning" (Collier and Lakoff 2014: 22). Indeed, one early site for development of vital systems security as a mode of operational practice was strategic military planning in the context of World War I. Assessing urban vulnerabilities required an expert rationality of determining which systems were indeed vital—a view of "the national economy as a complex of vital systems" (ibid.: 26) in which specific forms of expertise are developed to determine what infrastructures are critical given extensive systemic interdependency.

The vital infrastructures concept provides a tool for analysis of the political technologies of vulnerability surrounding issues like emerging infectious diseases, climate change, or terrorism (Aradau 2010; Grove 2014; Fearnley 2008). Climate change vulnerabilities, like other hard-to-anticipate emergent threats, can be viewed as a constitutive process of urbanization to the extent that they bear on the built form of the city, whether through direct impacts or strategies of planned preemption. Vital infrastructures, with their clear biopolitical stakes, therefore provide a useful contrast with discussions of vernacular infrastructural materialities (e.g., Graham and McFarlane 2015). Collier and Lakoff would concur with the view of "infrastructure not just as a 'thing,' a 'system,' or an 'output,' but as a complex social and technological *process* that enables—or disables—particular kinds of action in the city" (Graham and McFarlane 2015: 1). However, the issue here is not to describe a "kind of mentality or way of living in the world" (Larkin 2013: 331) in which daily life is structured by built form but rather to describe biopolitical dependency as part of the urbanization process. Major environmental disasters like the Bangkok flooding of 2011 or the devastation of Tacloban, Philippines, by Typhoon Haiyan, demonstrate the "relational infrastructures" described by AbdouMaliq Simone (2015: 20), and their limits, in which people must use "the very bodies of household and kin to hedge against uncertainty." If infrastructure composes a repertoire of possibilities, vital infrastructure is a repertoire for the maintenance of biopolitical life carefully guarded by a security apparatus and yet conspicuously inadequate in certain catastrophic events.

Vulnerabilities are built into cities both for how vulnerability planning systematically modifies the urban landscape and for how urban systems render specific populations vulnerable.[2] Vital systems security involves a different technology of risk analysis than social insurance in the sense of a risk probability distribution. *How* pervasive vulnerabilities are constituted as problems is essential to engaging with those vulnerabilities. Nuclear preparedness was among the first of a series of catastrophe planning situations that required simulation or scenario-based reasoning about potential futures with no analogies in past experience. Emergency preparedness, environmental disaster, critical infrastructure vulnerabilities, and infectious disease preparedness all formed fields of biopolitical power in which "managing uncertain threat[s]" required "the imaginative enactment of a catastrophic future event using scenario-based exercises" (Collier and Lakoff 2014: 26). Put differently, infrastructure design and planning, and its modes of anticipating uncertain futures, provides a diagnosis of the political stakes of climate change itself.

In this article, I place Singapore's climate strategy within the context of the island nation's postcolonial urbanism and its history of perpetual environmental transformation. Singapore's climate policy is orchestrated through the National Climate Change Secretariat and a prominent interministerial committee. The national strategy takes its public form in a comprehensive 2012 document (NCCS 2012) that justifies the limited approach to mitigation combined with interest in high-tech business opportunities and its thoughtful adaptation efforts, including the water infrastructure programs I discuss below. There is, of course, much to be commended in Singapore's typically thorough approach to comprehensive planning, even though its "clean and green" self-image and rhetoric of sustainability is thick and typically subordinate to business interests. The city is also regularly hailed as a model for forward thinking on urban adaptation (e.g., Arnold 2007; Mydans and Arnold 2007), including celebrated comments from the powerful, nationalist leader Lee Kuan Yew on the urgency of urban climate risks. Here I explore the significance of water infrastructure planning through interviews and archival work to assess the extent to which vital systems security provides an adequate framework for understanding the government's continued commitment to modernist infrastructure.[3]

2. On the former, see Grove 2014; Braun 2014; Bulkeley and Broto 2013; Collier 2008. On the latter, see Fjord 2007; Roberts and Parks 2006; Jabareen 2013; Smith 2006; Sims 2009.

3. My analysis is based partly on interviews and discussions with approximately twenty-five people who broadly fall into two groups: those with specific expertise on climate change or environment in Singapore, such as long-term academic observers, biologists, and other environmental scientists, policy experts, and planners, and two prominent diplomats with significant environmental expertise; and those with long-term experience in Singapore and a casual or public nonspecialist

That commitment rests on a distinctive environmental rationality. Victor Savage (1992) has argued that the governmentality of environment in Singapore depends on an ideology (his term) of *environmental possibilism* comprising two main features. First, it entails that Singapore's strategic geopolitical position can never be taken for granted, and hence basic environmental factors must be constantly guaranteed according to a logic of security—water and food supply, disease control, and urban hygiene are constantly invoked within a security framework. Second, environmental possibilism means that environment is wholly open to design transformation, and spatio-environmental relations are the staging ground for a kind of intensive, anthropogenic nature. If nothing can be taken for granted, the corollary is that Singaporeans are expected to accept perpetual transformation of the urban environment with an unsentimental attitude (certain forms of nostalgia are increasingly permitted). Many commentators have noted Singapore's relatively superficial invocation of the logic of green design in which Singapore is construed as a "city in a garden." What that critique misses is that Singapore is willing to wholly remake spatial and environmental features of the island nation regarding design prerogatives.

Yet Singapore's approach to climate change planning fails to assess what can be understood as a third feature of environmental possibilism, what I call pluripotent climate futures. While predictions for long-term changes at the global scale are relatively stable (but still uncertain), there is an essentially chaotic element in forecasting, especially for such a small area as Singapore. Forecasting cannot take into consideration nonlinear climatic changes or compounded sociopolitical and economic changes. Nonetheless, the Singapore government views the potential threat of climate change in terms of a gradual transformation of base climate variables (temperature, rainfall, etc.), while planning for a large increase in national carbon emissions. In effect, it is far too confident that it knows what climate change holds in store, with the result of limiting its apprehension of the future to a small number of constrained variables. Singapore's approach to climate change planning can be adequately understood in terms of the vital systems security concept. However, its commitment to an artificial remaking of environment through a rationality of control fails to appreciate the pluripotency of climate change futures, evident in its reliance on forecasting rather than a more expansive assessment of climate risk.

interest in environmental issues. The research also benefited from site visits and official tours, opportunistic conversations with Singaporeans, and four years teaching climate change to Singaporean undergraduates.

Singapore's climate change planning can be tied to its long-term commitment to urban planning only in the historical context of decolonization and Cold War militarization. The country is often referred to as a city-state for the fact that its small land area is mostly urbanized, and its form of planned urbanization stretching back to the immediate postwar 1950s has involved envisioning a cityscape that encompasses the whole island (B. Wong 2004). Its geographical status as an island—which in other respects is comparable to, say, Manhattan—is significant primarily because its political independence compounds a sense of national exceptionalism that routinely denies the regional context. Chua Beng Huat (2011) has argued that Singapore should be understood as an island nation rather than a city-state because its urban policy cannot really be separated from national policy and political exigency. A constant refrain in national political address following the separation of Singapore from postcolonial Malaysia in 1965 has been the strict scarcity of territory and economic hinterland and hence the necessity of technologically clever ways of maximizing available territory. Its aggressive social policies were linked to the anticommunist emergency politics of the 1950s and 1960s. Water supply and coastal protection have been at the center of Singapore's security apparatus since the water supply was cut during the Japanese invasion of World War II, leaving a stark memory of the island's vulnerability. This geopolitical dynamism led to postindependence Singapore's aggressive water supply, coastal protection, and flooding drainage policies.

Geographers Rodolphe de Koninck, Juliet Drolet, and Marc Girard (2008) call this unique mode of territoriality Singapore's perpetual territorial transformation. The willingness to manipulate any available spatial option has led to visually spectacular architecture such as the massive enclosed biospheric glass domes and ecologically motivated, apocalyptic "supertrees" that are an iconic signature of Singapore's central downtown waterfront (see Myers 2015). Far more strategically relevant has been the expansion of some 25 percent of the total national land area through infilling of the coastal zones through a bona fide process of geoengineering national territory (Koninck, Drolet, and Girard 2008: plate 4; P. Wong 2005, 2010) (fig. 1). Desalinization, recycling of used water, and the near optimal control of the island's watersheds have come to minimize the need for imported water. To add one last example, the country's use of underground and even underwater space is highly sophisticated (Amir 2015), taking to an extreme what Braun (2000) calls the vertical production of territory. While observers have both lauded and criticized the sustainability effectiveness of Singapore's visually spectacular

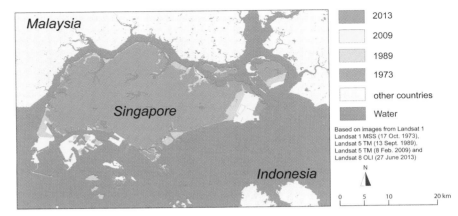

Figure 1 Infilling of coastal zones. In 1991 the elevation of new land was set to 1.25 meters above the highest-recorded high tide. In 2011 it was raised to 2.25 meters for new construction. Source: Peduzzi, Pascal. 2014 "Sand, Rarer Than One Thinks," *Environmental Development* 11, 208–218

"green" design features, such debates are overshadowed by the spirit of pervasive manipulation and reconstitution of nature.

In conjunction with terraforming and the production of underground space, Singapore's commitment to a "clean and green" urban environment since the 1970s cannot be dismissed out of hand. The early impetus to clean up Singapore came directly from colonial-era concerns with hygiene and focused on crowded, dilapidated housing concentrated in the city center, Chinatown, and the shipping quays. Much of the early effort centered on cleaning waterways in part through prohibiting raising of livestock, especially pigs. Cecilia Tortajada, Yugal Joshi, and Asit K. Biswas, among others, have described the process of public health education and enforcement that has been folded into both the formal education system and a form of neighborhood-based environmental governmentality focused on awareness building and community involvement. The Public Utilities Board (2011: 9) discusses "the ongoing Active, Beautiful, Clean Waters (ABC Waters) Programme, which tries to bring water closer to people's hearts by making water part of their lifestyle." These programs "covered a wide range of issues including pollution, food hygiene, infectious diseases, waste management, sanitation, anti-spitting, anti-littering, river clean-up, and global environmental issues" (Tortajada, Joshi, and Biswas 2013: 144). Disease vector control is one notable case, since mosquito-borne dengue fever remains a problem on the island and the dengue season is accompanied by mandatory policing by the National Environment Agency

(NEA) including entering people's homes in affected areas. When a dengue outbreak occurred in my neighborhood in 2014, NEA officials politely but firmly entered my apartment to inspect for any possible mosquito habitat and asked me to store upside down an empty vase under my kitchen sink to avoid collecting water.

The cityscape is remarkably green, and Singapore is promoted as a city in a garden. Many of the main roads are lined with trees whose broad branches arch over the roadway. Major parts of the island's interior remain forested, and other large areas also remain covered with plants. Whether any of this has any ecological significance is a completely different question. Something like 70 percent of the coastline is artificial—whether infilled land or protected sea barrier—and all the major estuaries have been converted into freshwater reservoirs as part of the water supply infrastructure. Singapore is green in the sense promoted by celebrated Singaporean architect Tay Kheng Soon, whose approach to what has become a dominant theme in large-scale building design incorporates all kinds of green elements. For Tay the tropical city involved an architectural critique of colonial urban forms. According to critic Bobby Wong (2004: 166), Tay's premise was that "when urban schemes or buildings incorporate [his] recommendations—including rainwater collection and recycling, vertical landscaping, aesthetics of shadow rather than platonic volume and plane, connectivity, synergistic mix of uses and social choreography and more—the designs will produce tropicality." Air-conditioning is a powerful metaphor and perhaps the predominant middle-class vernacular relation to climate. Lee Kuan Yew famously articulated a climatological theory of national development in terms of air-conditioning. "Before air-con, mental concentration and with it the quality of work deteriorated as the day got hotter and more humid. . . . Historically, advanced civilisations have flourished in the cooler climates. Now, lifestyles have become comparable to those in temperate zones and civilisation in the tropical zones need no longer lag behind" (Lee quoted in George 2000: 14). In connection to mosquitos and the periodic burning of peat forests for Indonesian palm oil plantations that inundates the city with smoke, it's not uncommon to hear, as in this comment from a young Singaporean, that "Singapore needs to build a huge air-conditioned dome around the country." In Singapore's postcolonial urbanism, Savage (1992) identifies this array of commitments to an artificial nature as an ideology of pragmatic environmental possibilism. This possibilism is double-edged. First, in the broader geopolitical environment, any threat is possible, and the nation and all of its citizens must maintain constant vigilance. Second, no possibilities are foreclosed, and anything remains open, at least hypothetically, so that natural relations become the occasion for futuristic manipulation.

Vigilance: Public Water Supply

Large infrastructure dominates the national imagination. As one informant put it, "The Singaporean view of nature is very infrastructural"—by which she meant that natural relations are heavily managed, capital-intensive, and allowed only in controlled spaces. Another, a lifetime environmental educator in the Singapore public school system, called attention to the shift from a technocratic infrastructural approach to a more "human-centered" approach, which, however, "is unable to let go of the engineering fetish" even though there has emerged a host of thin participatory attempts to get citizens involved in conservation efforts. Others routinely brought up the emphasis on "brown" environmental issues—hygiene, pollution, water and air quality—at the expense of "green" ecology or conservation efforts. This highly public emphasis on infrastructure as a practice of state, as Brian Larkin (2013: 336) has argued, forms a powerful critique of the idea that infrastructure only becomes visible when it breaks down. Nowhere is the emphasis on the visibility of vital infrastructures more apparent than in the context of public water supply, which has remained in prominent public view since the island's political separation from Malaysia in the immediate postcolonial period. "Water security has been a *permanent* consideration of the city-state's leadership," argue Tortajada, Joshi, and Biswas (2013: 18; my emphasis). The political narrative of infrastructure has increasingly become linked with climate adaptation.

Currently, seventeen major reservoirs capture runoff from some of the island's land area. The rapid expansion in water storage capacity since 1965 was the primary development approach to securing relative independence from imported water resources from Malaysia, which continued to be a diplomatic and security concern as late as 2011. "Due to water shortages the government was very nervous about water in the Mahathir years," one seasoned observer of the country's environmental politics told me, referring to the sometimes confrontational Malaysian prime minister Mahathir Mohamad. "The reservoirs had nothing to do with climate change." Most of the reservoirs are dammed former coastal tidal estuaries, which, like the infilled land, essentially eliminate native ecological habitat. One government marine biologist hesitated when I asked him if coastal infilling simply eliminated the existing ecology and replied, carefully, that species colonization of new aquatic habitats was very rapid. Another, also cautious, described the demise of a large mangrove forest when a major brackish estuary was converted to a freshwater reservoir.

Historically, such territorial and littoral appropriation of space provided the main expansion of domestic water supply until technological advances pushed forward water recycling and desalination in the 2000s. Nonetheless, interest in water recycling and desalination began as early as the 1972 Water Master Plan (Tortajada, Joshi, and Biswas 2013: 20). Of these "four national taps"—imported water, captured local rainfall, desalination, and recycled water—the last two are now described as "climate independent" for adaptation planning purposes. In this context, the security concerns of the independent and vulnerable nation have become translated into the language of resilience, and planners readily acknowledge that the pioneer efforts of the 1970s and 1980s provided continuity of policy focus now reframed as climate resilience.

Efforts to conform water supply technology to the requirements of Singapore's ecological situation have pushed the limits of its territorial and technological imagination, and water recycling efforts must have seemed pretty futuristic when the first pilot plant was built in 1974. Early efforts were curtailed due to cost, although the technologies worked, and were not revitalized until the late 1990s with dual-membrane reverse osmosis and ultraviolet disinfection technologies. Although predominantly used for industrial water demand, branded NEWater has been accepted cautiously by the public and has been the source of major marketing investment. While directly potable if necessary, recycled water is commonly mixed into existing reservoirs and then treated again before entering the domestic water supply. With four processing plants, the country currently has installed capacity of 60 million gallons per day, with plans to meet 55 percent of water demand by the expiration of the country's water treaty with Malaysia in 2061 (Public Utilities Board 2014b). "The political conviction is for water self-sufficiency . . . not strictly for security but also for general diplomacy," noted one academic observer. That mind-set is very much part of the "common sense," in Antonio Gramsci's language, of infrastructure in the context of the country's logic of vital systems security.

Desalination of seawater is the other "climate-independent tap." It provides 25 percent of public water supply and has been the source of government-subsidized, private industry development and test bedding for new technologies. The Singapore Economic Development Board considers the country to be a "global hydro-hub" for major investment partnerships including sustained research centers developed with local universities and a substantial number of corporate partners including Siemens and General Electric (SEDB 2011; NEWRI 2014).[4] Water technology investment has been the basis of the public-private partnership with Hyflux

4. Government research and development investment in water technology was some S$470 million from 2006 to 2012 (Balakrishnan 2012).

to build two desalination plants using "design-build-own-operate" construction and financing arrangements. Hyflux, a major Singaporean water technologies firm, experienced a meteoric annual growth rate of 30 percent from 2001 to 2009, and its CEO was a nominated minister of Parliament during that time (*Wikipedia* 2015; Hyflux 2009). Ong (2005) theorizes this characteristic approach to strategic state investment as the creation of "ecologies of expertise." It is safe to say that Singapore refuses to take water supply for granted as a matter of public investment and private-sector capabilities development.

The very idea of the island as a sealed system demonstrates why vital systems security can be described as a rationality or logic of rule. Nowhere is that clearer than in the context of national water supply. At the heart of the conceptualization of these "four national taps" is the aspiration that "in Singapore, the complete water cycle is managed" (Symenouh 2013: 15). The idea is that the water system, augmented by recycling, can be understood as a semiclosed loop in which the key variable is the total capacity of the whole system at any given time, rather than simply the availability of stored freshwater (fig. 2). The Public Utilities Board manages freshwater, storm drainage, and used water as an integrated whole. The water in domestic sewage pipes and toilet bowl tanks is effectively part of the usable water capacity of the island. To this end, one of the main achievements of water supply infrastructure is the massive deep tunnel sewage system that supplies the water reclamation plants. The current phase of this project, operational in 2009, comprises forty-eight kilometers of tunnels up to six meters in diameter, thus forming a substantial volume of stored capacity.

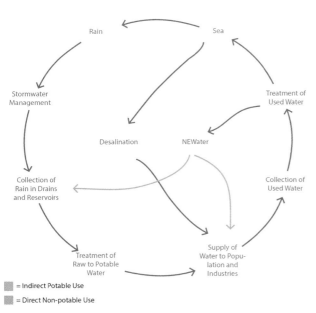

= Indirect Potable Use

= Direct Non-potable Use

Figure 2 Singapore's water system as a semiclosed loop. Note that the two "climate-independent taps" are at the symbolic center of the circle meant to bypass rainfall and storm water management as natural variables. Illustration by the author based on Public Utilities Board 2014a.

Even while recycled water has needed to be supplemented by a major marketing campaign, the express visibility of vital security infrastructure is nowhere more apparent than with the Marina Barrage. The sophisticated tidal gate system forms a reservoir in the heart of the financial district to capture catchment runoff from approximately one-sixth the area of the island; it is routinely mentioned in connection with climate change adaptation. The barrage spans the 350-meter-wide mouth of the Singapore and Kallang Rivers, which were conjoined through land infilling that extended the shoreline several kilometers, to form a 240-hectare (600-acre) bay. The barrage incorporates variable control gates and high-capacity water pumps designed to regulate the balance between storm drainage and tidal inundation. The reservoir level is kept below the regular high tide to allow for more rapid drainage of storm water, which is then pumped into the sea. As the sea level rises over the coming decades, the multifunction design maintains freshwater supply, more rapid drainage for monsoon flooding, and protection from higher sea levels.

The prominent design of the barrage at the heart of the city also integrates urban environmental concerns, in aesthetic, recreational, commercial, and functional registers, that echo the postcolonial emphasis on martial security. Historian Lai Chee Kien has argued that Marina Bay itself mimics the colonial form of the *padang*, which was central to British displays of military power. The *padang* was a flat, open parade ground amid central administrative buildings that served as "an exemplary space for surveillance, military drill display and governance" (Lai quoted in Koh 2014: 166). Lai has argued that Marina Bay, which forms the stage for fighter jet flyovers and military parachute drops for annual displays of national patriotism, now serves as the country's most prominent "padang"—a liquid *padang* that unites Singapore's monumental prestige architecture, the extensive infilled land surrounding the reservoir, and the deliberate prominence of the country's water infrastructure (cited in ibid.: 183).

The routine invocation of Singapore's military vulnerability due to constrained water supply demonstrates the subtext of vigilance and emergency central to the country's modernist infrastructure-oriented urbanization. Whereas the government enjoys effective hegemony regarding security discourses, the emphasis on infrastructure speaks to the heterogeneous, intimately managed sociotechnical processes through which population security is achieved and maintained. However, as the government makes clear, climate change adaptation planning is not the primary motivation for water infrastructure development. Rather, existing postcolonial concern over water security has meant that climate-related vulnerabilities were easily folded into existing water policy when the former were taken into consideration in the late 2000s. Climate change has become an explicit part of vital systems logic of population security.

Emergency: Coastal Protection

The clearest specific climate adaptation policy change has been a legal requirement that the platform level of newly infilled land shall be set to a height of 2.25 meters above the highest tide observed before 1991. The requirement is unambiguously due to concern about climate change. It is also costly, since Malaysia and Indonesia have both banned export of sand on the grounds that it is an export of national territory itself (Comaroff 2014). However, most of the coastal areas designated for reclamation have already been developed, and the rule is not retroactive. Beyond the immediate implications of a higher platform level, the new rule calls attention to the vast concentration of shipping, refinery, petrochemical, and luxury development on artificial coastal land. Coastal protection implies a distinction between population vulnerability and the vulnerability of industrial infrastructure, and the radical transformation of much of Singapore's coastal zone has led to a rationalization of space dividing the relatively protected urban population from global economic infrastructure that may or may not remain vulnerable. That historical process of coastal resettlement hinges on the anticommunist emergency of the immediate postwar period.

In the late colonial period, many of the largest of numerous small islands surrounding the southern coast of Singapore were settled by largely Malay-speaking Muslim fishing communities. With a population of over three thousand and a light police presence, the islanders formed a new political constituency when the British decentralized control to the city-state prior to decolonization. There was an active effort to develop the islands with government-sponsored improvements. In a human interest article on government-led development in 1961 a journalist wrote that "the future of the Southern Islands is bright for the government is doing everything possible to eradicate the peoples' problems and make the places productive" (Richards 1961: 6). This effort to improve was made against the backdrop of a socially complex border geography. Mobile fishing communities worked among some fifty-odd offshore islands, while closer to shore extremely busy ports relied on labor-intensive portage. "Floating hawkers" serviced shipping boats with supplies but posed a threat of theft and pilfering. Just across one of the busiest shipping passages in the world, the Riau Islands in Indonesia were considered dangerous sources of piracy, kidnapping, training of armed insurgents, and smuggling.

By the early 1970s, water pollution became a serious concern, and the highly polluted Singapore River was singled out as a target for remaking space. Nearby islands had been slated for acquisition for shipping, oil refining, and petrochemicals, while farther out the military appropriated islands for demolition training and live firing exercises, and specific islands were earmarked for recreation development. Resettlement proceeded apace, including dismantling mosques and schools, while numerous islands were combined or obliterated through land infilling in a process of wholesale rationalization of space. Jack Meng-Tat Chia (2009) shows the cultural history for one of these islands, now owned by Sentosa Resorts and still home to two important temples that receive large numbers of annual pilgrims every October even though the island is basically depopulated. Semakau Island, once home to over eighteen hundred people, was conjoined with Sakeng Island to form Singapore's incinerator waste landfill, while numerous smaller islands became subsumed by the infilling process for shipping, oil refining and petrochemical joint ventures. Once rocky shoals, brackish estuaries, and mangroves, the depopulated military and industrial coastal zone is now some 70 percent artificial coastline.

Depopulation of the coastal landscape occurred within the context of resettlement as perhaps the central feature of Singapore's program for population control and social entitlement. Housing has been the centerpiece of the city's emphasis on total planning, social engineering, and surveillance, with some 80 percent of the population living in government high-rises that also form the backbone of their retirement assets with an ownership ratio of some 94 percent. Gregory Clancey (2004: 38) describes the late colonial anticommunist emergency, which forms a critical part of Singapore's national political imagination, as "one of the greatest forced re-housings in the history of modern colonialism, or for that matter in the history of East and Southeast Asia." He argues that public housing was an essential expression of anticommunist counterinsurgency, which then became a "permanent emergency" for the purpose of population control. For Chua Beng Huat (1991), housing was both a radical reorganization of society and a real enfranchisement of Singaporeans vis-à-vis the state. Resettlement of the coastal population into high-rise government apartments has been part of a larger popular nostalgia and cultural memory of old Singapore. Regardless, it is clear that population vulnerability to climate-related disasters was already sharply reduced through the complete remaking of the island's coastal zones.

Infrastructure vulnerability in the coastal zones is a more complex matter due to what appears to be a strict separation between publicly accessible civilian urban planning and rigorously maintained secrecy on military matters for these zones. Climate adaptation planning likely incorporates a parallel but invisible military chain of command. Both chairs of the Inter-Ministerial Committee on Climate Change (IMCCC), current deputy prime minister Teo Chee Hean and previous deputy prime minister Shunmugam Jayakumar, were concurrently coordinating minister of defense, and Teo was formerly minister of defense. Singapore promotes climate governance through what it calls a "whole of government approach," but, aside from the position of chair of the IMCCC, there is no public documentation of any military involvement in climate adaptation planning. For the military and industrial coastal zones, one can only speculate on how climate adaptation planning is approached.

More problematically, official technical assessments of Singapore's climate vulnerability are off-limits, including any discussion of methodologies used. I quickly learned that the Official Secrets Act made inaccessible any more detailed, off-the-record information as contracted researchers and city planners declined requests for interviews. (Even if I accessed such information, I could be prosecuted for making it public.) Disaster response or management is not taken into consideration by the working group on climate change adaptation, confirming a construction of risk that discounts out of hand the possibility of tropical cyclones. It is widely believed that Singapore is not especially exposed to deadly natural disasters (G. Chua 2013). The meteorological argument is that typhoons are unable to form so close to the equator due to the lack of a Coriolis effect. It may be true that the island has never experienced a typhoon in recorded history, but in 2001 Typhoon Vamei made landfall about sixty kilometers north along the Malay Peninsula. Vamei was in fact the first-ever-observed typhoon within 1.5 degrees of the equator and is considered a 1-in-400-year event (Chang and Wong 2008). In Singapore the peak storm surge was approximately twenty centimeters (Tay 2010: 35). Serene Hui Xin Tay further shows that only 13.5 years of extreme wind data were available and demonstrates that storm surges could reach 1.6 meters for a small cyclone (ibid.: 69). Kumaran Raju et al. (2012) have shown modest coastal risks due to sea level rise on infilled land. Other potential vulnerabilities like regional migration of climate refugees or political or financial instability are not considered, while food security and infectious disease risks are given brief mention. Any public discussion of Singapore's risks is filtered through the careful communications mechanism of the National Climate Change Secretariat, which, with minor exceptions, only raises issues related to slow linear changes in rainfall, sea level rise, and temperature. As one interviewee put it, there is no need to press the panic button if climate change is seen as a long-term issue, especially if it risks scaring investors.

Given the importance of shipping, petrochemical, and refinery infrastructure central to Singapore's status as a global trade hub, it perhaps comes as no surprise that the discursive construction of risk makes it seem like the small island can easily adapt to modest ecological changes. In the meantime, prominent Singaporean economists argue that based on cost-benefit analysis it makes no sense for Singapore to go to much effort to reduce its emissions. The national policy advertises an 11–16 percent decrease in carbon intensity by 2020, while real greenhouse gas emissions will increase by at least 60 percent, to sixty-five metric tons, by 2020. Given the extreme exposure of regional cities Jakarta, Bangkok, Manila, and Yangon, not to mention smaller centers that make up a highly urbanized region, the biopolitical implication of protecting Singapore's national population at others' expense becomes clear. The historical depopulation of the coast through a process of dispossession was central to the politics of emergency through which the postcolonial city became pivotal to global capital. The apparent split between a biopolitics of population and the preservation of military and industrial interests in the coastal zone draws into relief Singapore's politically conservative approach to emissions reductions and vulnerability assessment.

Prediction and Control: Monsoon Flooding

Monsoon flash flooding has been a constant feature of postcolonial urban management and was routinely at stake in the politics of resettlement during the 1950s–1970s. Flash flooding is the most publicly visible climate change impact and an issue where the government is especially responsive to public opinion. Climatically, the city is subject to intensely focused tropical downpours and, more rarely, extended, multiday rain events that dump a tremendous volume of water in a very short period of time. Concern with drainage goes back to antimalaria campaigns of the 1910s but was especially prominent during resettlement beginning in the 1950s. A prominent flooding event in 2011 captivated the public imagination and is routinely brought up in discussions of climate change. A major downpour swamped the city's most famous shopping district, rapidly flooding malls and carparks and provoking a public outcry over inadequate government control over the situation. It demonstrated that Singapore's technocratic government is not allowed to fail without being subject to intense public criticism—the flip side of which, of course, is that it can't be criticized on more fundamental grounds. Urban monsoon flooding best exemplifies the rationality of obsessive prediction and control in which the only response to a changing nature is more technology.

As with coastal vulnerability and public water supply, adaptation needs for flooding are nonetheless minimal due to long-term investment in public infrastructure. Newspaper archives show that public demand for drainage infrastructure has been high since at least the 1950s, with major investments closely paralleling the

431

massive push for decentralized public housing. Potong Pasir was one notable area, first home to sand quarrying activities, that became settled by Cantonese farmers before being converted to government-built housing blocks in the early 1980s. Another was Bedok, a major colonial resettlement area that was hit with a series of major floods in 1954, including one that brought almost thirteen inches (thirty-two centimeters) of rain over twenty-four hours. While colonial and postcolonial resettlement proceeded apace, drainage became a key locus of permissible public complaint—effectively a backstory to the social entitlement and population control strategy. After the December 1954 floods, the "Bedok problem" obliged the colonial government to promise rehabilitation while denying any possibility of compensation for flood victims, even while it was acknowledged that they were moved "under protest," and the colonial secretary promised "vigorous action" on drainage (*Singapore Free Press* 1954; *Straits Times* 1954). Following a major 1978 flood, often hailed as the largest in Singapore's records at 512 millimeters (20 inches) in twenty-four hours, Potong Pasir was quickly subject to wholesale redevelopment under the directorship of the minister of defense, even while the offending river was subject to millions in investment to dredge and canalize it. But Singapore's rivers were offending not only for flooding's financial damages, occasional loss of life, and inconvenience. In news stories from the late 1970s, Singapore's rivers are the source of tales of crime, pollution, unidentified corpses, waste from pig farms, derelict lighter boats, and industrial debris—already explicitly contrasted with the city's "clean and green" urban landscape (A. Wong 1979).

Major public debates about drainage have persisted, and there are clearly periodic flooding events that exceed current drainage capacity. The average number of days when rainfall exceeds seventy millimeters per hour has doubled since 1980 (NCCS 2012: 76). The response has been a combination of engineering and sophisticated "nowcasting" of rainfall events with text message and e-mail warnings. In public debates, officials are at pains to show both that they are doing whatever is feasible and that there are limits to what can be done to drain such torrential downpours especially during high-tide events. Drainage canals have been equipped with gates to block the tides, while the Marina Barrage can pump storm water to the sea at a capacity of 280 cubic meters per second (billed as the "world's largest pumps"; Channel NewsAsia 2007). Singapore's integrated drainage / water supply system has increasingly relied on innovative mixed-use designs that reconfigure drainage infrastructure as recreational and tourist destinations for enjoying technically enhanced nature. A case in point is the Active, Beautiful, Clean Waters Programme, with a vision of drainage as a site for urban leisure, exercise, and environmental cleanliness—for the same river that, in 1979, was routinely referred to as heavily polluted and the favored dumping ground for victims of organized crime.

Even while planners and experts whom I interviewed remained convinced that engineering solutions were perfectly adequate, they present their own risks. The Marina Barrage project, completed in 2008 at a cost of about US$150 million, had to be defended against public speculation that it had contributed to the highly visible 2011 flooding—including "technical analysis" by self-styled vernacular experts (e.g., Tan Kok Tim 2011) and awkward claims by the Public Utilities Board that what occurred was not really flooding but simply "ponding." Whereas flooding presents massive compound problems for Southeast Asian cities like Bangkok or Jakarta, Singapore's highly engineered concrete waterways are a paradigm of infrastructural modernization. Nonetheless, as Chua Beng Huat (2011: 32) argues, "failure haunts success. . . . Fear of failure keeps the government constantly in search of the next niche for development thrown up by shifts in global capitalism"— and all the more so for potentially chaotic shifts in climate. In a context where much criticism is strictly curtailed, the technocratic imagination can lead to a kind of reductio ad absurdum in which the claim to predict and control nature is always already a political vulnerability because it directly relates to authorizing claims of Singapore's postcolonial rule.

Anticipating erratic, spatially localized tropical downpours demonstrates a kind of Deleuzean intensiveness to the prediction and control approach, especially apparent in the recurring emphasis on information and communication. The Tropical Marine Science Institute, a university research body that contracts for much of the government's climate change modeling, has developed computation-intensive nowcasting for three-hour periods that show imminent rainfall intensity in different quarters of the island (fig. 3). Using another web-based app, citizens can engage in their own island-wide flood surveillance using government-installed closed-circuit television cameras and flood gauges (excluding military and industrial areas). The Public Utilities Board also documents flooding events on its website with depth and duration data—with the same "finding" repeated for each and every event: "Intense rain caused flooding at this location." Bobby Wong has argued that Singapore's urban planning has repeatedly returned to the close-up image of the island completely abstracted from regional neighbors, which establishes a "virtual plane" that, in the country's independence, constituted the new nation territorially, ecologically, and in its urbanism. For Wong (2004: 173), the repeatedly framed close-up of Singapore—the intensified representation of the island, forty-four by twenty-three kilometers—is akin to Gilles Deleuze's understanding of the close-up image of a face in cinema: "an intensity 'that tears the

433

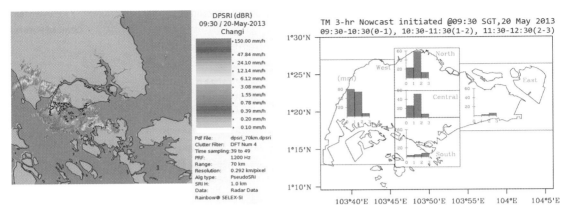

Figure 3 Nowcasting provided by the Tropical Marine Science Institute. The radar image on the left shows Singapore in the regional context of the Malay Peninsula (north) and Indonesia's Riau Islands (south). The right-hand image shows expected rainfall intensity in different parts of the city for the subsequent three-hour period.

image away from its spatio-temporal coordinates,' or its historicity." It is also infrastructural rationality that tears Singapore away from its spatiotemporal coordinates. The technopolitics of environmental possibilism demonstrates Singapore's historicity and the limits of its infrastructural reason. For instance, there seems to be little evidence that these high-tech responses to potential flooding are especially used or valued by citizens; they represent the logical conclusion of a process of intensification rather than any practical utility.

Conclusion: Pluripotent Climate Futures

I have argued that Singapore's approach to climate change adaptation closely tracks long-standing elements of its postcolonial urbanism, namely, its rationality of environmental possibilism and perpetual territorial transformation. Ultimately an approach to population security, water infrastructure as vital systems security bears out Singapore's biopolitics of vigilance, spatial emergency, and intensified prediction and control over nature. But it is precisely the predictability of climate change futures that remains in question. To maintain that adaptation will be possible without mitigation, the island nation must assume that the impacts of climate change will be limited to modest linear changes in base climatic variables. Viewed from a certain perspective, Singapore's climate change policy is comprehensive and duly integrated into many aspects of its economy and society without much of the hand-wringing that frequently accompanies climate-related infrastructure investment. Meanwhile, it has planned for a radical increase in emissions by some 60 percent from 2005 to 2020 and routinely touts the increase as an emissions reduction (e.g., NCCS 2012: 35). In its modest risk assessment and its commitment to increased emissions, Singapore's climate policy seeks to safeguard its small national population at the expense of regional neighbors while maximizing its position in fossil energy–based accumulation. In a context of increasingly unpredictable, nonlinear climatic changes, Singapore's forecast of modest linear climatic changes amounts to a bold wager that adaptation is possible without substantial global mitigation of greenhouse gas emissions.

Singapore's commitment to the artificial remaking of environment through a rationality of prediction and control fails to appreciate the pluripotency of climate change futures. I use the biomedical metaphor from pluripotent stem cell research, avidly funded in Singapore, to underscore the highly divergent climate change outcomes that may be unpredictably localized in any number of regional contexts. While the government acknowledges scientific uncertainties due to limitations in data and modeling resolution, it nonetheless limits its apprehension of the future to a kind of forecasting. Yet long-term climate modeling is not forecasting, and even less does modeling account for compounded effects through which climate, long taken for granted within the complexity of human sociotechnical systems, permeates manifold future possibilities. Collier and Lakoff argue that vital systems security hinges on a kind of threat analysis that goes beyond probability assessment utilized for social welfare and insurance models of risk assurance. Climate change, like terrorism and emerging infectious diseases, implies an anthropogenic future in which predictability itself is not a realistic assumption.

Climate change adaptation planning fits neatly within Singapore's strategy of environmental possibilism. Savage (1992) describes environmental possibilism as holding, on the one hand, that any threat is possible within the geopolitical and territorial environment of the small, independent island nation and, on the other, that natural relations, including environment and territory, can be wholly remade according to modernist technological aspirations. Futuristic manipulation of the island's natural parameters, which serves to abstract the nation from its regional context, is one signature of Singapore's urbanization strategy. Its infrastructural modernity has been a crucial feature of governmental claims to its uniqueness in the region, and Singaporeans are well aware of their prosperity and ecological security relative to other major Southeast Asian cities. Furthermore, it is a mistake to interpret its approach as a recapitulation of Euro-American urbanism. On the contrary, its urbanization process is distinctive for its perspicuous strategic assessment of the country's geopolitical potential. Singapore's climate adaptation planning fits within this tradition of environmental possibilism.

However, the politically conservative commitment to fossil energy futures and a modest interpretation of climate risk demonstrates an inadequate understanding of the kinds of uncertainty at stake in planning for climate change futures. There is no reason to assume that either localized climatic variables or modest linear changes in those variables will be the primary driver of climate change–related threats. Already, in the case of Syria, there is a major demonstrated case of climate change–induced drought helping drive a protracted and bloody civil war and prompting a major regional geopolitical shift (Kelley et al. 2015). Geopolitical militarization in the Arctic has been driven not only by unexpectedly precipitous ice loss but also by the risky, opportunistic exploration of new fossil energy reserves by Russia, Norway, and Canada (Huebert et al. 2012). In Southeast Asia, the large-scale flooding of Thailand's industrial estates in 2011 demonstrated Singapore's financial sensitivity to climate impacts happening elsewhere in the world. When adaptation is narrowly construed as a response to variation in temperature, sea level, and rainfall, with some potential for further knock-on effects, it may seem as if modest infrastructural improvements can effectively protect a city from adverse effects of climate change. Singapore views adaptation in such naturalistic terms, and indeed it must if it is to believe in predictability. Yet the problematic of climate change is constituted by uncertainty in such a way that predictability itself cannot be taken for granted. The effects of climate change already permeate complex social and technical arrangements in unpredictable, nonlinear ways, and its chaotic effects are all the more apparent when human anticipation of future climates is part of its present-day impact.

Urbanization and its related planning practices increasingly hinge on a moment in which planetary-scale ecology and the biopolitics of population security are dynamically and mutually interrelated. The shift in perspective in the 2000s, from climate change as a relatively distant future trend to an increasingly complex problem bearing immediately on urban infrastructures, has become part of a situation in which cities are increasingly the de facto scale for assessing climate risk. Whether a revitalized modernist trust in infrastructure is up to the task remains to be seen, even while climate change is repeatedly used to justify and legitimate a major shift to large-scale infrastructure investment especially in the global South. Cities are paradigmatic of a unique historical conjuncture that brings together planetary ecology and global capitalism with localized, dramatic urban ecological changes. These localized changes, such as land subsidence in Jakarta or Bangkok, very often constitute the immediate vulnerabilities exacerbated by climate change. In Singapore's case, it is probably safe to say its long-term investment in water infrastructure has made planners' jobs incomparably easier. But infrastructure is the built form of its own vulnerabilities—think of the vast areas of the city resting on artificial land just over a meter above sea level—and the government's deterministic, engineering approach to the prediction and control of nature suggests it hasn't taken seriously the pluripotency of its climate futures.

References

Amir, Sulfikar. 2015. "Manufacturing Space: Hypergrowth and the Underwater City in Singapore." *Cities* 49: 98–105.

Aradau, Claudia. 2010. "Security That Matters: Critical Infrastructure and Objects of Protection." *Security Dialogue* 41, no. 5: 491–514.

Arnold, Wayne. 2007. "Vulnerable to Rising Seas, Singapore Envisions a Giant Seawall." *New York Times*, August 29. www.nytimes.com/2007/08/29/world/asia/29iht-Dikes.2.7301576.html.

Balakrishnan, Vivian. 2012. Speech by Minister Vivian Balakrishnan at the opening ceremony of Hyflux Innovation Centre, Singapore, July 3. Ministry of the Environment and Water Resources. app.mewr.gov.sg/web/contents/contents.aspx?contid=1677 (accessed February 5, 2015).

Barry, Andrew. 2001. *Political Machines: Governing Technological Society.* London: Athlone.

Beck, Ulrich. 1992. *Risk Society: Towards a New Modernity.* Translated by Mark Ritter. Thousand Oaks, CA: Sage.

Braun, Bruce. 2000. "Producing Vertical Territory: Geology and Governmentality in Late Victorian Canada." *Cultural Geographies* 7, no. 1: 7–46.

———. 2014. "A New Urban Dispositif? Governing Life in an Age of Climate Change." *Environment and Planning D: Society and Space* 32, no. 1: 49–64.

Bulkeley, Harriet, and Castán Broto. 2013. "Government by Experiment? Global Cities and the Governing of Climate Change." *Transactions of the Institute of British Geographers* 38, no. 3: 361–75.

Chang, C.-P., and Teo Suan Wong. 2008. "Rare Typhoon Development near the Equator." In *Recent Progress in Atmospheric Sciences: Application to the Asia-Pacific Region*, edited by Kuo-Nan Liou and Ming-Dah Chou, 172–81. Singapore: World Scientific.

Channel NewsAsia. 2007. "Marina Barrage Will House World's Largest Water Pumps." August 29.

Chia, Jack Meng-Tat. 2009. "Managing the Tortoise Island: Tua Pek Kong Temple, Pilgrimage, and Social Change in Pulau Kusu, 1965–2007." *New Zealand Journal of Asian Studies* 11, no. 2: 72–95.

Chua Beng Huat. 1991. "Not Depoliticized but Ideologically Successful: The Public Housing Programme in Singapore." *International Journal of Urban and Regional Research* 15, no. 1: 24–41.

———. 2011. "Singapore as Model: Planning Innovations, Knowledge Experts." In *Worlding Cities: Asian Experiments and the Art of Being Global*, edited by Ananya Roy and Aihwa Ong, 29–54. Malden, MA: Wiley-Blackwell.

Chua, Grace. 2013. "Cyclone Unlikely to Hit Singapore, Experts Say." *Straits Times*, October 22.

Clancey, Gregory. 2004. "Toward a Spatial History of Emergency: Notes from Singapore." In *Beyond Description: Singapore Space Historicity*, edited by Ryan Bishop, John Phillips, and Wei-Wei Yeo, 30–59. New York: Routledge.

Collier, Stephen J. 2008. "Enacting Catastrophe: Preparedness, Insurance, Budgetary Rationalization." *Economy and Society* 37, no. 2: 224–50.

Collier, Stephen J., and Andrew Lakoff. 2008. "Distributed Preparedness: The Spatial Logic of Domestic Security in the United States." *Environment and Planning D: Society and Space* 26, no. 1: 7–28.

————. 2014. "Vital Systems Security: Reflexive Biopolitics and the Government of Emergency." *Theory, Culture and Society* 32, no. 2: 19–51.

Comaroff, Joshua. 2014. "Built on Sand: Singapore and the New State of Risk." In "Wet Matter," *Harvard Design Magazine*, no. 39. www.harvarddesignmagazine .org/issues/39/built-on-sand-singapore-and-the-new-state-of-risk.

Daniell, James, et al. 2013. "Typhoon Haiyan / Yolanda." Report no. 2, Focus on Philippines. November 13. Potsdam, Germany: Center for Disaster Management and Risk Reduction Technology. quakesos.sosearthquakesvz.netdna-cdn .com/wp-content/uploads/2013/10/CEDIM_FDA_Haiyan_Rep2.pdf.

Fearnley, Lyle. 2008. "Signals Come and Go: Syndromic Surveillance and Styles of Biosecurity." *Environment and Planning A* 40, no. 7: 1615–32.

Fjord, Lakshmi. 2007. "Disasters, Race, and Disability: [Un]seen through the Political Lens on Katrina." *Journal of Race and Policy* 3, no. 1: 46–66.

Foucault, Michel. 2007. *Security, Territory, Population: Lectures at the Collège de France, 1977–1978*. Edited by Michel Senellart and translated by Graham Burchell. New York: Palgrave Macmillan.

George, Cherian. 2000. *Singapore: The Air-Conditioned Nation; Essays on the Politics of Comfort and Control, 1990–2000*. Singapore: Landmark Books.

Goh, Kian. 2014. "Making Room for Water: Urban Adaptation and Uneven Development in Jakarta." Unpublished manuscript, last modified October 24. Microsoft Word file.

Graham, Stephen, and Colin McFarlane. 2015. Introduction to *Infrastructural Lives: Urban Infrastructure in Context*, edited by Stephen Graham and Colin McFarlane, 1–14. New York: Routledge/Earthscan.

Grove, Kevin. 2014. "Biopolitics and Adaptation: Governing Socio-ecological Contingency through Climate Change and Disaster Studies." *Geography Compass* 8, no. 3: 198–210. doi:10.1111/gec3.12118.

Huebert, Rob, et al. 2012. *Climate Change and International Security: The Arctic as Bellwether.* Arlington, VA: Center for Climate and Energy Solutions.

Hyflux. 2009. "Hyflux Still Expanding." Press release. *Asia Biotech* 13, no. 2: 57. www.asiabiotech.com/publication/apbn/13/english/preserved-docs/1303/0057 _0057.pdf.

Jabareen, Yosef. 2013. "Planning the Resilient City: Concepts and Strategies for Coping with Climate Change and Environmental Risk." *Cities* 31: 220–29.

Kelley, Colin, et al. 2015. "Climate Change in the Fertile Crescent and Implications of the Recent Syrian Drought." *Proceedings of the National Academy of Sciences* 112, no. 11: 3241–46.

Koh, Hong Teng. 2014. *Last Train from Tanjong Pagar.* Singapore: Epigram Books.

Koninck, Rodolphe de, Julie Drolet, and Marc Girard. 2008. *Singapore: An Atlas of Perpetual Territorial Transformation.* Singapore: NUS Press.

Larkin, Brian. 2013. "The Politics and Poetics of Infrastructure." *Annual Review of Anthropology* 42: 327–43.

Mayer, Maximillian. 2012. "Chaotic Climate Change and Security." *International Political Sociology* 6, no. 2: 165–85.

MEWR (Ministry of the Environment and Water Resources). 2014. "Factsheet: Study of Long Term Impact of Climate Change on Singapore." Singapore: MEWR. app.mewr.gov.sg/data/ImgCont/1386/6.%20Factsheet%20-%20Climate%20 Change%20Study%20%5Bweb%5D.pdf (accessed August 26, 2014).

Mydans, Seth, and Wayne Arnold. 2007. "Lee Kuan Yew, Founder of Singapore, Changing with the Times." *New York Times*, August 29. www.nytimes.com /2007/08/29/world/asia/29iht-lee.1.7301669.html.

Myers, Natasha. 2015. "Edenic Apocalypse: Singapore's End-of-Time Botanical Tourism." In *Art in the Anthropocene: Encounters among Aesthetics, Politics, Environments, and Epistemologies*, edited by Heather Davis and Etienne Turpin. London: Open Humanities Press.

NCCS (National Climate Change Secretariat). 2012. *National Climate Change Strategy.* Singapore: NCCS.

NEWRI (Nanyang Environment and Water Research Institute). 2014. *The Power of Water.* June. Singapore: NEWRI. newri.ntu.edu.sg/aboutus/Documents /NEWRI%20Brochure_June%202014.pdf.

Ong, Aihwa. 2005. "Ecologies of Expertise: Assembling Flows, Managing Citizenship." In *Global Assemblages: Technology, Politics, and Ethics as Anthropological Problems*, edited by Aihwa Ong and Stephen J. Collier, 337–53. Malden, MA: Wiley-Blackwell.

————. 2011. "Introduction: Worlding Cities, or the Art of Being Global." In *Worlding Cities: Asian Experiments and the Art of Being Global*, edited by Ananya Roy and Aihwa Ong, 1–26. Malden, MA: Wiley-Blackwell.

Peduzzi, Pascal. 2014. "Sand: Rarer Than One Thinks." *UNEP Global Environmental Alert Services* (March): 1–15.

Public Utilities Board. 2011. *Water: Vital, Valued, Vibrant.* Annual Report 2010–2011. Singapore: Public Utilities Board. www.pub.gov.sg/mpublications/Lists/Annual Report/Attachments/16/PUB_AR2011.pdf (accessed November 18, 2015).

————. 2014a. "Closing the Water Loop." August 29. www.pub.gov.sg/about/p.s /default.aspx#ctw.

————. 2014b. "NEWater." May 30. www.pub.gov.sg/about/historyfuture/Pages /NEWater.aspx.

Raju, Kumaran, et al. 2012. "Future Sea Level Rise Implications on Development of Lazarus Island, Singapore Southern Islands." *Contributions to Marine Science*, edited by K. S. Tan, 23–31. Singapore: Tropical Marine Science Institute, National University of Singapore.

Richards, Arthur. 1961. "Our Island Neighbours." *Singapore Free Press*, November 10.

Roberts, J. Timmons, and Bradley Parks. 2006. *A Climate of Injustice: Global Inequality, North-South Politics, and Climate Policy.* Cambridge, MA: MIT Press.

Savage, Victor. 1992. "Human-Environment Relations: Singapore's Environmental Ideology." In *Imagining Singapore*, edited by Ban Kah Choon, Anne Pakir, and Tong Chee Kiong, 210–39. Singapore: Times Academic Press.

SEDB (Singapore Economic Development Board). 2011. "Tap into Singapore's Pool of Resources." Singapore: SEDB. www.edb.gov.sg/content/dam/edb/en /resources/brochuresnew/Global-Hydrohub-Brochure.pdf.

Simone, AbdouMaliq. 2015. "Relational Infrastructures in Postcolonial Urban Worlds." In *Infrastructural Lives: Urban Infrastructure in Context*, edited by Stephen Graham and Colin McFarlane, 17–28. New York: Routledge/Earthscan.

Sims, Benjamin. 2009. "Disoriented City: Infrastructure, Social Order, and the Police Response to Hurricane Katrina." In *Disrupted Cities: When Infrastructure Fails*, edited by Stephen Graham, 41–53. New York: Routledge.

Singapore Free Press. 1954. "The Bedok Problem." December 23.

Smith, Neil. 2006. "There's No Such Thing as a Natural Disaster." In *Understanding Katrina: Perspectives from the Social Sciences*, by the Social Science Research Council (SSRC). New York: SSRC. understandingkatrina.ssrc.org /Smith.

Straits Times. 1954. "Vigorous Action on Drainage: Goode." December 15.

Symenouh, Ginette. 2013. International Enterprise Singapore. November 22. Unpublished document in author's possession.

Tan Kok Tim, 2011. "Technical Analysis of Why the Marina Barrage Is the Cause of Recent Floods." *Temesak Review*, June 15. www.temasekreview.com/2011/06/15 /technical-analysis-of-why-the-marina-barrage-is-the-cause-of-recent-floods/.

Tay, Serene Hui Xin. 2010. "Typhoon-Induced Extreme Water Levels near Singapore: A Numerical Model Investigation." MSc thesis, Delft University of Technology.

Tortajada, Cecilia, Yugal Joshi, and Asit K. Biswas. 2013. *The Singapore Water Story: Sustainable Development in an Urban City-State*. New York: Routledge.

Whitington, Jerome. 2013. "Fingerprint, Bellwether, Model Event: Climate Change as Speculative Anthropology." *Anthropological Theory* 13, no. 4: 308–28.

———. 2016. "Carbon as a Metric of the Human." *Political and Legal Anthropology Review* 39, no. 1.

Wikipedia. 2015. "Hyflux." en.wikipedia.org/wiki/Hyflux (accessed February 5, 2015).

Wong, Alice. 1979. "Taking a Slow Boat up the Singapore River." *Straits Times*, November 27.

Wong, Bobby [Wong Chong Thai Bobby]. 2004. "The Tropical City: Slippages in the Midst of Ideological Construction." In *Beyond Description: Singapore Space Historicity*, edited by Ryan Bishop, John Phillips, and Wei-Wei Yeo, 165–75. New York: Routledge.

Wong, Poh Poh. 2005. "Reclamation." In *Encyclopedia of Coastal Science*, edited by Maurice L. Schwartz, 791–94. Dordrecht: Springer.

———. 2010. "Singapore." In *Encyclopedia of the World's Coastal Landforms*, edited by Eric C. F. Bird, 1129–34. Dordrecht: Springer. doi:10.1007/978-1-4020 -8639-7_19.3.

....

Jerome Whitington is an anthropologist whose research focuses on anthropogenic climate change and its constitutive uncertainties as a generative impulse for emerging sociocultural practices. His recent works include "Carbon as a Metric of the Human" (*Political and Legal Anthropology Review*, forthcoming); "The Terrestrial Envelope: Fourier's Geological Speculation" (in *A Cultural History of Climate Change*, edited by Tom Bristow and Thomas H. Ford, forthcoming); and "Fingerprint, Bellwether, Model Event: Climate Change as Speculative Anthropology" (*Anthropological Theory*, 2013). He is based at the National University of Singapore.

See inside front cover
for ordering information.

"Like an antidote to amnesia, Scott's meticulous, granular
research vividly recreates the political weather of the 1970s.
Here is a sidelined architecture history that returns as a
missing link — eccentric stories in the emerging development
of those networks, technologies, media, and advocacies
of global governance that are of most consequence today."
—KELLER EASTERLING, YALE UNIVERSITY

"Essential reading for anyone with activist stakes in the contemporary history of insurgent habitats and militarized space."
—EMILY APTER, NEW YORK UNIVERSITY

FELICITY D. SCOTT

Outlaw Territories

Environments of Insecurity/
Architectures of Counterinsurgency

$39.95 hardcover, 544 pages, 6 x 9,
104 b&w illus., ISBN 978-1-935408-73-4

Zone Books are distributed by the
MIT Press. Online at zonebooks.org

ZONE BOOKS

;lim Fashion
:emporary Style Cultures
IA LEWIS
ustrations (incl. 17 in color),
r, $28.95

k Matters
he Surveillance of
kness
ONE BROWNE
ustrations, paper, $23.95

cing Freedom
rtheid, Squatter Politics,
the Struggle for Home
E-MARIA MAKHULU
ustrations, paper, $23.95

Spectral Wound
ual Violence, Public
nories, and the
gladesh War of 1971
ANIKA MOOKHERJEE
ustrations, paper, $26.95

**Asians Wear Clothes on
the Internet**
Race, Gender, and the Work
of Personal Style Blogging
MINH-HA T. PHAM
38 illustrations, paper, $24.95

Reel World
An Anthropology of Creation
ANAND PANDIAN
51 illustrations, paper, $26.95

Dilemmas of Difference
Indigenous Women and
the Limits of Postcolonial
Development Policy
SARAH A. RADCLIFFE
20 illustrations, paper, $27.95

Save **30%** with coupon
code **P15PC**

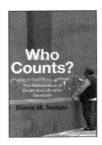   

Who Counts?
The Mathematics of Death
and Life After Genocide
DIANE M. NELSON
35 illustrations, paper, $25.95

Emergent Ecologies
EBEN KIRKSEY
72 illustrations, paper, $25.95

Alchemy in the Rain Forest
Politics, Ecology, and
Resilience in a New Guinea
Mining Area
JERRY K. JACKA
*New Ecologies for the
Twenty-First Century*
39 illustrations, paper, $25.95

Ontopower
War, Powers, and the
State of Perception
BRIAN MASSUMI
1 illustration, paper, $24.95

How Would You Like to Pay?
How Technology Is Changing
the Future of Money
BILL MAURER
51 illustrations, paper, $19.95

A Nervous State
Violence, Remedies, and
Reverie in Colonial Congo
NANCY ROSE HUNT
41 illustrations, paper, $26.95

Gesture and Power
Religion, Nationalism, and
Everyday Performance in Congo
YOLANDA COVINGTON-WARD
*Religious Cultures of African and
African Diaspora People*
17 illustrations, paper, $25.95

   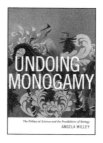

addicted.pregnant.poor
KELLY RAY KNIGHT
Critical Global Health
34 illustrations, paper, $25.95

Metrics
What Counts in Global Health
VINCANNE ADAMS
Critical Global Health
paper, $24.95

Islam and Secularity
The Future of Europe's
Public Sphere
NILÜFER GÖLE
Public Planet Books
paper, $24.95

The Ghana Reader
History, Culture, Politics
**KWASI KONADU &
CLIFFORD C. CAMPBELL, editors**
The World Readers
53 illustrations, incl. 12 in color, paper,
$27.95

Biocultural Creatures
Toward a New Theory of
the Human
SAMANTHA FROST
paper, $22.95

Undoing Monogamy
The Politics of Science and
the Possibilities of Biology
ANGELA WILLEY
9 illustrations, paper, $23.95

Plastic Bodies
Sex Hormones and Menstrual
Suppression in Brazil
EMILIA SANABRIA
Experimental Futures
12 photographs, paper, $24.95

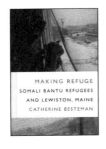

Making Refuge
Somali Bantu Refugees
and Lewiston, Maine
CATHERINE BESTEMAN
Global Insecurities
32 illustrations, paper, $26.95

After War
The Weight of Life at Walter Reed
ZOË H. WOOL
Critical Global Health
17 illustrations, paper, $24.95

Memorializing Pearl Harbor
Unfinished Histories and the
Work of Remembrance
GEOFFREY M. WHITE
30 illustrations, paper, $26.95

Performance
DIANA TAYLOR
74 illustrations, paper, $23.95

Edgar Heap of Birds
BILL ANTHES
95 illustrations, paper, $24.95

Race Becomes Tomorrow
North Carolina and the
Shadow of Civil Rights
GERALD M. SIDER
13 illustrations, paper, $24.95

Sensing Sound
Singing and Listening as
Vibrational Practice
NINA SUN EIDSHEIM
Sign, Storage, Transmission
26 illustrations, paper, $24.95

Save **30%** with coupon
code **P15PC**